ETHNIC CONFLICT AND DEVELOPMENT:
THE CASE OF FIJI

The United Nations Research Institute for Social Development (UNRISD) is an autonomous agency that engages in multi-disciplinary research on the social dimensions of contemporary problems affecting development. Its work is guided by the conviction that, for effective development policies to be formulated, an understanding of the social and political context is crucial. The Institute attempts to provide governments, development agencies, grassroots organisations and scholars with a better understanding of how development policies and processes of economic, social and environmental change affect different social groups. Working through an extensive network of national research centres, UNRISD aims to promote original research and strengthen research capacity in developing countries.

Its research themes include Crisis, Adjustment and Social Change; Socio-Economic and Political Consequences of the International Trade in Illicit Drugs; Environment, Sustainable Development and Social Change; Ethnic Conflict and Development; Integrating Gender into Development Policy; Participation and Changes in Property Relations in Communist and Post-Communist Societies; Refugees, Returnees and Local Society; and Political Violence and Social Movements. UNRISD research projects focused on the 1995 World Summit for Social Development included Rethinking Social Development in the 1990s; Economic Restructuring and New Social Policies; Ethnic Diversity and Public Policies; and The War-torn Societies Project.

A list of the Institute's free and priced publications can be obtained by writing: UNRISD, Reference Centre, Palais des Nations, CH-1211, Geneva 10, Switzerland.

This book forms part of a wider research project on Ethnic Conflict and Development sponsored by UNRISD. Covering 15 countries in Africa, South Asia, the Middle East, Central America and Eastern Europe, where ethnic conflicts have exploded with great intensity in recent years, the project is concerned with the nature of conflict among ethnic groups in the process of development, and with the implications of such conflict for the international relations of states. The origin and background of the conflicts are analysed, and the interests and motives of the major actors are explored; the relationship between particular conflicts and the broader development process is studied; and attention is given to the nature of external interests and to the internationalization of conflict. At same time, the project specifically attempts to provide comparative analysis of the solutions which have been set in place in different circumstances, including assessment of the procedures through which particular solutions have been found.

Ethnic Conflict and Development: The Case of Fiji

RALPH R. PREMDAS
Department of Government
The University of the West Indies
St Augustine, Trinidad and Tobago
and
Visiting Professor
Department of Political Science
University of Toronto
Toronto, Canada

Avebury

Aldershot • Brookfield USA • Hong Kong • Singapore • Sydney

Published by
Avebury
Ashgate Publishing Limited
Gower House
Croft Road
Aldershot
Hants GU11 3HR
England

Ashgate Publishing Company
Old Post Road
Brookfield
Vermont 05036
USA
Reprinted 1996

British Library Cataloguing in Publication Data

Premdas, Ralph R.
    Ethnic Conflict and Development: Case of
    Fiji – (Research in Ethnic Relations Series)
    I. Title II. Series
    305.80099611
ISBN 1 85628 979 6

Library of Congress Catalog Card Number: 95-78511

Printed in Great Britain by
Antony Rowe Ltd, Chippenham, Wiltshire

Contents

Tables		vii
Abbreviations		viii
Preface		x
Introduction:	Ethnicity and Development	1
I	The Making of a Multi-Ethnic Mosaic	8
II	The Politics of Representation, Land and Jobs	19
III	Erosion of the Balance and an Attempt at a Government of National Unity	37
IV	The Elections of 1987 and Military Intervention	55
V	The Coup d'Etat, Racism and Abridgement of Human Rights	67
VI	The Grievances and Demands of Fijians and Non-Fijians	91
VII	Ethnonationalist Supremacy under a New Constitutional Order	117
VIII	The Elections of 1992 and 1994 and the Assumption of Power by Rabuka	140

IX   Ethnic Conflict and Development: The
Political Dimension   152

X   Ethnic Conflict and Development: The Economic,
Cultural and Psycho-Social Dimensions   164

Bibliography   185

Tables

Table 1.1	Population of Fiji, 1987	9
Table 2.1	Representation	23
Table 2.2	Communal and National Rolls	25
Table 2.3	Representation in the Senate	25
Table 2.4	Land Ownership	27
Table 2.5	Examination Pass Rate by Ethnicity	30
Table 2.6	Examination Pass Rate by Ethnicity (per cent)	30
Table 2.7	Numbers Qualified in Selected Professions, 1958	30
Table 2.8	Civil Service Personnel by Ethnicity, 1974	31
Table 2.9	The Police Force Personnel by Ethnicity, 1974	31
Table 2.10	Fijian Armed Forces	32
Table 2.11	Trade Offs	33
Table 7.1	The House of Representatives	119
Table 7.2	The Senate	121
Table 8.1	Fijian Seats	142
Table 8.2	Skewed Allocation of Voters on the Fijian Rolls	142
Table 8.3	Party Results in the Fijian Constituencies	146
Table 8.4	Results in the Indian Constituencies	146
Table 8.5	General Voters Seats	146
Table 10.1	Composition of Sugar Cane Growers, 1990	167

Abbreviations

ACP/EC	-	African-Caribbean-Pacific/European Community
ALTO	-	Agricultural Landlord and Tenants Ordinance
ANC	-	All Peoples National Congress
BLV	-	Bose Levu Vakaturaga (Fiji Council of Chiefs)
BOMAS	-	Business Organization and Management Unit
CIAC	-	Constitutional Investigatory and Advising Committee
CRC	-	Constitutional Review Committee
FA	-	Fijian Association Party
FBC	-	Fiji Broadcasting Corporation
FCC	-	Fiji Council of Churches
FIC	-	Fiji Indian Congress
FILP	-	Fiji Indian Liberal Party
FINS	-	Fiji International News Service
FIS	-	Fiji Intelligence Service
FLP	-	Fiji Labour Party
FNP	-	Fijian Nationalist Party
FNUF	-	Fijian National United Front
FRMF	-	Fiji Royal Military Forces
FS	-	Fiji Sun
FT	-	Fiji Times
FTL	-	Fiji Times Limited
FTUC	-	Fiji Trade Union Council
GARD	-	Group Against Racial Discrimination
GCC	-	Great Council of Chiefs
GVP	-	General Voters Party
IBI	-	Islands Business
JPH	-	Journal of Pacific History
NFP	-	National Federation Party

NFU	-	National Farmers' Union
NLTB	-	Native Land Trust Board
PCC	-	Pacific Conference of Churches
PIM	-	Pacific Islands Monthly
PJT	-	Pacific Journal of Theology
RFMF	-	Royal Fijian Military Force
STV	-	Soqosoqo ni Taukei ni Vanua
SVT	-	Soqosoqo ni Vakavulewa ni Taukei
UN	-	United Nations
UNESCO	-	United Nations Educational, Scientific and Cultural Organization
VAT	-	Value added tax
WUF	-	Western United Front

Preface

In a contemporary world engulfed by ethnic turmoil that has wreaked havoc on the lives of millions of people and threatens to trigger wider international conflicts, this study on Fiji aims to offer an empirical analysis of how these conflicts emerge, develop, and manifest themselves. In particular, an attempt is made to show not only the contours of communal conflict but to point to the political, economic and socio-psychological effects it tends to generate on the development efforts in most of the Third World. Most Third World countries are polyethnic, some with a few cleavages and others with numerous deep divisions, but in nearly all cases, religious, linguistic, regional, and customary factors have unleashed centrifugal forces that threaten the unity and development efforts that are undertaken. Since attaining independence, Fiji has been bedeviled by communal divisions that have prevented the state from optimizing the use of its scarce material and human resources for the benefit of all citizens. The state has been constantly struggling to maintain harmony and equity among the country's inhabitants. At times, the effort has found solutions in modes of conflict regulation that have lasted for a few years.

Peace in polyethnic states is a fragile affair and can easily succumb to the least provocation, throwing the entire society into a tailspin of almost uncontrollable conflict and turmoil. In Fiji this has occurred at the instigation of outbidders in an open competitive democratic process for votes and political gain. Is democracy the culprit in ethnic and communal conflicts? Or are there particular aspects of democratic practice that are more conducive to ethnic strife than others? Are there effective and acceptable modes of ethnic conflict regulation available to apply to the numerous cases of communal strife that currently afflict the world? In this case study, these questions are raised. How Fiji managed its ethnic conflict is very instructive for other instances of communal strife and offers both positive and negative lessons. Above all, the raw materials of the Fiji case can present important comparative insights into the workings of the ethnic phenomena and may contribute to the forging of public policy aimed at limiting and controlling the adverse effects of ethnic strife. For the Third world in particular, although ethnic conflict is by no means limited to this region, the frustration of development plans by poorly understood communal struggles is at stake. Communal conflict stands as a major source of poverty and injustice in the world today.

I began the present work in February 1973 when I made my first visit to Fiji, thus commencing a long trek of research that has extended into the present. Except for one year in 1981 when I was at the University of Ife in Nigeria examining ethnic conflict there, I was present in Fiji at least twice every year. The importance of over two decades of continual research in Fiji has been the opportunity it gave me to observe first hand the communal strife as it developed. While I was examining Fiji and writing on it, there were other cases which interested me and which I also researched. These included Guyana, Trinidad, Suriname, Sri Lanka, Mauritius, South Africa, Nigeria, Papua New Guinea, Irian Jaya, Vanuatu, the Solomon Islands and Quebec. In most of these cases, I have written and conducted field work. This work is my first full length treatment of Fiji, although I wrote several pieces earlier in which many of my ideas were developed.

I wish to thank several persons who have aided me over the past two decades in my research effort on Fiji. These include R.S. Milne, Dharam Ghai, Jeff Steeves, Cynthia Enloe, Mike Howard, Simione Durutalo, Claire Slatter, Ropate Qalo. Vijay Naidu, Ahmed Ali, Wadan Narsey, Karai Vuibau, Jay Narayan, Jone Dokavalu, Brij Lal, Stephanie Lawson, Peter Larmour, William Sutherland, Robbie Robertson, Norm Meller, John Chick, Paul Grocott, Ron Crocombe, Ahmad Ali, Alex Mamak, Raymond Firth, Rodolfo Stavenhagen, and Jackie Leckie. This list deliberately omits the names of numerous politicians from all parties and many citizens of Fiji who have been generous in sharing with me their views of life in Fiji. The list is too long to enumerate, but my sincere thanks go to all. The work on Fiji continues.

For Justin

Introduction: Ethnicity and Development

In the multi-ethnic states of the Third World, planned political change for development cannot succeed unless conceived through the prism of ethnicity (Enloe, 1973; Melson and Wolpe, 1970). Development change cannot follow a simple unilinear path driven by neutral factors such as capital and technology without being mediated through social processes, in particular the recognition of ethnic interests. The ethnic factor is a fundamental force in the Third World environment and must be incorporated into any strategy of development that is adopted. Ethnic pluralism cannot be ignored, nor can it be reduced to an epi-phenomenon that will disappear when change transforms the environment. The ethnic factor is integral to the environment; it is at once both the subject and the object of change. If it is accepted that the ethnic variable is and must be an integral part of the process of planned change, then one would expect to find it occupying a central role in the many strategies of development that have been designed and implemented in the Third World. Yet this is not the case. In the orthodox models of economic and political development from which strategies have been adopted for Third World transformation, the ethnic factor has generally been neglected. The obstacles that have been identified have come to define the nature of the development task. In the economic sphere, they are lack of capital, entrepreneurial and organizational expertise, infrastructure etc.; in the political realm, they are problems of participation, power, mobilization, etc.; and in the social field, they focus on institutional structures, minimum standards of education, nutrition, maternity care, housing, etc. Different ideologies of development vary in the degree of importance they attribute to these factors in interpreting and facilitating change.

Regardless of whether they are founded on Marxist class analysis or capitalist *laissez-faire* market claims, interpretations of change tend to put aside the political-cultural claims of ethno-national groups, deeming these as residual factors which would in due course be assimilated or eliminated in the

1

process of developmental change. The results of this lack of emphasis of the ethno-cultural factor by the different ideologies are devastating. From Lebanon in the Middle East to Guyana on the South American continent, from Northern Ireland to Azerbaijan and Bosnia in Europe to Quebec in North America, from the Sudan and South Africa to Sri Lanka and Malaysia, the assertion of the ethnic factor has made a shambles of development objectives and social peace everywhere, on all continents, in both under-developed and industrialized societies. But particularly in the multi-ethnic states of the impoverished Third World, the ethnic resurgence, like an unrestrained monster, has devastated all those promising plans for change, built on sophisticated economic and other models. The 'ethnic bomb', now exploded, has diverted enormous amounts of scarce resources for security and stability. Formerly a neglected and peripheral factor, the ethnic variable has now emerged as one of the paramount forces of Third World change (Young, 1993; Stavenhagen, 1989; Smith, 1981).

The environment of cultural pluralism and ethnic diversity is now grudgingly but generally acknowledged as a critical variable that must be incorporated in designing new strategies for development. We know little about this factor, however, and only in a general way - not with the sort of sure-minded confidence that goes with the manner in which an established body of knowledge is handled. The reason for this ambivalence is clear. Systematic knowledge of ethnicity in the operations of social structure and, in particular, with reference to development, is desperately deficient. The ethnicity domain is a frontier which only recently received systematic exploration (Schermerhorn, 1970; Banton, 1967; Isaacs, 1975; Young, 1976; van den Berghe 1978, 1981; Glaser, 1975; Barth, 1969; Esman, 1977; Enloe, 1973; Connor, 1972, 1973). Questions on the nature of this phenomenon are as plentiful as settled answers are lacking. Many contemporary theorists and researchers are generating new insights into ethnic relations (Rex and Mason, 1986; A.D. Smith, 1986; Hobsbawm, 1992; Young, 1993; Andersen, 1983; Breuilly, 1982; Hecter, 1975; Gellner, 1983; Armstrong, 1982; Banton, 1983; Keyes, 1981; Stone, 1977; Milne, 1982). There is an urgent need to discuss the relationship between ethnicity and development in all its manifold political, economic, and social dimensions.

The task is daunting. The fruitfulness of many designs of development involving billions of dollars and the fate of millions of poor people may rest on its outcome. The aim of this work is to offer some empirical evidence and to generate some theoretical insights into the behavior of the ethnic factor in the developmental experience of one Third World country. The effort is undertaken in the belief that data derived from individual case histories can offer important building blocks towards constructing a wider theory on the connection between ethnicity and development. The project was stimulated and sponsored by the United Nations Research Institute for Social

2

Development, which convened a group of scholars in the late 1980s and early 1990s to examine the issue. Each participant produced one or more works on the ethnicity factor in relation to development in the country of his/her expertise. The present work is on Fiji. We must begin however with a discourse on and a definition of ethnicity.

Individual analysts define ethnicity in different ways to suit individual research needs. The sense in which I use this term incorporates three components: 1] collective consciousness; 2] bases of affinity; and 3] behavioral effects. Above all, ethnicity refers to a collective group consciousness, that is, a shared sense of identification with a larger community; it pertains to the perception that one at once shares a common identity with a particular group and, in turn, one is also perceived as such by others. Ethnicity is akin to nationalism (Kohn, 1944; Hayes, 1948; Kedourie, 1960) and for this reason, ethnic consciousness may be referred to as ethno-nationalism so as to point to the fact that many states contain several sub-communities with a sense of consciousness distinct from that of other similar groups (Connor, 1972,1973; Emerson, 1966; Premdas, 1977). The second component of ethnicity points to certain putative commonalities such as common language, religion, region, tradition, etc. or a multiple coincidence of several of these cleavages which together have contributed to deep divisions in a state. Clifford Geertz referred to these factors as 'primordial' (Geertz, 1963 p.109). The primordial factors such as religion, race, language, custom, etc. may be regarded as 'objective' features which underlie ethnic identity and facilitate collective consciousness (Premdas, 1993). It is not important that scientific evidence bear out the accuracy of group claims to these commonly apprehended bases of identity. Neither is it significant that the boundaries of these cleavages be always maintained consistently. What is crucial, as Shibutani and Kwan noted, is that an ethnic group consists 'of those who conceive of themselves as being alike by virtue of their common ancestry, real or fictitious, and who are so regarded by others' (Shibutani and Kwan, 1965 p.47). Equally important to note is that ethnic boundaries are socially constructed and reproduced in relation to these symbolic and instrumental needs of a group. As Barth pointed out, they are almost entirely 'subjectively-held categories of ascription and identification by the actors themselves' (Barth, 1969). The maintenance of the boundaries is situationally determined, may shift over time and context, and generally serves to differentiate members dialectically and oppositionally from other groups in terms of 'we-they' antipathies. The third feature of ethnicity refers to the behavioral effects of this variant of group membership. Specifically, ethnic group membership, as a politically self-aware entity, confers symbolic solidarity satisfactions as well as instrumental and material advantages (Rothchild, 1981).

The important point here is that ethnicity is a politically charged

3

phenomenon whose consciousness is stimulated into existence by certain 'triggers' such as group contact, decolonization, modernization, and policy choices by the state which in turn precipitate defensive group quest as well as initiatives for symbolic and material gains. Consequently, ethnic group formation is expressed behaviorally as rival claims to those of other groups. Ethnic group identity is relational and conflictual. It is often marked in the pursuit of an objective by an intensity of emotion that is at once community-building, when moderately expressed and self-annihilating when fanatically followed (Young, 1993). The sentiment of ethnic solidarity bears its own internal logic, compelled by its own formative needs, but once it picks up momentum, it can rarely be denied. To some, it is a marauding monster while to others it embodies the finest creative spirit of a community. It easily ignites into uncontrollable violence out of all proportion to the rational goals that impelled it to act in the first place. Critical to this phenomenon from a behavioral perspective is the element of comparison and competition that is found in the irrational behavior of ethnic groups. Social psychologist Henry Tajfel pointed to the propensity for group loyalty to be sustained intensely and irrationally not for 'greater profit in absolute terms' but in order 'to achieve relatively higher profit for members of their ingroup as compared with members of the outgroup' (Tajfel, 1970). Ethnic groups are not, however, always negative social entities as their well-reported outbursts suggest. They are more frequently very rational bodies which act as pressure groups in pursuit of the programmatic interests of their members. They may seek limited ends following legal procedures and provide a host of solidarity services for their members (Horowitz, 1989).

The importance of Fiji consists of a demonstrated case where multi-ethnicity engenders sectional consciousness which in turn renders efforts at development difficult if not impossible. Few empirical instances exist where the contours of the aroused ethnic phenomenon have been so available for open scrutiny as the Fiji case. The phases of the Fiji experience are almost a paradigmatic model that generally describes a familiar pattern in the life of ethnic conflict from its inception in the colonial migration of different peoples leading to the creation of a plural society. Once these diverse peoples are implanted in the state, the emergence and hardening of multiple cleavages in residence, religion, race, and culture tend to occur. Often, this is followed by the arousal of collective group consciousness, typically through contact, colonial manipulation, and/or modernization (Deutsch, 1966). The introduction of democratic practices at some point thereafter often abets unrestrained inter-ethnic rivalries for control of the state. In a context of zero-sum party politics, competition for values and resources as well as protection of communal identity generally leads to periodic bouts of ethnic riots and violence. Attempts at inter-communal reconciliation are followed by the rise of ethnic 'outbidders' who ignite the latent fires of ethnic fears, often culminating in the failure of the first inter-ethnic compromises and accords. Self-serving analyses and justifications of intransigent communal claims and the blaming of the other side for perfidies of various sorts become abundant. A new level in the rising crescendo of inter-ethnic tensions and the loss of rationality are experienced, fueled by the alleged violation of sacred communal symbols. In the intensifying ethnic struggle, through one means or the other, be it legal or illegal, one group often seizes control of the state and commences a policy of ethnic repression, discrimination and systematic human rights violations (McGarry and O'Leary, 1993). Mass migration follows threats of genocide. The new power wielders deploy immense amounts of scarce state resources for national security and surveillance of entire ethnic communities (Lustick, 1979; Smootha, 1980; Premdas and Hintzen, 1982). This tends to thwart national efforts at development and to encourage the persistence of debilitating divisions and the creation of a garrison state, overseas refugee communities, and the internationalization of the conflict (Premdas, 1990b). The upshot is the entrenchment of a pattern of poverty shared by victims and victimizers alike and the collective helplessness of the ethnic state caught in an unending quagmire of misery.

There are many variations to this sequence of ethnically-propelled events from country to country. The Fiji case captures nearly all of these phases and for this reason deserves close analysis which may yield insights into the behavior of ethnic conflict. There are many theories of ethnic conflict stretching from Darwinian and socio-biological postulates (van den Berghe, 1981; Wilson, 1975) to psychological propositions (Tajfel, 1970) and economic hypotheses (Cox, 1948). In this work, the Darwinian and socio-biological explanations are not useful except where they point to the role of racist perceptions that the respective groups in Fiji hold of each other. By and large, inter-group stereotypes are socially and culturally constructed categories in Fiji and are examined as such. A psychological theory that has value in the Fiji context refers to the relative deprivation hypothesis (Taylor and Mogahaddam, 1985; Runciman, 1966; Korpi, 1974; Ashan, 1988). It is clear that a good part of the sectional conflict in Fiji derives directly from the feelings of deprivation that indigenous Fijians hold vis-à-vis other groups. In turn, this explanation evokes the use of another theory pertaining to equity and rightful shares (Taylor and Mogahaddam, 1985; Despres, 1975; Rothchild, 1986). Relative deprivation and equity theories are brought into play by examining the data of ethnic conflict in Fiji mainly in an auxiliary role in support of a larger explanatory view. There is also an economic hypothesis that seeks to address communal strife pointing to the critical and determining role of material and property relations (Cox, 1948; Miles, 1980; Bonacich, 1980; Melson and Wolpe, 1988; Bolaria and Li, 1988). In the present work,

5

the economic variable is not given the pre-eminent role and is used more as a support hypothesis in illuminating aspects of the ethnic strife in Fiji. Instead, the theoretical thrust is focused on group boundaries in a plural society and the role of outbidders, as well as the concept of balance in structuring the nature and form of ethnic strife in Fiji (Furnivall, 1948; M.G. Smith, 1965; Despres, 1967; Rabushka and Shepsle, 1972; Rex, 1958; Jenkins, 1988). These ideas are more fully developed in the handling of the data as a whole.

This work differs in important ways from other texts on Fiji that have appeared since the military intervention in 1987 (Howard, 1991; Lawson, 1991; Sutherland, 1992; Robertson and Tavanisua, 1981; B. Lal, 1988; V. Lal, 1990; Scarr, 1988). First, it seeks to address the impact of communal strife on efforts aimed at development. The political, economic, and socio-psychological dimensions of the persistent communal struggles in Fiji are explored at length. The manner in which this is done suggests a mode of analysis for similar studies that examine the connection between ethnic conflict and development. Second, the text takes up a theory of ethnic conflict that focuses on the critical role of outbidders in a plural democratic society, examining in the process the value and limitations of the conflict regulating mechanism of 'balance' in the distribution of ethnic shares. It is thus open to the objections of economic determinists who dismiss the role of group boundaries and inter-group competition examined by Tajfel, Barth, M.G. Smith, Furnivall and others as epi-phenomena. In this study, the ethnic strife in Fiji is examined in its multi-dimensional aspects involving social, cultural, economic, and ethical features, giving more importance to the cultural factors than to the economic ones. Finally, the work examines at length the human rights effects of the ethnic conflict in the establishment of an inegalitarian constitutional order. To do this, the work has had to comprehend a stretch of time that covers not only the immediate post-coup period, but also events that led up to the 1992 and the 1994 general elections. The fact that Indians have been the main victims of human rights violations does not imply that this community has moral virtues superior to those of other communities. The victims in this case just happen to be Indians but structurally the victims could be any ethnic community that has become subordinated to the power of another, as illustrated in Bosnia, Rwanda, South Africa etc. The important category is not Indians but any group that happens to be at the receiving end of an ethnically repressive order. The Fiji case only illustrates some of the characteristics of human rights violations in situations of ethnic strife. In some ways, it is rather unfortunate that ethnic conflict in Fiji involves an indigenous group that has acquired power. Indigenous groups are more frequently the victims of racist and ethnic policies that have reduced first nation peoples to exploited and peripheralized communities. What is more important than the special claims of any group, indigenous or otherwise, is not their ethnic

6

identity but the idea of a just order. In the long run, it is this perspective that will best benefit all oppressed peoples, including indigenous groups. No group has a monopoly over good or evil. The Fiji case examined in this work focuses on the nature of ethnic conflict, its emergence, form of manifestations, attempts at conflict regulation, causes of democratic failure, and the overall impact of communal strife on the efforts of the multi-ethnic states of the Third World to transform the conditions of their survival.

I The Making of a Multi-Ethnic Mosaic

Communal politics in Fiji are fraught with tension. Inter-ethnic animosity pervades the system. Open expressions of mutual contempt by members of the communal sections in daily intercourse are subtle and restrained, but periodically spill over into public discourse. Practically no one in Fiji's multi-ethnic social setting is free from the corrosive ravages of sectional stereotyping that attend cross-cultural interaction. Paradoxically, no one disagrees with the harm that the atmosphere of malaise creates for inter-community cooperation. But the same person who openly condemns the prejudices displayed in routine inter-communal exchanges proceeds, in the privacy of his or her own home and community, to participate in its enactment. Hypocritical professions of concern for one's cross-communal compatriot are as endemic in the system as rabid ethno-centrism itself. It is a deadly game of serious self-deception.

On a number of occasions in recent years, collective communal violence has spilled over into the public arena, threatening to envelope the entire fragile system in conflagration. In particular, the year 1968 is remembered in this regard; electoral competition cultivated sectional sentiments to unprecedented heights. The fear that one day all restraints would be removed in a confrontation had haunted political leaders. It happened finally in May 1987 when the Fiji military forces executed a coup d'état that removed the duly elected government of Dr. Timoci Bavadra. Unprecedented communal violence ensued. The event that triggered the military intervention was the removal via the electoral process of Fijian High Chief Ratu Mara and his Alliance Party from power after a decade and a half of uninterrupted rule. Lt. Colonel Sitiveni Rabuka, the architect of the coup d'etat cried 'Fiji for Fijians' in removing the Labour-Federation Party from power. The critical issue in the coup turned on inter-ethnic relations.

Politics in Fiji have had a built-in potential for recurrent instability stimulated in part by the country's ethnically plural socio-cultural structure

8

(Table 1.1). The two dominant groups, the indigenous Fijians and the Indians (India), constitute over 94 per cent of the total population. These two groups live side by side, but each is uncomfortablewith if not hostile to the other. They do not share basic cultural institutions and neither is economically independent. Their economic resources and productive facilities are different and complementary rendering economic exchange necessary. Until independence granted by Britain in October 1970, these two cultural sections were kept together in outward harmony by the colonial government which served as an 'umpire'. As independence approached, they engaged in deeply divisive disputes concerned directly or indirectly with ethnic domination. In all these respects, Fiji conforms uncannily to the plural society model postulated by J.S. Furnivall (Furnivall, 1948).

Table 1.1
Population of Fiji, 1987

	Per Cent
Fijian	46
Indian	48
European	1
Part-European	2
Chinese and Part-Chinese	1
Other Pacific Islanders	2
Total	100

Source: *Notes on the Commonwealth*, Commonwealth Secretariat, London, 1987

Unlike homogenous and heterogeneous societies which are fundamentally integrated (M.G. Smith, 1965), plural societies lack an underlying consensus of basic values and are perennially exposed to strife stimulated by ethnonationalists. Political moderation is a vital but scarce commodity; even where it exists by compromise and special arrangements worked out by inter-communal elites, social equilibrium can be easily disrupted by ambitious politicians who manipulate stereotypical inter-ethnic fears for support. Called 'outbidders' in the jargon of plural society analysts, they disrupt the fragile political order, charging that the moderate leaders have sold out to the other side or that they have designed conspiracy arrangements which serve their interests to the detriment of their unsuspecting followers (Rabushka and Shepsle, 1972). Events a decade earlier illustrate the fearsome power of outbidders prior to the military intervention in 1987. On October 9, 1975, Mr. Sakiasi Butadroka, a member of the Fiji House of Representatives, introduced

9

a motion calling for the expulsion from Fiji of all persons of Indian origin, that is, about half of the country's population. Ethnic Fijian sympathy for the motion was widespread (*PIM,* 1975). Indians felt insecure notwithstanding constitutional guarantees giving them full citizenship. The prejudices of Fijians and Indians are two sides of the same coin; each is frustrated by the other's presence. In this chapter, I discuss the emergence of Fiji's polyethnic structure and the patterns of inter-ethnic relations. In the following presentation, 'Fijian' will refer to indigenous persons who have descended from the original inhabitants of Fiji; 'Indians' will refer to descendants of persons who came to Fiji from India.

A. The ethnic groups in the making of a plural society

Fiji is an archipelago of some 844 islands lying virtually at the center of the South Pacific. Two islands, Viti Levu and Vanua Levu, account for approximately 87 per cent of the total land area of 7,055 square miles. Viti Levu (4,010 square miles) is the larger of the two islands, nearly twice as large as Vanua Levu (2,137 square miles) and generally dominates life in Fiji. It contains 73 per cent of the total population and the most productive economic facilities such as sugar fields, factories, hotels, and commercial houses as well as the capital city, Suva. Indians constitute about 55 per cent of the population on the two islands, while Fijians make up only 38 per cent. The surrounding islands, some 100 of which are permanently inhabited, are populated predominantly by indigenous Fijians who subsist mainly from traditional agriculture, fishing and copra harvesting.

Fiji was colonized on October 10, 1874 when Chief Cakobau ceded the islands to Britain. The Deed of Cession bound Britain to protect the Fijians from European commercial interests and to preserve the Fijian way of life. To halt the steady decline of Fijian customs, Sir Arthur Gordon, the first British governor of Fiji, initiated three policies that laid the cornerstone of communalism. First, all land which was not yet alienated to Europeans, consisting of nearly 90 per cent of the country, was to remain under Fijian ownership. Although temporarily breached by legislative fiat between 1905 and 1911 when free land transactions were once again permitted, this policy curtailed economic development of the islands because growth depended on the availability of Fijian land for commercial exploitation. Land, then, became an issue.

The second policy was the importation of labour to substitute for Fijians. Protection of the Fijian way of life required not only that their land, which was an integral part of the traditional culture, be kept from alienation, but also that the people be free from the labour impositions of European plantations. If this policy was to be pursued, however, then Fiji as a financially self-supporting colony needed an alternative source of labour for the plantations. The colonial government depended heavily upon the profits of plantations for its revenues.

Plantations cannot survive without cheap and abundant labour (Williams, 1964). Denied this source from among the indigenous population, Governor Gordon recommended the importation of Indian coolies from India as had been done successfully in British Guyana, Mauritius and Trinidad. From 1879 when the labour indentureship was inaugurated to 1916 when it was terminated, about 60,537 Indians were introduced into Fiji (Ali, 1973). About one-half returned to India, the rest remaining under a scheme that allowed them to become legal residents 'with privileges no whit inferior to those of any other class of Her Majesty's subjects resident in the colonies' (Gillion, 1977 pp.70-71). The Indian population grew steadily so that by 1945 they outnumbered the Fijians for the first time. From the policy of labour immigration, then, a new community was 'grafted' onto Fiji.

The final policy was the establishment of a separate Native Fijian Administration through which the British governed the Fijians indirectly (Lasaqa, 1984). The Fijian hierarchical political structure was recognized and Fijian chiefs continued to govern their own people (Nayakalou, 1975). While this policy substantially preserved the traditional Fijian culture by virtually establishing a state within a state, it so protected Fijians that they were almost wholly unprepared to compete effectively with the Europeans, Chinese and Indians once their circle of interaction had enlarged beyond the village. The result was the institutionalization of Fijian economic inferiority and the implantation of racist conceptions of inherent Fijian capabilities. Towards the end of the twentieth century, some 40 per cent of the Fijians still subsist mainly from villages. The typical Fijian worker in the monetized modern sector tends to maintain tight material connections with his or her village. The Fijian community continues to own about 83 per cent of the land which is held communally by over 7,000 mataqali groups. Fijians who no longer rely on their villages for their income are employed by the government as policemen, army officers, teachers, nurses, medical officers, office workers, etc. From the government services has sprung a well-to-do Fijian middle class. Fijians regard the government bureaucracy as their pre-eminent domain in much the same way as Indians regard the commercial and sugar sectors (Report, 1967). Fijian penetration of the business sector has been generally unsuccessful even when special programmes have been established to initiate them into the commercial world. The nature of Fijian culture, which is communal, non-competitive and non-profit oriented, has been blamed for the poor performance (Watters, 1969). Fijians own very few businesses which are almost totally in Indian, European and Chinese hands. Because of the tight competition they face in other sectors, Fijians have found it necessary to

11

protect ownership of their land which is their main resource base from which they can bargain politically with other groups in Fiji society.

Most Indian immigrants to Fiji came as indentured labourers. They came from many parts of India, from different language and religious groups and, in general, without their families (B. Lal, 1983). Indians who remained in Fiji leased or bought land on which they planted their own cane. By the end of World War II, they had practically taken over the entire sugar growing business. Today, some 80 per cent of cane farmers are Indians. However, most of the lands are leased from Fijians rendering what would normally be a powerful political base into a tinder box of communal conflict. Sugar is the most significant crop in the economy providing more than half of Fiji's foreign reserves (Fisk, 1970). About 3-6 per cent of the Indians came as free settlers, mainly Gujaratis, who by 1936 numbered about 2,500 (Ali, 1973). They established businesses but were later joined by other Indians who left the sugar fields to start small stores and tradeshops. In contemporary Fiji, most small and intermediate size commercial operations are in Indian hands. The government bureaucracy was soon challenged. In the professions - law, medicine, engineering, etc. - Indian incursion into traditional European areas also became significant (Census, 1966). Hence, at all levels Indians represented an economic threat to the two other major groups. To the Fijians, Indians who were mainly rural dwellers and demanded more land on secure tenure posed a land threat. They were also moving into the Fijian preserve of the public service. The Europeans, with their prestige as the group with a monopoly over expert skills in government and the professions, were challenged by an increasingly educated and trained Indian population (Gillion, 1977). There was, furthermore, a political area where Indians confronted European and Fijian political power, but more will be said of this later. What is important here is that the seeds of ethnic strife were germinating from the contest over resources and power compounded by negative stereotypical perceptions that these groups held of each other.

Many Indians and Fijians have migrated to urban areas such as Suva and Lautoka. As in the rural areas where Indians and Fijians live apart (Fijians live in small concentrated nucleated villages while Indian farming units are dispersed on sprawling leased *matagali* land), in the towns such as Suva similar ethnic residential self-selectivity occurs thereby rendering districts either predominantly Fijian or Indian (Walsh, 1978). Indeed, Census reports revealed that in four-fifths of the enumerated areas on the two main islands, there was a 70 per cent majority of either Indians or Fijians (Ibid.). However, there are several middle income neighbourhoods, especially in Suva, notable for their ethnic mix.

Cultural features also separate the two major communities. While English is the cross-communal language, Indians speak Hindi among themselves while

Fijians speak their indigenous language. The radio stations carry separate programmes in Hindi and Fijian and, until recently, pre-university educational institutions were segregated. Finally, most voluntary social and economic organizations such as sports clubs and trade unions are predominantly uni-ethnic (Mamak, 1978; Rae, 1979). Inter-marriage between Fijians and Indians is practically non-existent.

Europeans, although numerically insignificant, have dominated the direction of the colony. First, the traders and planters stamped a capitalist economy onto Fiji (Legge, 1958; Knapman, 1987). Second, missionaries converted the Fijians to Christianity (Garrett, 1983). Finally, the Europeans, who at first served as instigators of Fijian inter-tribal conflict, won political domination of Fijian society through the Deed of Cession in 1874 (Derrick, 1966). The political imprint was a form of government which, at independence in 1970, was a variant on the Westminster parliamentary model. The overall social impact has been the de facto establishment of English ways as the measure of excellence. The *lingua franca* is English. A strong ethnic dimension has been added to the emerging class system. Privileges and rewards are skewed in favour of those who are English or who have acquired English cultural traits. Consequently, Europeans are generally over-represented as managers, supervisors, professional and skilled workers (Census, 1966). Constituting less than 1 per cent of the population, they command high status and income many times over their proportional share. Today, most non-government European workers are employed in high executive positions in foreign multinational corporations. Many big businesses remain in the hands of Europeans and European-owned companies (Rokotunivuna, 1974). The remaining population categories are the Chinese, Mixed Races and other Pacific Islanders. The Chinese are mainly small businessmen and skilled professional workers. They enjoy a middle socio-economic well-being and are among the most urbanized of Fiji's population. The other Pacific Islanders refer mainly to the Rotumans who belong to the adjacent island, Rotuma, which is part of Fiji's territory, and to Solomon Islanders and other nearby island groups who were originally recruited to serve on European plantations. These Pacific Islanders identify politically with indigenous Fijian interests.

B. Ethnic conflict and social stereotypes

Ethnic conflict is endemic in plural societies. Objective conditions generally provide supportive bases for stereotypical images held of each community. However, these stereotypes serve as crude shorthand summations of diverse traits that simplify and distort reality. While they may also serve as defence mechanisms against other groups, they lend themselves quite easily to manipulations by demagogues who make scapegoats out of these groups (Levine and Campbell, 1972). These basic characteristics of stereotypes provide some insight into the structure of Fijian-Indian relations (Coulter, 1967; Premdas, 1978). Fijians generally regard Indians as frugal, profit-oriented, unscrupulous and aggressive. Substantially, this image is derived from Indian commercial activities, even though only a small minority of Indians own or manage businesses. Most Indians are sugar and rice farmers, many of whom are in debt. The Fijian's economic relationship to the Indian is played out mainly in three areas. First, the Fijian *mataqali* group leases land to Indians for which rent is paid; the Fijian-controlled Native Land Trust Board negotiates the rental price on behalf of a *mataqali* so that room for rental irregularity is minimal. Second, the Fijian may work seasonally as a labourer on the land which his *mataqali* leases to the Indian. Third, and most significantly, the Fijian may use part of the wages earned to buy food, clothes and other articles from Indian stores. More than likely, this latter type of interaction at the market place where private self-interests predominate is the source of the image that Indians are profit-oriented and unscrupulous. In defense, some Indians point out that the Gujaratis, who came as free settlers are predominantly Indian businessmen; the typical Indian who is a descendant of indentured labourers is honest and hardworking and may be as much the victim of unscrupulous entrepreneurs as Fijians. Overall, the behaviour ascribed to Indians has led Fijians to fear that they will eventually be overrun by an 'alien' group in their own native country. Many Fijians believe that Indians are contemptuous of Fijian culture and that alleged Indian disrespect has its roots in cultural arrogance and even feelings of racial superiority.

The Indian stereotype of the Fijian is that he or she is lazy, unambitious, inferior and manipulable. Indian achievements in cash cropping (sugar), commerce and many professions stand in stark contrast to Fijian achievements. Production for subsistence and not for profit is the critical feature of Fijian traditional economy. Most Fijians have not sought to accumulate savings for investment (Spate, 1959; Watters, 1969). Over several decades of sharing the same state, the result of the differential Indian-Fijian approaches to wealth has reverberated in visible disparities in standards of living.

C. Coinciding and conflicting ethnic cleavages

Despite the fact that stereotypical categories put Fiji's communities into almost rigid ethnic compartments, objective evidence points to important internal divisions within each communal segment as well as cross-sectional overlaps that have had significant bearing on inter-communal relations. In Fiji, cleavages between the two dominant groups are erected around six major criteria: (1) race, (2) language, (3) religion, (4) culture, (5) occupation, and (6) residence.

Race, language, religion and culture may be regarded as more enduring givens or primordial differentiators between the two groups, while occupation and residential patterns are secondarily acquired traits (A.D. Smith, 1991; Premdas, 1993b). Gross racial and phenotypical differences serve as the first signals in identifying relationships of ethnic affinity (M.G. Smith, 1993). It is easy at first sight to tell an Indian from a Fijian. Colour is not necessarily a part of the physical differentiators; many Fijians and Indians share the same pigmentation. Religion is a major divider with practically all Fijians adhering to Christianity while Indians overwhelmingly adhere to Hinduism or Islam. Language is also a pervasive separator, for when in their own company, Fijians and Indians speak their own tongue. Cultural practices such as rituals and observances around religion, diet, marriage and family matters separate the two groups literally into worlds apart. Hence, racial, linguistic, religious and cultural cleavages fall one on top of the other in a pattern of parallel and coinciding reinforcements separating Indians from Fijians. To be sure, there are areas of sharing such as education and attire. However, culture in Fiji encapsulates in a meaningful sense the essential differences between the two groups. After over a century of sharing the same country and colonial master, cultural convergence has been minimal. The secondary cleavages such as the occupation and residential patterns are acquisitions from colonial adaptation. Most Indians are rural dwellers who cultivate sugar cane and live in individual homesteads. Most Fijians are also rural residents but they live in nucleated villages and plant food crops primarily. In towns where Fijians and Indians meet, they live in predominantly Indian or Fijian residential neighbourhoods and hold jobs in occupations predominantly staffed by Fijian and Indian personnel (Walsh, 1978). But even here, the occupational and residential structures are not cast in exclusive compartments. Especially in the civil service, Indians and Fijians work side by side. This happens less so in stores and factories. A policy of deliberate cross-communal hiring has, in a number of cases, created a mixture of Indian and Fijian workers. Urbanization and migration patterns point to increasing Indian-Fijian interaction and residential mixing, but not much of this penetrates into the separated cultural systems.

Several cross-cutting cleavages, a few of which are mentioned above, have moderated the effects of the ethnic compartments in Fiji's plural society. In the same areas of primordial segmentation, important instances of cross-cutting experiences co-exist. Specifically, in the language area, most Fijians and Indians speak English which is the language of communication between the two groups. Additionally, a number of Fijians speak Hindi and Indians speak Fijian, although this cross-linguistic competence is not very extensive. In the cultural sphere, all Fiji citizens share common educational facilities and

15

teachers in primary, secondary and tertiary institutions. Separate language schools have only recently been abolished. In the areas of residence and occupation, especially in towns as pointed out earlier, many cross-cutting experiences are enacted daily. In sports, Indians and Fijians play cricket and soccer together (but not Rugby which is almost entirely Fijianized). In many clubs and associations, especially in Suva which contains nearly a fifth of the country's population, Fijians and Indians alike are members. Alexander Mamak traces out in empirical detail the numerous areas where Indians and Fijians share common membership such as unions, clubs, neighbourhood groups, recreational, and professional bodies (Mamak, 1978). To be sure, trade unions are still preponderantly uni-ethnic in Fiji, including the two unions representing Fiji teachers. And most associations remain primarily, but not exclusively, subscribed by one ethnic group.

While major cleavages divide the ethnic groups into cultural compartments, each segment in turn is not monolithically unified. The degree of internal divisions within the Fijian and Indian communities has risen in the last decade. Within the Indian group, there are Muslims and Hindus with the former constituting about 15 per cent of the Indian population. A further division exists between North and South Indians as well as separate sub-identities such as Punjabis, Gujaratis, etc. The politics of this internal differentiation were seen in the support of certain Indian sub-groups in whole or in part for the old Fijian-dominated Alliance Party, as will be discussed below. Traditional Hindu-Moslem antipathy has had political reverberations in Fiji's Indian politics with many Muslims actually joining the Fijian Alliance or sympathizing closely with it. Many Gujarati businessmen were also covert supporters of the old Fijian-dominated Alliance Party. Within the Fijian section, internal regional and linguistic divisions compounded by coinciding economic disparities have split Fijian political solidarity. In part, these divisions have influenced the formation of significant groups such as the Fijian Nationalist Party and the Western United Front. With only one vote in the House of Assembly, the Fijian Nationalist Party voted with the Indian Federation Party in a vote of no confidence to oust the Fijian Alliance from office after the March 1977 elections. The Fijian-dominated Western United Front was a coalition partner of the Indian Federation Party. The Indians in the Alliance and Fijians in the Federation Party, however, were a very slender and shifting minority and did not constitute a powerful enough force to modify Fiji's deeply bifurcated society. The numbers were too marginal to radically restructure the watershed which separated the communities. An overview of the major dimensions of Fiji's ethnic cleavages - coinciding, cross-cutting and internal divisions, shows that the commonly shared forces are not powerful or pervasive enough to mold a national Fiji hybrid man or woman.

16

D. The problem of balance

In subsequent chapters, a number of issue areas will be examined in detail to see how the contest for resources and policy favours is conducted among the ethnic elements in Fiji. We shall see how ethnic identity originated in the colonial order and came to influence the claims to niches of power and privilege, and how, in a circular dynamic of reinforcement, the struggle stimulated and intensified competition and ethnic antagonism, justifying further assertions for a system of distribution sensitive to ethnic fears. Specifically, we look at the perennial problems of political representation - land, and the allocation of employment opportunities in the private and public sectors. To understand how ethnic claims to privileges and power are legitimated, it is crucial to look at the concept of 'balance' in the Fiji polity. Until the military intervention of 1987, the idea of balance prevailed, however imperfectly, as the mode of ethnic conflict regulation in Fiji.

While not a written constitutional law, the idea of balance was embedded in Fiji's multi-ethnic politics by practice, whereby sectoral pre-eminence was distributed as follows: (1) The Fijians controlled the government, in particular, the Prime Minister's office, and they also owned 83 per cent of all the land; (2) the Indians dominated the sugar industry and small and intermediate size business; and (3) the Europeans controlled the very large businesses, such as banks, hotels, factories, etc. This distributive sectoral 'balance' was not a rigid formula for the sharing of power in all its detail. Room existed for one ethnic group to penetrate and participate in another group's domain. For instance, the Alliance Government (1970-87) used subsidies to encourage the entry of Fijians into businesses, while the Prime Minister, a Fijian, deliberately appointed several Indians to his Cabinet. Fijians leased their land to Indians and others. In the end, this limited 'mix' had moderated the sharp edges and virtual monopoly rights of the 'balancing' concept. At various times in the recent history of Fiji, the balance was in danger of being upset, leading to efforts to rectify the disequilibrium. For example, when Indian population growth threatened to overwhelm the demographic balance, the government informally initiated two effective policies to offset it: (1) a vigorous birth control and family planning programme more oriented to the Indian than to the Fijian population, and (2) a policy enabling Indians to emigrate from Fiji, taking their assets with them.

'Balance' assumed asymmetrical areas of dominance and sustained sectoral equality by requiring reciprocity. Such exchanges were, however, not imposed by sentiments of love for another community but were informed by self-interest. Each group needed the resources of the other group to survive and maintain its standard of living. Each group was its brother's keeper in a mundane, practical, self-interested sense. It was no more in the interest of the

Fijians to deny Indians access to land than for Indians not to pay taxes to the Fijian-dominated government. 'Balance' was an evolving act constantly needing nurture by inter-communal consultation and cooperation. It was not a rigid or written agreement but a dynamic concept that required revisions and adaptations to be made in contemplation of changes in society. However, 'balance' could only be a short-term solution for inter-communal conflict and its sustenance revolved around amicable relations among intersectoral elites. The balancing act was bound to face assault sooner or later by chauvinistic outbidders who, at a moment of opportunity, wanted to instigate fellow communal chauvinists not to accept part of the pie but to seize all of it. 'Balance' in such a situation could be displaced by 'hegemony' and all the consequences this entailed, or it could trigger civil conflict that would destroy the society. In the face of rapid social change, 'balance' was not easily applied to new areas of activities. Cross-communal coalitions could emerge to challenge the balancing concept or technological breakthroughs could bestow overwhelming benefits to one ethnic group leaving others behind. In the following chapters, we shall see how the 'balancing' concept evolved and note the difficulties it confronted in the absence of an explicit formula for its application. In discussing 'balance' in relation to representation, land and employment, Indians and Fijians enunciated their own ideas of balance to assert dominance and to prevent encroachment on their claimed territory. In effect, 'balance' was repeatedly evoked to justify an ethnic claim; its meaning, however, was so manipulated that it instead served to legitimate self-interest.

II The Politics of Representation, Land and Jobs

In the making of Fiji's multi-ethnic mosaic, several perennial problems came into play, bedeviling relations between Fijians and Indians. In particular, communal conflict evolved around issues of (1) representation, as the British colonial authorities began to introduce an element of popular participation in collective decision-making; (2) insecurities over the ownership and control of land, a scarce commodity that was critical to the survival of Fijians and Indians alike; and (3) the distribution of public service jobs and budgetary allocations for development projects. In this chapter, these issues are examined showing why they evolved, what constituted their essential features, and how they were resolved in the Independence Constitution of 1970. Underlying the issues was a fierce but subdued contest between Fijians and Indians for the protection of their communal interests. Frequently, this struggle assumed the form of a threat of ethnic domination. Fijians propounded a doctrine of paramountcy to assert and safeguard their interests. Indians sought a system of equality under which they could be allocated what they regarded as an equitable share of the values of the polity and economy. The struggle was often cast in zero-sum terms so that the ethnic strife that was triggered seemed intractable. At various times, an informal concordat of balance in the distribution of communal claims was struck. At other times, inter-communal understandings were challenged and ethnic conflict loomed large and imminent.

A. Representation

(i) Fear of Indian domination and the demand for Fijian political paramountcy

To obtain a firm grasp of this complex issue, it is necessary to go back to the time when the Fiji islands were annexed by Britain in 1874 under the Deed of Cession. Fijians regard the Deed of Cession of 1874 as their Magna Carta, the fundamental document which they perceive as the safeguard of their rights as an indigenous people both from internal threats such as loss of land and external interferences such as further colonization. Most importantly, over the years since 1874, the doctrine of 'Fijian paramountcy' has emerged among Fijians as a proper interpretation of the Deed (Lawson, 1991; Premdas, 1990a). Lacking precision and even literary authentication within the Deed of Cession itself, 'Fijian paramountcy' evolved as a mystique of imagined claims (Hagen, 1987; France, 1969; Durutalo, 1986). However, starting with Governor Gordon and periodically invoked in subsequent parliamentary debates, the imaginings of these claims soon acquired concrete form, developing credibility by being repeatedly invoked. 'Paramountcy' itself is not mentioned in the Deed. It was used first in regard to Fijian demands for protection of their customs and land from European claims. Later, in the twentieth century, with the advent of Indians, it was interpreted to embody a new inter-group political dimension with increasing alarm and stridency. Fijian paramountcy as an anti-Indian counter-claim then came later as a doctrine of theFijian assertion of political pre-eminence. It emerged as a reaction to the perceived threat of Indian domination of Fiji.

The paramountcy of Fijian interests, although not firmly documented, developed life and authority by repeated usage. Adversaries of the paramountcy idea tend to point to its flimsy historical roots with a view to nullifying its contemporary use. What is significant about the paramountcy doctrine is that as a counter-claim, it became valid, as it could be enforced. Clearly, it is a power concept camouflaged as a legal or moral right. It may have been empty and innocuous at first and was beyond implementation until a much later date. It would take the Fijian Armed Forces to give it reality. Power legitimates doctrine in its raw use. The doctrine offered the coat of legitimacy to cover the dark designs of a power grab. However, this is not the entire story but only one side of the argument. It is true to say that even adversaries often begin, directly or indirectly, to accept the legitimacy of an untenable doctrine which they may have previously explicitly debunked by conforming to its demands. It is noteworthy in this regard that the paramountcy claims which, by Fijian convention, became linked to the Deed of Cession found their way by interpretation into the preamble of the 1970 Fiji Constitution. The preamble cited the Deed of Cession as conferring special position to the indigenous Fijians. It was inevitable that, at least to Fijians, this meant that the political paramountcy idea was recognized and accepted by the constitutional Founding Fathers.

The paramountcy doctrine then assumed its political form in a particular context. It contained its own paradoxes and absurdities. While the British governed, paramount rights were conceived as consistent with Fijian political subjugation to European rule. When the Indians came to Fiji and eventually demanded equal representation with Europeans in public decision-making, the assertion of Fijian paramount rights emerged as a counter-claim to the threat of Indian dominance. It has since retained this particularistic ethnicized connotation. It may even be regarded as a contrivance instigated by European interests to contain the expansive political and economic threat posed by the Indians (Meller and Anthony, 1967; Gillion, 1977).

At the outset of British colonial rule in 1874, no concession was made for direct popular participation in collective decision-making. When an element of popular representation was first introduced in Fiji in 1904, the colonial council included six elected Europeans, two nominated Fijians, and ten European official members. In effect, the two nominated Fijians represented an indigenous population of 92,000, while six elected Europeans represented a white population of 2,440. The 22,000 Indians were completely without representation (Ali, 1975). The different ethnic communities did not mingle or mix so that the idea of forging a consensus of popular opinion was effectively discouraged. One scholar depicted this practice of socio-political apartheid as follows: 'For its part, the government pursued no policy to achieve integration or even bring the races into a close relationship. In the compartmentalised world of colonialism, social intercourse between ethnic groups was discouraged' (Ali, 1980 p.178). The exclusion of the Indian sector, however, was only temporary. By 1916 when a new council was introduced, Indians were allocated one nominated representative after agitating for the franchise. The impetus for Indian representation came from recently-arrived Indian immigrants, mainly Gujaratis, who emulated the nationalist struggle of the Indian Congress in India for equal rights. As British subjects, they demanded equal representation with the white section of the population. Indian agitation for equal rights would soon become a persistent practice in the racially-oriented colonial system. It would engender the assertion of political paramountcy by indigenous Fijians for fear of domination by 'an alien, Asiatic race'.

The European settlers reacted against Indian demands arguing that European superior representation was justified on the basis of "their large stake in ... developing the economy of the islands" (Meller and Anthony, 1967 pp.11-12). Up to this point, Indians were highly regarded by Europeans, especially for their labour. Intersectional conflict was primarily between the Europeans who wanted land and labour, and the Fijians who wanted to preserve their way of life. The arrival of Indians forged an informal alliance between Indian labour and European capital against the Fijians. But with the intensification of Indian prospects for equal representation, the old Indian-European intersectional alignment altered, and a new era of European-Fijian collabouration was inaugurated. The Indian immigrant became the common enemy of both the Fijians and the Europeans (Gillion, 1962).

Indian demand for electoral equality was couched in terms of 'common' roll (one man, one vote) as distinct from the 'communal' roll (sectional representation). Because the Fijians were governed under a separate native administration, the Indian demand for a common roll challenged European control of the colonial council and was interpreted as an attempt to introduce Indian political domination of Fiji. The equation of the demand for a common roll with the alleged desire of Indians to politically dominate the entire society has since become a pervasive theme in the communal politics of Fiji. When the Indian population surpassed that of the Fijian in 1946 and became a clear majority in the entire population by 1966, the menace of Indian hegemony became as ominous as it was allegedly real. The growing Indian economic and educational ascendancy compounded the problem and seemed to provide the foundations for an effective takeover. At any rate, these social and demographic facts provided the raw materials for a form of invidious inter-ethnic comparisons.

To the Fijians, their perception of the threat of Indian domination contravened the Deed of Cession, which accorded them supreme authority above all other sectional interests. Fijian 'paramount right' then was seen as threatened only by Indians in their demand for common roll. Accordingly, Fijians shared the European view that common roll would cause a fundamental alteration in the distribution of political power and privileges in Fiji. Indians viewed the alternative to 'common roll' as the continuation of communal representation and the institutionalization of inequality. In 1929, when an enlarged third colonial council was established, Indians were given three seats, but 'almost immediately after taking their seats, they demanded the introduction of common roll' (Meller and Anthony, 1967 p.14). The upshot was that the 'European members strongly attacked the Indian demand for a common roll on the grounds that it would contribute to a "definite and absolute breach of faith and honour to the coloured race (the Fijians) which the British government was supposed to protect and care for"'; (Ibid., p. 28). The voting was 33 to 3 against the common roll. The Indian members promptly resigned their seats. When again in 1933 a new council was composed under the old communal formula, Indian members again demanded common roll and again resigned from the Council. Over the following years, common roll 'in the

22

minds of European and Fijian members (had) become synonymous with an attempt at political domination by Indians, and each proposal had been voted down' (Ibid., p.15) No significant alteration in the mode of representation was made until 1966. Prior to this date in 1963, universal adult suffrage was introduced. It was in 1963 also that Fijians were first allowed to directly elect their representatives from among the Fijian people. Previously, Fijians were nominated to the council. (Burns, 1960). In 1966, a new legislative council in which elected representatives constituted a majority was inaugurated and a ministerial-member system under which elected members were given Cabinet supervisory responsibilities came into effect. The "wind of change" inspired by the post-World War II anti-colonial movements in Africa and Asia had reached the Fiji islands. The wheels of political change were turning rapidly, making their most significant impact in the transfer of the government to local leaders. A full-blown party system came into existence by 1966 consisting of two major parties, the National Federation Party (NFP), supported predominantly by Indians, and the Alliance Party supported mainly by Fijians, Europeans, Chinese and others (Alley, 1973). What did not change under the new political order of 1966 was the communal system of representation as Table 2.1 shows:

Table 2.1
Representation

Communal Group	Population	Seats
Fiji-Indians	272,040 (50.8%)	12 (33.4%)
Fijian and Pacific Islanders	244,364 (45.7%)	12 (38.9%)
Europeans, Chinese Mixed Races	18,822 (3.5%)	10 (27.8%)

The table depicts the inequities of the communal system. The Europeans, Chinese and Mixed Races, for example had only 3.5 per cent of the total population in 1966, but had been allocated 27.8 per cent of all elected seats. For the first time, however, the European section obtained fewer seats than were assigned to Fijians or Indians. Nevertheless, Fijians and Indians remained under-represented. The struggle to correct these inequities and the debate over the relative merits of the common versus the communal system of representation was, after 1966, carried on mainly by the two political parties representing communal interests. Essentially, as self-government approached, the contest for power shifted from the Indian versus European-cum-Fijian configuration to a bipolar Indian versus Fijian confrontation. The British presence would remain salient until independence, but increasingly, the definition of political and constitutional relations devolved to Indian and Fijian party leaders in preparation for independence. The issue of the new emergent local leaders reconciled Indian claims for common roll against the 'paramount' rights of the minority Fijians had to be settled, as did that of land, through the political process of bargaining and compromise (Vasil, 1972).

Although the Fijians initially resisted independence, fearing Indian designs to dominate Fiji, they gradually came to accept it as inevitable. The results of the 1966 elections in particular heartened the Fijians since they gave the Fijian-dominated Alliance Party an overwhelming victory against the predominantly Indian National Federation Party. Observed one scholar: 'The emergence thus of the Alliance as the most important political force in the country lessened the Fijian fear for further constitutional advance. Their constitutional supremacy having been established not only through the 1965 constitutional arrangement but now through the general elections of 1966, reduced their resistance to rapid advance to independence' (Vasil, 1972).

The Alliance Party which represented the non-Indian voter was actually a 'federal' party. It consisted of three groups, namely: (1) the Fijian Association representing the Fijian people; (2) the General Electors Association representing Europeans, Chinese and Mixed Races; and (3) the Indian Alliance, representing a very tiny splinter Indian group. The Alliance was led by Ratu Sir Kamisese Mara, a prominent Fijian Chief. The NFP, on the other hand, was a 'unitary' organization; it grew out of the Indian trade union movement that agitated for better working conditions in the sugar industry. The leader of the NFP was A. D. Patel who died in 1969 and who was succeeded by Siddiq Koya, a Fiji-born Muslim Indian. Independence meant that the country required a new constitution, and this in turn implied that the outstanding issues which separated Fijians and Indians had to be reconciled. Between August 1969 and March 1970, the representatives of the NFP and Alliance met to work out a constitutional solution for Fiji. We shall discuss here the negotiations related to the issues of representation, citizenship, and land.

On the system of representation, the Alliance accepted the common roll as a long term objective and acceded to the NFP demands that (1) A Royal Commission be established sometime between the first and second elections after independence to re-examine the entire issue of common versus communal roll, and (2) common roll elections be held for the municipalities of Suva and Lautoka. In the meantime, a system of communal and cross-communal voting continued. The lower House in the proposed a bicameral Parliament was composed as shown in Table 2.2:

Table 2.2
Communal and National Rolls

Group as % of Population	Communal Roll	National Roll	Total
Fiji-Indians (50.8)	12	10	22(42.3%)
Fijians/Pac.Is (45.7)	12	10	22(42.3%)
Europeans, Chinese, Mixed Races (15.4)	3	5	8(15.4%)
Total	27	25	52

Parity of representation was accorded to the Fijian and to the Indian communities, while the European, part-European and Chinese sectors referred to as 'General Electors', although constituting only 3.5 per cent of the population, continued to be overrepresented with 15.4 per cent of the seats. On paramount rights for Fijians, the NFP conceded that additional 'weightage' should be allocated to Fijian interests. The device through which this was to be implemented was a second chamber, a Senate.(See Table 2.3)

Table 2.3
Representation in the Senate

Fijian Great Council of Chief's nominees	8
Prime Minister's nominees	7
Opposition Leader's nominees	6
Council of Rotuma's nominees	1
Total	22

The power of the Senate resided not only in the representation of superior numbers of Fijians, but in the amending procedure which entrenched Fijian land and custom. It did this by requiring a two-thirds majority in each chamber in order to alter the constitution. Here, it must be noted that the Fijian Great Council of Chiefs had 8 out of 22 seats, that is, more than a third of the seats, and was thus capable of blocking any constitutional change without its consent. Summing up the impact of these special provisions conceded to Fijian paramount rights, one observer noted that 'none of the continuing imbalances in Fiji's parliamentary representation can be rectified without the concurrence of the traditional Fijian leadership' (Grocott, 1976 p.20).

On the issue of citizenship, the Indian negotiators successfully won acceptance of full Indian citizenship. It was agreed that all citizens be called Fijians. To underscore that this citizenship implied equality and freedom from discrimination, a Bill of Rights was agreed upon to prohibit discrimination on 'grounds of race, place of origin, political opinions, colour or creed.' This was a rather curious provision in light of the 'paramountcy' doctrine. In exchange, certain concessions were demanded by the Fijian negotiators with regard to independence and the Deed of Cession. Specifically, it was agreed that (1) after independence, Fiji would retain dominion status within the Commonwealth; and (2) there be a definite reference to the Deed of Cession in the constitution so that 'if there was a threat to their position through constitutional changes, they [the Fijians] would invoke the Deed' (Norton, 1978 p.103).

(ii) The safeguarding of Fijian land

The land issue is perhaps the most significant triggering point of Fijian-Indian inter-group conflict. Fijians own most of the country's land under a system of traditional communal tenure that prohibits private individual alienation to non-Fijians. They equate ownership of land with their heritage and identity. In a modern cash economy dominated by Europeans and Indians, land constitutes the Fijians' most powerful pillar of political bargaining. Being mainly farmers, Indians view land as the indispensable means for their survival. Since they own very little of it, however, they require predictable access to land use since alternative avenues of employment are very limited. The struggle, then, between Fijian owners and Indian lessees is cast in terms of vital needs over a very limited resource generating unusual emotional intensity around the issue (Premdas, 1991c; Esman, 1977; Norlinger, 1972).

Fiji has about 4,505,000 acres of land. At the time of Cession, the Europeans had claimed about 1,000,000 acres. A land commission subsequently recognized as legal only 415,000 acres. Nevertheless, these tracts represent the best agricultural land in Fiji. Since 1874, apart from a brief period between 1905 and 1911 when an additional 100,000 acres of Fijian land were alienated, land policy has remained very tight (Lloyd,1982). Essentially, the government intervened to terminate all private sales in an effort to preserve the Fijian way of life. Land ownership in Fiji is distributed as shown in Table 2.4 (Spate, 1959).

The freezing of the tenure pattern has bequeathed a legacy of wide disparities in land ownership among the communities. Fijians, constituting about 48 per cent of the population, retain ownership over 83.8 per cent; less than 10 per cent of this is cultivable. Europeans, constituting about 3 per cent of the population, own in freehold 5.5 per cent of prime commercial land. Indians,

26

forming about 48 per cent of the population, own 1.7 per cent. The overwhelming majority of Indians are tenants and sub-tenants who depend on Fijians for leased land. About 62 per cent of the leases issued by Fijians are held by Indians. Indians utilize the land mainly for sugar farming; about 80 per cent of the sugar farmers are Indians who continue to demand more land preferably on 99-year leases. Interestingly, up to Word War I, Europeans were the most insistent on the release of more land for commercial development causing antagonistic relations with Fijians (Narayan, 1984). Thereafter, with the termination of the Indian indentureship system and the adoption of Fiji as their home, the pressure for more land came from Indians. This latter fact has launched Fijians and Indians on a collision course that continues to the present.

Table 2.4
Land Ownership

	Estimated Acres	% of Total
Fijian communal land	3,714,990	82.16
Rotuman communal land	11,000	24
Freehold	368,000	8.15
Crown lands combined	377,420	9.45

Fijian fear of losing their land as well as their desire to retain land unencumbered by long leases for future use led to the enactment of the controversial Land Reserves Policy in 1940. Called the Native Land Trust Ordinance, this legislation established the Native Land Trust Board (NLTB) to administer the leasing of Fijian land and to terminate leases where necessary so as to create 'reserves' for future Fijian use. The architect of this legislation, Ratu Sir Lala Sukuna, viewed the reserves policy as the embodiment of Fijian vital interests. Indians did not share Ratu Sukuna's views of the NLTB and especially the land reserves policy. The selection of land for reserves has yet to come to a completion. For over four and a half decades, year after year, land leased to Indian families who had no alternative source of income was taken out of cultivation and placed in reserves. Bitter Indian reaction stemmed form three consequences of the reserves policy. First, many farms which went into reserves were not cultivated; they soon reverted to bush (Unispac, 1969). The Indian family who suddenly became landless was forced into a large pool of farm labourers available for hire. Second, because the length of leases under the new NLTB regulations was erratic with no guarantee of renewal, the insecurity of tenure provided little incentive for the Indian farmers to develop a care for the land. Third, as more land was placed in reserve, the country lost revenues from taxes, fewer people were employed, and more persons moved into already overcrowded urban areas in search of jobs.

Fijians defend the land reserves policy, pointing out that the availability of land may provide the incentive for them to cultivate the soil commercially. Because of long leases, many Fijians may not have the opportunity to use their land during their lifetime. Further, they argue that the overwhelming majority of leases are renewed so that the commotion and criticisms over non-renewal are exaggerated and unfair (NLTB, 1977). Indians are not happy, especially with the first of these rebuttals, because Fijians already have more than an adequate supply of land, much of which is not cultivated. Consequently, the reserves policy is seen by many Indians as an expression of the Fijian jealousy of growing Indian prosperity and fear that, in the long run, Indian economic power may be translated into political power.

Caught between the expansive needs of Indians for long-term secure leases and Fijian demands for more reserves, the British colonial administrators oversaw the passage of the Agricultural Landlord and Tenants Ordinance (ALTO), which required the NLTB to offer tenants an initial lease for 10 years, plus two further 10-year periods if the land was not needed by Fijians. This legislation was a balancing compromise that temporarily stabilized Indian-Fijian relations over land. Fijian interests in land were safeguarded in the 1970 independence constitution which validated all Fijian claims to 83 per cent of the country's land and entrenched Fijian land rights by requiring two-thirds of the Great Council of Chiefs in the Senate to alter the land-related aspects of the constitution. Indian access to land was further strengthened in 1976 by an amendment to ALTO (1966) giving leases for an initial period of 20 years instead of 10 years, conceivably to be followed by further extensions. The deterioration of Fijian-Indian relations following the military intervention in 1987 has thrown the renewal of these leases in the mid-1990's into an incendiary zone of uncertainty.

(iii) Competition for jobs in the public services

Employment, especially in the public sector, has emerged as a vicious arena in which competitive claims for ethnic shares have attained a special intensity. While the two areas, representation and land, were bound by colonial precedent and yielded to formal compromises, jobs from the modern commercial sector and from the public bureaucracy (both spheres expanding significantly in the post World War II period) were left wide open for competition by the ethnic communities. In the absence of an explicit formula, each group staked its own claims guided by its own interests. Later, the idea of balance would serve to legitimize Fijian pre-eminence in reciprocal exchanges in other sectors with Indians. More than any other area, the public service emerged as the arena in which ethnic competition over resources assumed tangible force (Despres, 1975).

Civil service, the professions and private business represent the modern monetary sectors in Fiji. It was from jobs in these activities that stable and high incomes were earned and access to modern urban-type services was acquired. The quest for these positions by Fijians and Indians, acculturated to European ways and trained in skills, conferred dignity and status not only to the individual incumbents of these positions but also on the respective communities. Hence, symbolic gratification as significant as the monetary rewards was attached to them. Employment opportunities in the modern non-agricultural public and private sectors were, however, limited. It was in this crucible of scarcity for a very highly prized value that government policy played a pivotal part in determining the distribution of benefits.

Public service, including the education service, has become the largest single source of employment in Fiji. Until independence, the highest posts were occupied by European personnel. To gain access, the non-white population needed European education and training. English language schools, however, were not set up until 1916: 'Prior to 1916, the government took little interest in Fijian and Indian education. In those days, the two state-aided public schools were restricted to children of European descent' (Mamak, 1978 p.86). Under the Education Ordinances of 1916, the colonial regime initiated policies to assist the development of schools for Fijians and Indians. These schools were segregated into exclusive Fijian, Indian and European institutions. Separate facilities were, however, not equal. European schools were better equipped and staffed while 'the facilities and opportunities provided for education of children of other races ... contrasted greatly' (Narayan, 1984 p.73). To attain a reasonably high standard, Indian and Fijian schools depended on their own resources. Because of their lack of land and insecure leases, Indians spent heavily on upgrading their schools. To them, education was the only alternative to land scarcity; it held the promise of employment in the emerging modern public and private sectors. Indian expenditures in education were reflected after World war II in the steady incremental displacement of many Europeans in position that required skills. Fijian educational achievement was retarded by comparison. A government inquiry assigned the reasons to 'the geographical scatter of the Fijians, the isolation of the rural Fijian teacher from much intellectual stimulus, the shortage of Fijian primary school teachers, rural poverty, social distraction and other less tangible and psychological factors...' (B. Lal, 1986 p.18). Fijian education, however, did grow, even if at a slower rate than the Indian pace, and many Fijians would qualify to compete with Indians for positions, especially in the government bureaucracy.

By Independence in 1970, large numbers of Indians and Fijians were attending elementary and secondary schools, but Indians predominated as Table 2.5 shows. Fijian students also suffered a greater rate of attrition as they moved to high grades in school; this was bound to adversely reflect in their effort to obtain post-secondary qualifications essential for high paying and senior echelon ranks.

Table 2.5
Examination Pass Rate by Ethnicity

	Fijians	Indians	Europeans	Others
Primary schools				
1958	1,251	29,778	2,867	5,384
1968	5,404	8,581	2,945	3,982
Secondary schools				
1958	642	1,751	324	862
1968	3,356	7,268	511	860

Table 2.6
Examination Pass Rate by Ethnicity (per cent)

	Fijians	Indians	Others
Secondary School Entrance Examination, 1967	39.7	61.9	67.2
Cambridge School Certificate Examination, 1967	44.8	65.4	67.2
New Zealand University Entrance Examination	25.0	30.0	44.7

Table 2.7
Numbers Qualified in Selected Professions, 1958

	Fijians	Europeans	Indians	Others	Total
Lawyers	--	17	38	1	56
Doctors	1	51	12	2	66
Dentists	1	6	8	--	15
Total	2	74	58	3	137

It was almost inevitable, then, given the trend in Indian education, that most university positions would go to Indians. In 1968, out of 643 graduates with university degrees, 464 were Indians, 77 Fijians, 63 Chinese and 33 others (See Table 2.6; See also Vasil 1984 p.195). Indian employment in the professions underlined an emergent preponderance especially after many European expatriates left after independence (Table 2.7).

As the state undertook an increasing number of development projects and more services were extended to citizens, the public bureaucracy expanded. In a scheme where merit determined appointments, the public service was swamped by educated Indian personnel. But the concept of balance entered into the picture. After independence, a Fijian-dominated government offset Indian preponderance in the private business sector by higher Fijian employment in the public bureaucracy. Examining the evidence, Professor R. S. Milne concluded:

The current level of Fijian recruitment, therefore, is based not primarily on qualifications but rather on a policy of 'racial balance' which in practice results in recruiting slightly more Fijians (Milne, 1982 p.143).

Table 2.8
Civil Service Personnel by Ethnicity, 1974

Fijians	5,414
Europeans	440
Indians	4,716
Oters	490

Table 2.9
The Police Force Personnel by Ethnicity, 1974

Fijians	628
Europeans	5
Indians	448
Others	55

In Tables 2.8 and 2.9, it can be seen that soon after independence was attained Fijians outnumbered Indians in the civil service as well as in the police force by a small margin.

In the armed forces, lopsided Fijian representation evoked vehement protests against the government which was charged with obliquely guaranteeing Fijian

31

paramountcy by the threat of an ethnic army (Table 2.10). Fijian leaders countered that Indians did not prefer the military for a career (Enloe, 1980).

Table 2.10
Fijian Armed Forces

	Fijian	Indian	Others	Total
Regular Force	372	5	19	396
Territorial Force	502	29	32	563
Naval Squadron	59	2	10	71
Total	933	36	61	1,030

During 1975, in the Ministry of Fijian Affairs and Rural Development, there were 51 Fijians, 4 Indians, and 1 other; and in the Ministry of Fijian Affairs, there were 35 Fijians only (Ali, 1980). In the 1980s, Fijian dominance of the public service had become very lopsided especially at the senior echelon levels. This compelled the Indian Opposition Leader to accuse the government of implementing a policy designed to ensure that all strategic levels of government were staffed by Fijians who were placed in positions of command (Premdas, 1990a). Reddy contended that 'there was little multiracialism at work' and that this was 'reflected in all aspects of governmental work and activities, from its composition, its development strategies, appointments to boards, promotions in the Civil Service, its Crown lands policy, everywhere' (Ibid., p. 10). For Fijians, however, public service employment was the primary access route to middle class well-being and status. Fijians argued that their disproportional numbers were balanced by Indian preponderance in the private sector. Fijians made up only about 2 per cent of the entrepreneurs in the country. Europeans controlled the largest businesses while Indians predominated in middle-sized enterprises. Many attempts were made to remedy Fijian under-representation in business by a government policy of affirmative action such as existed in its Business Organization and Management Unit (BOMAS) which trained Fijians in business practices, and also through extending interest-free loans from the Fiji Development Bank. Other programs of official 'positive discrimination' have been pursued to promote 'Fijians in Business' (Milne, 1982 p.144). Prior to the military intervention in 1987, the former Alliance government acted in other major areas to aid Fijians. Foreign aid for capital projects was directed mostly to Fijian regions or to activities benefitting mainly Fijians. Examples include the pine wood industry and its predominantly Fijian-staffed Pine Commission, the tuna fisheries project, and the sugar cane Seaquaqua scheme in Vanua Levu.

B. Constitutional understandings and 'balance'

Along with the written compromises, the 1970 constitution contained two far-reaching extra-constitutional features:
(i) A societal-wide power and resources distribution formula encapsulated in the word "balance"; and (ii) Comity agreements. Without these informal understandings, the written agreements in the constitution could not be smoothly implemented.

(i) Balance

In chapter one, the concept of 'balance' was introduced pointing to the existence of an informal mechanism for ethnic conflict regulation and resolution. As pointed out, the idea of 'balance' essentially embodied an asymmetrical system of sectoral sharing. A graphic summary of the exchanges that occurred in the spheres of representation, citizenship, and land is sketched in Table 2.11.

Table 2.11
Trade Offs

Representation:
Fijian gains/losses:
(a) Gain of concession of a Royal Commission to examine the electoral system at a further date;
(b) Gain in relation to the communal system of representation by which they were relatively over-represented vis-a-vis Indians;
(c) Gain by Senate provisions that entrenched protections against Fijian land and customary interests.
Indian gains/losses:
(a) Gain in provision of Royal Commission to examine the electoral system;
(b) Loss of equality in conceding communal representation.

Citizenship:
Fijian gains/losses:
(a) Gain: Fiji's presence in the Commonwealth;
(b) Gain: insertion of Deed of Cession in constitution.
Indian gains/losses :
(a) Gain: full citizenship.
(b) Gain: Bill of Rights barring discrimination; protecting of equality.

continued ...

Land

Fijian gains/losses:
(a) Gain: recognition of their ownership of 83 per cent of Fiji's land.
(b) Gain: entrenched Senate provisions against loss of land.
Indian gains/losses:
(a) Gain: longer tenure of land lease.
(b) Loss of long-term guarantee of land for lease.

It bears repeating that as a conflict resolution mechanism, 'balance' was an informal, unwritten understanding. It implied exchanges and territorial demarcations. It was fundamentally an unstable formula that depended on 'comity', to which we now turn briefly.

(ii) Comity

While constitutional agreements provided the broad structural bases for cooperation in Fiji, some other factor was necessary to link the leadership of the two parties so that they could consult each other and collaborate informally in running the government. Stated differently, constitutional agreements without the benefit of informal friendly ties between communal elites, built upon mutual recognition of each side's problems, could easily collapse into acrimonious interpretations of the constitutional document. We use the term 'comity agreements' to refer to the varieties of informal devices by which communal leaders work out a *modus vivendi* to accommodate each sections' interests. 'Comity agreements' are the mortar which provides the effective linkages, prescribed constitutionally, between the segments of a plural society. Without 'comity agreements', a constitution could become a source of conflict and continuous communal animosity.

The term 'consociational democracy' was used by Arend Lijphart to refer to the condition under which elites in a plural society collaborate to manage a democratic polity (Lijphart, 1985). We do not use the phrase 'consociational democracy' because government by 'elite cartel' rarely is democratic (Barry, 1991; Premdas,1986b). A great deal of privacy is required by elites to hammer out differences and forge new compromises to meet changing conditions. Often if the masses are consulted or constantly kept informed of negotiations in progress, outbidders and ethnic chauvinists may seek to inflame ethnic passions over particular items being negotiated, thereby sabotaging inter-communal peace. Law and order is of sufficient value to the stability of plural societies that democracy may have to be sacrificed. Plural societies often have to choose between an undemocratic peace and a turbulent consultative democracy.

In Fiji, the leadership of the NFP and the Alliance party in the persons of

34

Mr. Koya and Ratu Mara respectively worked out comity agreements by which they consulted each other privately about running the Fiji government. In an important article on the subject, Professor R. S. Milne pointed to the prerequisites which were necessary for such a collaborative relationship (Milne, 1975). At least two of these factors need to be isolated out here. First was the realization, based on experience, that communal conflict was intolerable. In 1968 such an event occurred when Fijians and Indians were on the brink of inter-communal civil war over the results of a by-election. Reminiscing about that event, Ratu Mara said 'those [were] the days when we sailed close to the rocks... we came so near to the edge of the abyss that we could see with unmistakable clearness the dangers that lay there if we did not change course' (Ibid.). The sentiments were evidently shared by Koya and his associates who proceeded to initiate moves conducive to inter-ethnic peace. The hovering omnipresence of civil war provided the ever-constant reminder that the price of inter-elite conflict may be the destruction of the society itself.

The second factor concerns 'personality'. Both Koya and Mara were practical politicians with congenial personalities. Before Koya acceded to the NFP leadership, A.D. Patel who led and directed the Indian community's relationship with the Fijian section used varieties of tough uncompromising confrontation methods to bargain for his demands. A.D. Patel had the reputation as a charismatic, intense, forthright, and uncompromising political leader. He led the NFP delegation which negotiated with the Alliance in the early rounds of constitutional talks in 1969. Then Patel died in October 1969 while the negotiations were stalemated. When Koya ascended to the NFP leadership, the stalemate over such issues as independence and common roll was dramatically broken almost immediately. Many observers noting the overwhelming role individual personalities play in developing countries in determining the direction of a community, attribute, rightly in this opinion, the change in NFP-Alliance relationships generally to the compatible personalities of Ratu Mara and Siddiq Koya.

For over five years, Mara and Koya consulted each other and cooperated in running Fiji, bringing a remarkable amount of basic peace to the plural society. The leaders' rapproachment evidently spilled over to lower levels of the NFP and Alliance leadership echelons. The image projected was that varieties of comity agreements, although personalized, had served not only as a buffer between the raw nerves of the Indian and Fijian communities, but as a positive device that led to many constructive individual inter-communal events. Above all, inter-communal elite harmony precluded any thought of military intervention.

But, as pointed out earlier, a comity arrangement faces dual danger from outbidders and criticisms alleging conspiracy between elites. In late 1975, Siddiq Koya and Ratu Mara faced intense pressures from these two danger

35

points. Mara was challenged by Sakiasi Butadroka who claimed that the Alliance party presided over a government that was inimical to indigenous Fijian interests and promoted continued Indian economic progress in Fiji. Similarly, Koya faced a challenge from R. Patel, brother of A. D. Patel. R. Patel quit the NFP, abandoned his position as Speaker of the House, resigned from parliament, and encouraged moves to start a new party which would challenge Koya. While Butadroka received a resounding vote of disapproval in the Parliament for his anti-Indian motion and R. Patel was defeated in a by-election in Ba against a NFP candidate, the criticisms made by these challengers exemplify the dangers which continuously bedevil a plural society even where constitutional and comity agreements serve to integrate the polity. Towards the end of 1975 and early 1976, it appeared that the criticisms by outbidders against Koya had started to have the effects desired. To answer the charge that he had sold out, the Opposition Leader, Koya, began an open attack on Mara and his Fijian colleagues for allegedly encouraging Butadroka who sought mass expulsion of Indians from Fiji. Ratu Mara's public reply was a call for evidence that Koya's charges were correct. Throughout the exchanges it became clear that both leaders were under pressure to show that they had not 'sold out' to the other side. Regardless of whether the comity agreements persisted or not, the point remained that the informal working relationships between communal leaders were required to complement constitutional agreements in preventing centrifugal forces from splitting the society asunder.

III Erosion of the Balance and an Attempt at a Government of National Unity

The 1970 constitution represented a settlement in compromise of claims and counter-claims by the main communal interests in Fiji's society. Following the compromises, there was a remarkable period of friendly relations between the Fijian and Indian party leadership. The 1972 elections were conducted in a fairly amicable atmosphere and there was much talk of the Alliance and Federation parties forming a coalition government in the immediate post-constitutional period. Professor Milne described the ambiance of this cordial phase of Fiji's political history thus:

> The most obvious change concerned the possibility of a coalition. The moves for a coalition came to nothing, but relations between the leaders of the two parties were good in the early 1970's lasting even beyond the 1972 elections. A Legislative Council member who had left the Alliance observed that the country had a 'coalition government' in all but name (Milne, 1982 p.143).

The honeymoon that followed the making of the 1970 constitution and the elections in 1972 which confirmed the Alliance and Fijian political authority did not last long. Soon a basic challenge to the entire constitutional process emerged and while it was deftly, if only temporarily suppressed, it would lay the foundation for a more powerful movement for a revision, and even a rejection of the entire inter-ethnic accord written in the constitution. This came from the Fijian section of the population in the form of a newly-organized Fijian Nationalist Party led by Sakiasi Butadroka. The Butadroka challenge took aim at all of the major concessions constitutionally given to the Indian section, challenging even the continued presence of Indians in Fiji. Equally significant, it caused the Alliance's moderate multi-racial posture to change.

37

The Butadroka challenge would be followed by three critical events in the remaining part of the decade which saw the growth of new strains between the Alliance and Federation parties, throwing the entire set of understandings of the 1970 constitution into turmoil.

The first event came as part of the outbidding process with which the Butadroka Nationalists confronted the Alliance Party. In a similar manner, a faction within the Indian community decided to challenge Koya's leadership of the Federation Party, charging that he had sold out Indian interests at the 1970 constitutional talks. Hence, both Mara and Koya, moderate leaders within their own respective ethnic communities, were confronted by extremist outbidders whose actions pushed them to adopt extreme positions themselves to counter the challenge. When this happened, there was bound to be a resurgence of inter-communal malaise which deteriorated into outright Fijian-Indian animosity.

The second event occurred as a consequence of the March-April 1977 general elections when the Alliance lost to the Federation Party. Had the Indian-based Federation Party assumed power, it would have broken the expectations of continued Fijian political paramountcy and, in all probability, would have triggered military intervention, nearly a decade before it actually happened in 1987.

The final event pertained to the Royal Commission Report that reviewed the electoral system submitted in 1975. It was unceremoniously and unilaterally rejected by the Alliance government thereby foreclosing Indian demands for an electoral system based on 'one man, one vote'. We shall examine these events briefly to show how they contributed towards the undermining of the constitutional and especially the extra-constitutional compromises and expectations that were beaten out during the 1970 London constitutional talks. The Butadroka incident temporarily destabilized the inter-communal *modus vivendi* that the idea of balance had successfully implemented. Recognizing the grave dangers that inhered in open ethnic confrontation, the Fijian and Indian leaders entered into a discussion over a government of national unity This is covered in the second part of the chapter.

A. Butadroka and the Fijian Nationalist Party

On October 9, 1975, Mr. Sakiasi Butadroka, a member of the Fiji House of Representatives, introduced a motion in Parliament calling for the expulsion of Fiji's Indians, who constituted nearly half of the country's total population. The motion read:

That this House agrees that the time has arrived when Indians or people

38

of Indian origin in this country be repatriated back to India and that their travelling expenses back home and compensation for their properties in the country be met by the British Government (Premdas, 1980b p.1).

The motion was debated for an entire month as speaker after speaker arose to condemn it, praising at the same time the contribution of the Indians to Fiji's development. While Butadroka was isolated in Parliament, the debate, reported in sensational detail in both the press and radio, sent massive voltages of fear throughout the Indian community. Their very existence was threatened for they knew that indigenous Fijian sympathy with the motion was widespread. The Indian community felt that the issue of their permanent residence and full citizenship had been resolved at the London Constitutional Conference in 1970. The Fiji constitution does accord citizenship to Indians born in Fiji, but Mr. Butadroka questioned the legitimacy of this right, saying in Parliament:

The agreement (1970 Constitution) was made without direct consultation with the Fijian chiefs and people. We, the Fijians, who have been taught by the British Government during the 97 years of colonial rule, have almost been made a 'yes-man' type of our leaders (Ibid., p.2).

Continued Mr. Butadroka:

When independence came in 1970, the Fijians thought that the Indians would return ... as Gandhi and Nehru did in India with 'India is for the Indians'. But this was not the case in Fiji because the Fijian leader who (led) the constitutional talks was only thinking of his name and honour and sold the Fijian interests at the wholesale rate (Ibid., p.3).

The motto 'Fiji for Fijians' became the fundamental platform in Butadroka's new party, the Fijian Nationalist Party (FNP). In polyethnic states, moderate party leaders who attempt to maintain communal harmony by making concessions and compromises between inter-communal interests are always threatened by 'outbidders' such as Butadroka who seek to assert chauvinist claims to the entire national pie. A 'sell out' of communal interests is frequently made by extreme chauvinists. However, the success of an outbidder partly derives not only from the multi-ethnic unintegrated structure of communal societies, but from the existence of certain legitimate complaints. Often these complaints are part and parcel of a wider systemic crisis in the society (Gurr, 1970; Johnson, 1967). Disparities in living standards between the communities in Fiji constitute the objective basis of Fijian discontent. Generally, Fijians remain as preponderantly rural dwellers. Village life is subsistence-based and in this regard, the Fijian lives free from want. However, the contrast in facilities between rural and urban centers provides the fuel for higher expectations amoung rural dwellers. Large numbers of Fijians visit the urban areas for brief periods where they sample and participate in the 'good life'. Schools are available and better equipped; public mass transportation is reliable and inexpensive; entertainment and distraction plentiful, etc. The Fijian also experiences or witnesses better housing conditions, water supplies, and electricity in urban areas. In turn, the relatively deprived nature of rural facilities is reflected in lower educational performances and inferior qualifications for jobs. The rural Fijian is caught in a vicious circle of self-perpetuating poverty (Barr, 1990). He attributes the better facilities and conditions of life in the urban areas to greater government attention and budgetary expenditures for urban dwellers. Indeed, rural development is comparatively neglected. The rural Indian is in a different position from the rural Fijian. Most rural Indians are cane farmers who are highly motivated to improve their economic well-being (Mayer, 1963, 1973). Rural Fijians engage in some cash-cropping, but, by and large, they are less inclined to undertake economic production for the sake of profit. In the end, the rural Fijian with a highly urban-stimulated expectation level lacks the economic means to satisfy at least some of those needs. By contrast, the typical Indian family, more disciplined by insecurity, has more cash to save and spend. Over the years, these differences in work habits accumulate so that one communal section conspicuously appears materially better off than the other. This can easily breed jealously and discontent. The existence of a significant stratum of impoverished Indians as well as a sizeable group of well to do Fijians rarely attracts attention in the broader sweep of generalizing on the comparative economic wellbeing of Fijians and Indians.

Events between 1972 and 1975 in Fiji exacerbated the economic disadvantages of Fijians. Triggered by a world-wide recession and later re-enforced by the fuel crises, Fiji succumbed to a pattern of recession, inflation, unprecedented unemployment, industrial disputes, and falling revenues from decreased tourism. Unemployment had been steadily rising since 1966 and it stood by mid-1973 at 6.3 per cent; by mid-1975 it was estimated at 7.1 per cent. Inflation was the dominant feature of economic activity in the early 1970s, generating a major source of friction and personal hardship. By the end of 1972, inflation was running at a two-figure rate. The annual increase in cost of living rose to 14.4 per cent in 1974 (Ibid., p. 7). The tourist industry, which grew stupendously in the late 1960s and the first years of the 1970s to rival sugar as the main source of foreign exchange, suffered significant decreases in tourist visitors over the next ten years. In the late 1960s, tourism increased at a phenomenal annual rate of 20 per cent, but in 1974 the rate of increase fell to - 2.8 per cent. The decrease in tourist visitors depressed the building and construction industry and led to the loss of jobs in hotels, motels and allied activities. Thus, when mention is made of the objective factors which provided the background for widespread discontent among Fijians, two sets of data must be considered. First, the prevailing disparity in living standards between Fijians and others; and second, the exacerbation of these disparities by the economic crisis in the early 1970s. Since 1976, the Fijian economy had very slowly begun to recover, but not discernibly fast enough to give hope and optimism to the Fijian masses about their economic betterment. The objective bases of Fijian alienation did not, by themselves, provide the sufficient foundations for a protest or a revolutionary moment (Gurr, 1970). Leadership was vital. The ingredient was provided by Sakiasi Butadroka, the ex-Alliance parliamentarian who launched the FNP in 1974. It is easy to depict Butadroka as an ambitious and frustrated man who sought to manipulate Fijian discontent for his own narrow ends. The facts are very illustrative. Butadroka was expelled from the Alliance Party and his business as an independent bus operator failed. Both his political and business careers appeared to be at an end. Hence, given his desire for prominence, but aware of the bleak future ahead, he indulged in appeals to the base communalist sentiments and fears among a segment of the Fijian people, pretending to promote their interests while in fact merely promoting his own.

This hypothesis is quite credible, but does not provide an explanation for the most important point - that without an objective base of discontent among Fijians, Butadroka's movement would never have gotten off the ground. The Alliance government quickly suppressed the Butadroka nationalists who in turn decided to take their case to the Fijian Governor-General. We shall look briefly at the charges and complaints contained in the submission to the Governor-General, which would be re-invoked in May 1987 to provide much of the case for Fiji's first military coup. In fact, it can be argued that the submission contained most of the fundamental motifs of all subsequent Fijian ethno-nationalist charges against other communities in Fiji. In its submission to the Governor-General, the FNP claimed that it was an independence movement. It regarded both the Deed of Cession and the Independence Constitution as documents designed to serve foreign interests. On the Deed of Cession, the Submission argued:

In the trichotomy that existed during the colonial period, the Indians played the economic go-between role to the benefit of the white settlers and to the detriment of the native Fijians. The Indians were the catalyst for the transformation of traditional Fiji into a semi-European styled one. The westernization of Fiji was primarily for economic purposes only (Premdas, 1980b p.32).

41

The FNP's assault on the Deed of Cession, a document most Fijians regard as sacred, was revolutionary in significance. For the first time, the political economy of British colonization in Fiji was seriously interrogated by an indigenous group. The FNP's submission referred to the economic transformation of Fiji under colonial rule as motivated not by Fijian interests, but by imperial economic changes, as 'development' put in inverted commas, and to the British colonial presence as 'occupation'. In effect, the British promise to protect the Fijian way of life and to preserve the rights as written in the Deed of Cession amounted to an ideological smokescreen intended to camouflage the true purpose of the British 'occupation', namely economic exploitation.

What the FNP ideologists were attempting to do was to provide a theoretical justification to effectively underpin the idea of Fijian paramountcy. Specifically, the FNP attacked the concepts of 'democracy' and 'equality' as western values which had been 'the major obstacle in the true independence of Fiji. Citizen rights, equality and the inclusion of the Bill of Human rights were the cause of the draw-backs. 'The Bill of Human Rights...is an exposition by the Western powers' (Ibid., p.9). It saw inconsistency between the promise of 'paramountcy' on one hand and 'equality' and 'democracy' on the other. Indeed, the FNP posit that the latter negated the former. Underlying the condemnation of the principles of equality and democracy was the interpretation of the Deed of Cession to mean Fijian dominance in all areas of life. In their own country, they and only they should by the masters. Hence, when they turned their attention to the London Constitutional Conference of 1970, they critically revised the established view that the constitution and the Deed of Cession guaranteed the pre-eminence of Fijian rights. They found the independence document very wanting and totally in contradiction to Fijian primacy over all other communities. Two examples would serve to illustrate these points. On the question of representation, the FNP observed that under the constitution, the House of Representatives had 30 non-Fijians to 22 Fijians. Butadroka elaborated on this point in his election campaign radio broadcast:

It is quite obvious today that the Fijians are lagging behind in all spheres of life. Under the Colonial Government, Britain had promised that the Right of the Fijian people would always be protected and would always be foremost at all times. But when Britain withdrew in 1970 it gave the Fijians only 22 seats in the House of Representatives and 30 were given to other races - 22 to the Indians and 8 for the Europeans (Ibid., p.34).

He concluded that 'the Fijians have no power in the present parliament in Fiji today, and it is the foreigners that actually rule' (Ibid.).

On the issue regarding citizenship and equality, the FNP condemned the

1970 constitution for extending a Bill of Rights and citizenship to Indians and Europeans and argued that 'it cannot accept the equality of other races' (Ibid., p.36). The FNP, therefore, viewed the London Independence conference as an attempt by 'foreigners', acting in collaboration with certain Alliance Fijian chiefs such as Ratu Mara, to institute a form of government which preserved domination of foreign interests and races in Fiji. The FNP challenged the legitimacy of the 1970 constitution and demanded that a new constitutional conference be called to establish 'a fully-Fijian Parliament' (Ibid., p.34).

B. The March-April 1977 general elections

Since general elections were introduced in 1966, the Fijian-based Alliance Party had won consistently over its adversary, the Indian-based National Federation Party. Upon winning the 1972 elections, the Alliance had scored three convincing victories leading observers to predict that the Alliance would win all foreseeable elections in Fiji, including the upcoming March-April 1977 general elections. But this felicitous anticipation was predicated on the prevailing structure of the two-party system as well as the vicious infighting prevailing within the Federation Party at the time. Furthermore, no one expected a splinter party to emerge to challenge the Alliance, especially with its base within the Fijian section. But it was exactly this that occurred in the March-April election when the Fijian Nationalist Party competed for the votes of Fijians. While the Nationalist Party won only one seat, it drew substantial numbers of Fijians away from the Alliance, reducing its support from 83 per cent obtained in 1972 to 67 per cent in March-April to allow the National Federation Party to score victories in at least six of the nine seats that the Alliance had lost in 1977 (Premdas, 1980a). To be sure, the Nationalists did not act alone. In a number of cases the Federation Party paid the nomination fees of Nationalist candidates so as to split the Fijian vote in Indian and Fijian National seats thereby providing a critical margin for victory. Further, where the Nationalists did not have a candidate in these National seats, it encouraged Fijians sympathetic to its views to vote for Federation candidates or to destroy or mismark their ballots. In one of the major ironies in these elections, the fact that the Nationalists sought to expel Indians from Fiji while the Federation Party mobilized to prevent this, did not inhibit these two groups from temporarily collaborating to defeat the Alliance. At the last minute, the internal schism in the Federation Party was closed and Indians voted so overwhelmingly for the Federation Party that its 25 per cent support for the Alliance in 1972 fell to 16 per cent in 1977. A combination of unique factors then caused the Alliance majority in the House of Representatives to tumble from 33 to 24 in the March-April elections. The Federation Party won the elections with 26 seats. The Nationalists were jubilant and Butadroka claimed that God had favourably responded to his prayers. The Nationalists were happy because it was their purpose in participating in the elections to demonstrate that Fijian paramountcy was an Alliance-created illusion. By facilitating the Federation Party's victory, it demonstrated to Fijians that the independence constitution of 1970 did not guarantee that a Fijian would always be Prime Minister and that the Indians were likely sooner or later to take political control of the country, endangering Fijian rights. When the results were in, the Nationalists obtained 20,189 Fijian communal votes or 25 per cent of the total Fijian communal votes cast out of 80,369. The Alliance control of Fijian votes fell from about 90 per cent to 66 per cent. The FNP won only one seat, that belonging to its leader, Sakiasi Butadroka, but it attracted enough Fijian votes from the Alliance to allow the Federation Party to secure more seats than it usually garnered. Fortunately for the Alliance, the Federation Party won 26 out of the 52 seats in Parliament giving it only half of the total number of seats. The Alliance won only 24 seats and was clearly not the majority party in Parliament. After nearly four days of wrangling caused by an internal leadership struggle, the Federation failed to come forward with an unanimous candidate for Prime Minister upon which the Governor-General re-appointed Ratu Mara of the Alliance as Prime Minister (Murray, 1978). When the new government convened, the Alliance quickly lost on a vote of no-confidence requiring a new election to be called. The people of Fiji were called upon again, the second time in the same year, to vote into office the nation's political decision-makers. After the Alliance lost in March-April, it underwent a long and painful self-examination of its defeat. It re-vitalized its organization and opened a systematic assault on the Nationalists whom it regarded as its primary enemy. The FNP responded in turn by increasing its activities. However, its leader and main asset, Butadroka, was held in jail for six months for breaking the Public Order Act, while the President of the NFP was declared bankrupt by the courts. It was clear that the Alliance government had embarked on a course to persecute and eliminate the Nationalists from any future political contention for power. Even so, during the elections, the FNP activists were out in force. However, it became evident that while the Alliance neglected its grassroots in March-April, in September no resources were spared to resuscitate the old party branches and supporters from lethargy. When the results were in, the Alliance had won a resounding victory with 36 out of the 52 seats, reducing the Nationalist share of the Fijian communal votes from 25 per cent to 17 per cent. The total of the National votes overall fell from 11 to 8 per cent (Ibid.). The significance of the April-March elections pointed to the possibility that Fijian parliamentary and political superiority could be undermined by the correct combination of electoral circumstances and actors. It took a rather unusual act by the Fijian Governor-General to

44

overturn the victory of the Federation (Murray, 1978). In some ways, the act could be construed as the first 'coup' in Fiji's post-independence politics aimed at maintaining Fijian paramountcy at all costs. The April-March 1977 general elections signalled to Fijian leaders that their political paramountcy was no longer secure and acknowledged by Indians. An inter-communal struggle for power was now on. Systematic acts of discrimination by the Alliance government against Indians increased.

C. The Royal Commission on Electoral Reform of 1975

The conflict between Indians and Fijians over representation consumed most of the negotiation time of the NFP and Alliance delegates at the Constitutional Conference between 1968 and 1970, although the issues were only partly and temporarily resolved. As pointed out earlier, on the system of representation the Alliance accepted the common roll as a long term objective, and acceded to the NFP demands that a Royal Commission be established sometime between the first and second elections after independence to open and re-examine the entire issue of common versus communal roll. Indians lived in hopeful anticipation that some day they would receive electoral equity. In 1975, the Royal Commission was appointed. Submissions from all quarters were made. When the report of the commission was submitted for public scrutiny, it called for a modification of the current communal system of representation (Min. of Info., 1975). The changes recommended were more favourable towards Indian interests. Given the persistence of intransigent communal voting behaviour, if the recommendations were accepted by the Fijian-dominated government, the Indian communal party would probably wrest power away from the incumbents. This would upset the balance in the distribution of spheres of influence, in particular Fijian political control. The recommendation of the Royal Commission was therefore rejected outright by the ruling regime. With the rejection, a shadow of illegitimacy descended on the government. To Indians, the Fijian Prime Minister had broken his word for fear of losing power. To Fijians, it was the right thing to do in order to maintain balance in the system. What was more important however, was that the old problem of reconciling common roll with communal roll was once again on the political agenda. However unfair Indians felt that they were treated by the prevailing communal system of representation, the electoral process was the only non-violent mechanism available to them to effect a change of government. Subsequent elections, then, were bitterly fought, exacerbating ethnic relations between Fijians and Indians. In the 1983 elections when the NFP came close to winning over the Alliance, the Great Council of Chiefs threatened that 'blood will flow' if Indians persisted in their quest for political power. The 1986 elections would actually bring things to a test. Whereas in March-April 1977 and in the 1983 elections, a NFP victory was barely within reach, in the 1987 elections the NFP objective was actually attained. What is significant for us is that the failure of the Alliance government to accede to electoral reform, so as to satisfy Indian demands for electoral equity, led in part to a zero-sum struggle to win control over the government. While to Fijians the doctrine of political paramountcy legitimized future claims to govern in perpetuity, to Indians and other aggrieved Fiji citizens, the electoral mechanism had to be manipulated to force the Alliance out of power. A life and death outcome was now attached to elections.

An overview of the impact of the three preceding events points to significant challenges to all of the fundamental compromises that were reached and embodied in the 1970 constitution. The undermining of the consensus built in the constitution came from both Indian and Fijian dissidents. The Mara-Koya rapproachment following the signing of the 1970 constitution offered a temporary buffer against the immediate dismantling of the compromises in the constitution. But from 1975 onwards, all fundamental constitutional ideas from Fijian political paramountcy (seemingly guaranteed by expected Alliance victories in all foreseeable elections) to Indian citizenship were challenged by 'outbidders' coming from outside the leadership of the two major parties. Towards the end of the 1970s, the effects of outbidder sniping had their desired results. Mara and Koya had attacked each other bitterly to counter the 'sold out' charges against them. The rift between Mara and Koya grew and was never repaired. The comity factor which sustained the formal legal compromises in the constitution was destroyed. Thereafter, like a set of falling dominoes, all cross-communal agreements were functionally nullified as open hostility marked inter-communal relations. To be sure, the 1970 constitution remained formally intact, but it lacked the legitimacy and vibrancy that came from inter-communal support, especially among the leadership elite whose behaviour structured Fijian-Indian mass relations.

D. From ethnic chauvinism to a quest for a government of national unity

One decade later, the basic guaranteed rights enshrined in the 1970 Fiji constitution were put into doubt. Under Butadroka's challenges, the Indians' very right to reside in Fiji was questioned. Their access to land for lease was also placed in jeopardy, as was their equal treatment before the apparatus of the state. With regard to Fijians, the March-April elections of 1977 clearly demonstrated that their Alliance Party could not secure power for them in perpetuity. With the threat of loss of the state apparatus, Fijians feared that

Indian dominance over the entire society would be complete in just a matter of time. The restoration of Fijian political paramountcy in the September 1977 elections was not legitimate to Indians since the Governor-General had pulled the first Fiji 'coup' by denying office duly won by the Federation Party. Every major settled constitutional idea and compromise was in shambles by 1980. Neither Fijians nor Indians could be sure, constitutionally speaking, of their vital interests being protected and guaranteed. An unstable, fluid state of affairs existed throughout the first half of the 1980s which was exacerbated by growing inter-communal distrust. However, towards the end of the 1980s, one final attempt at forming a government of national unity was launched to rescue the ship of state from certain political disaster. This was an attempt at forming a government of national unity. By 1980, a new leadership had succeeded to the helm of the splintered Indian-based Federation Party in the form of lawyer Jai Ram Reddy. Momentarily, it appeared that a new era of comity was about to be inaugurated as Mara and Reddy launched a discourse into the unsatisfactory nature of inter-communal relations in Fiji. Prime Minister Mara expressed an interest in a scheme for a government of cross-communal unity. It is important for us to examine this proposal since it offers insights into the underlying issues that bedeviled Indian-Fijian relations.

(i) Proposals for a government of national unity

The proposal for a government of national unity was set forth by Fiji's Prime Minister, Ratu Sir Kamisese Mara. The ostensible reasons for the unification proposals were articulated in the Prime Minister's paper which was published in the local press on the subject (FT, 1980 p.2). The question of political legitimacy and parliamentary representation was assigned a pivotal role for Mara's overtures. Said the Prime Minister:

> The racial pattern of voting has hitherto given us a government where the community which does not support the ruling party is likely to be under-represented in the decision-making process for formulating national policy (Ibid.).

He argued that the lack of adequate representation cultivated disloyalty and frustrations among the communal group that lost the elections (Ibid.). Political discourse in a country that was communally divided tended to utilize ethnic identity as the measure of evaluating what was unsuitable for the country, Mara admitted: 'Issues are always discussed on the basis of which race will gain, not as to whether the country will benefit' (Ibid.). It was felt that over a period of time, this type of politics created conditions for total conflict among communal groups threatening 'destruction of what has already been achieved'

(Ibid.). He observed that because of the grip that communal identity had over national life, the society lived in tension fearing that one day inter-sectional confrontation would eventuate, plunging the state into civil war. A condition described by the Prime Minister as 'crisis prone' pointed to the general instability that characterized a government that failed 'to weld into a nation peoples with strong ethnic allegiances' (Ibid.). Overall, then, the Prime Minister viewed the persistence of communal politics as very undesirable and potentially destructive for Fiji.

When the Opposition Leader replied to the proposals, he agreed with the views that condemned the effects of communal politics. Pointing to some of the pragmatic negative effects of communally-bound government, Mr. Reddy noted that 'economic development cannot take place when the two communities which complement each other in the production of goods and services do not work in harmony. We must know that one community cannot prosper when another stands to perish' (Premdas, 1981 p.8). He went on to underscore the point that 'after ten years of independence, no nationalism exists, only communalism' (Ibid.). Mr. Reddy and Ratu Mara both predicted that if current trends continued, confrontation would be inevitable leading to open ethnic violence. The Opposition Leader decided to utilize the opening afforded by the dialogue to complain that the Alliance-run government had embarked on a systematic policy to staff the upper echelons of the government with Fijian personnel, while it publicly espoused a policy of multiracialism. Said Mr. Reddy:

While multi-racialism is still espoused, it is now very much a matter of slogans. There is very little multiracialism at work. This is reflected in all aspects of government work and activities, from its composition, its development strategies, appointments to boards, promotions in the civil service, its Crown lands policy, everywhere (Ibid.).

The two communal leaders arrived at almost identical conclusions regarding the detrimental effects of Fiji's sectional politics. They also agreed that the prevailing constitutional and political structure was inadequate in restraining communal sentiments in national political life. They concurred, again, that there must be institutional reforms if the effects of the deepening cleavages, which pointed almost inevitably to national catastrophe, were to be arrested. The Prime Minister proposed that the political solution to Fiji's persistent communal malaise resided in what he termed 'a government of national unity.' Institutionally, a government of national unity 'will be represented in a Cabinet which draws upon the best talents in the country having in mind, simultaneously, adequate representation of the various ethnic groups in Fiji' (*Fiji Times*, 1980 p.1). The National cabinet was the critical institution that was to be utilized in bringing together the two ethnic communities. An ethnic mixture of Indians and Fijians at the Cabinet level was viewed as the prime cure for Fiji's massive communal wounds. It was argued that through the Indian and Fijian leaders working together in a cooperative cabinet arrangement, a salutary example would be imparted to the entire population as a model of good inter-communal behaviour. However, the crucial issue of ethnic proportional representation in the cabinet required a solution. Mara proposed that the Indian-Fijian ratio should be guided by two factors: (1) the relative ethnic population size in the country, and (2) the percentage control by the various parties of seats in Parliament as a result of the previous general election. At that time Indians constituted about 50 per cent of Fiji's population, while Fijians were about 44 per cent. In the lower House of Parliament, the Alliance had 36 members, while the combined factions of the NFP had only 15 seats. One seat was held by an Independent member. Whatever the final numbers of Indians and Fijians would have been under this formula for a cabinet style government of national unity, its anticipated consequences were 'to ensure adequate participation by all communities in the decision-making processes' thereby nullifying...'a sense of alienation in anyone or more ethnic groups through apparent or real exclusion' (Ibid.). In opting for a government of national unity, Mara had explicitly rejected a coalition arrangement between the Alliance and the NFP. First, a coalition was described as only a temporary arrangement compelled by election results that gave no party a majority. Come election season again, each erstwhile coalition partner would engage the other in a bitter contest for votes. Each would blame the other for government failures while allocating praise to itself for all the accomplishments. In Fiji's communal context, such reversion to a contest was bound to exacerbate communal antagonism thereby defeating a major purpose for which the coalition was arranged, namely, to promote inter-ethnic harmony. Hence, according to this logic, a coalition between the Alliance and the NFP would be unsuitable to solve Fiji's problems of communal conflict. In prescribing a government of national unity, 'consensus' would be required for its operation. 'Consensus' was seen as a quality different from 'bargaining' that led to 'compromises'. In contrast to a consensus arrangement, a coalition system was regarded as bound by 'bargaining' and 'compromises', political traits described as undesirable in any sort of joint government between the Alliance and NFP. A cross-communal membership in cabinet would operate under a principle of consensus. Said Mara:

Solutions to the country's racial problem do not lie in resorting to compromises. Modification and bargaining for the sake of keeping power will not do so: they become ends in themselves....(Ibid.).

As events showed, the concept and the role of consensus, compromise and bargaining in Mara's proposals became a source of controversy as the exchange of views between the Prime Minister and the Opposition Leader developed momentum. The Opposition Leader's response to the Prime Minister's proposals was set forth at the NFP's annual convention held in October 1980 at the Western township, Ba. Mr. Reddy agreed that the solution to Fiji's communal politics resided in some form of joint government. To Reddy, whether the form was 'consociationalism', 'coalition', or 'government of national unity', it was subordinate to what he called 'any arrangement that is honorable' (Premdas, 1981 p.10). Evidently, the Opposition Leader was seeking to emphasize the proposition that a joint government could be forged only on a basis that permitted the NFP relatively equal leverage and representation with the other participant in the arrangement. However, this critical issue of specifying exactly the weightage of the two parties in the cabinet was left vague in the Prime Minister's proposal.

In his remaining Ba presentation, Mr. Reddy raised issues which related to land, discrimination in the public service, the lack of consultation with the opposition, and the need to bargain and compromise as preliminary processes to establish any kind of government of consensus. All of these items, but particularly that concerned with the government's action which converted crown land to native reserves, were to inflame subsequent discussions on the proposals for a government of national unity. However, Mr. Reddy also devoted much time to an analysis of Mara's rejection for a coalition arrangement. The Opposition Leader felt that 'compromise' and 'bargaining' were essential processes that would attend any attempt to constitute a form of joint or consensus government. Towards the end of his speech, Mr. Reddy called for inter-party discussions between the Alliance and NFP over the issue of a unified government. Negotiations to establish a new structure of government were likely to occur against the background of each party seeking minimally to preserve and promote its interests. Two immediate sets of Alliance interests were likely to be fulfilled by entering into a government of national unity. The first referred to the threat posed by the Fijian Nationalist Party to the electoral prospects of the Alliance in the next general elections due by 1982. In March-April 1977 when an untrammelled Nationalist Party competed for votes, it so split the Fijian bloc that the Indian-dominated Federation Party was able to win the general elections. The National Federation Party was the beneficiary of the split Fijian vote. Should the Nationalists be able to repeat this performance in the next elections, (and they openly admitted that their role was that of a spoiler intent on proving that the Alliance could not protect Fijian paramount rights), then the Alliance could be defeated again. The second possible motivation for the Prime Minister's proposal for a government of national unity was the proposal that the relative parliamentary strengths of the Alliance and NFP would feature as a criteria in forging a power-sharing formula for a new government. Clearly, this meant that the NFP would be a junior partner to a joint arrangement dominated by the Alliance. The timing of the Mara proposal coincided with the fact that the Alliance was at its most powerful parliamentary level in its history, while the Federation Party, plagued by internal dissension, was at the weakest in its existence. If Mara was negotiating from strength, Reddy was doing so from weakness. Mara could kill two birds - the Federation Party and the Nationalist Party - with the same stone if the unity proposals were accepted for a new political order. In the end, it seemed that the vital interests of the Alliance, namely the retention of power and the protections of Fijian interests, would be advanced, but those of its partner, the Federation Party, would still be locked up in a sphere of ambiguity.

Finally, it is necessary to examine another reason advanced by Mara as basis for his proposals. Since its inception, the Alliance had claimed that it was a multiracial party. The results of the general elections in 1972 showed that it had obtained about 25 per cent of the Indian vote, lending validity to its multiracialism claims (Ali, 1972; Chick, 1972). However, in the two general elections in 1977, on each occasion Indian support for the alliance was first reduced to 17 per cent in March-April, and then to 14 per cent in September. In a subsequent critical by-election in the Labasa-Ba national constituency, this figure was further reduced to 8 per cent. The claim of the Alliance government that it was multiracial was shattered. The international reputation of Ratu Mara as a moderate leader of a multi-racial party in a communally-divided society was partly tarnished. To add to this difficulty was the fact that three Indian recruits to Alliance cabinets had, in recent years, either resigned or been booted out, further reducing the government's multi-racial stance. All indicators pointed to the further deterioration of ethnic polarization in Fiji.

Crucially, as the Alliance became more and more reliant on mainly one ethnic section for its support, it correspondingly fell victim to extremist demands within the party for the further entrenchment and promotion of Fijian interests in the government. To the extent that the Alliance was multi-ethnic, the Prime Minister could argue for moderation, balanced representation of all groups in government, and for cross-sectional policies. But to the extent that it lost this mix in its make-up, it fell under influences that demanded that Fijian interests be preponderantly represented. Already the Alliance was bringing its rhetoric, policies and practices closer to that of the Nationalist Party. To free itself from this pressure, it sought a government of national unity. In this sense, the Prime Minister's proposals could be interpreted as an attempt to rescue the Alliance's multi-cultural image. The Leader of the Opposition was put in a quandary when the proposals for a Government of national unity were set forth. His party, which had been publicly split until September 1979, was

51

still recuperating from the self-inflicted wounds resulting from the infighting of the previous four years. Weak both in parliamentary numbers and in internal cohesion, it was challenged with what seemed a higher purpose of preserving communal peace in Fiji. Clearly, the Federation Party was not negotiating from a position of strength; it could not have been much weaker in parliamentary terms. It needed time to sort out its domestic problems and increase its parliamentary numbers before entering negotiations with the Alliance. As it stood, genuine fears were felt that a powerful Alliance machine would absorb the Federation Party, eliminating the latter's identity in a government of national unity.

The Prime Minister's proposals contained features that permitted Mr. Reddy to initiate a strategy of temporizing. The proposals lacked clarity on many main issues. They categorically rejected the process of 'compromise' and 'bargaining' as parts of any new political order. Mr. Reddy delved critically into these aspects of the proposal, but he did not stop there. He decided to raise some substantive issues which he felt required urgent attention if a joint government were to be agreed upon. Reddy then proceeded to attack the Alliance government for several policies which had allegedly sown the seeds of inter-ethnic discord in the country. In particular, he isolated one emotional item, land, for special attention. Reddy said that he had discovered that the Alliance government was embarking on a policy of reverting crown land to native reserves. Since ethnic Fijians owned about 83 per cent of Fiji's land, leaving only 17 per cent to others, the Opposition Leader felt that no policy should be enacted to further increase the size of the Fijian holding. What, in particular, worried the Opposition Leader was the fact that this government policy was never announced to the public.

The Opposition Leader was addressing an issue considered 'vital' to Indians in Fiji. Most Indians in Fiji were farmers who worked predominantly as tenants cultivating land owned by Fijians. The increasing Indian demand for more land to rent and to purchase so as to meet the needs of growing Indian population had become a very sensitive issue in inter-communal relations in Fiji. The land was as much a vital interest to ethnic Fijians as to Indians. In any form of joint government, this issue had to be reconciled to simultaneously meet the demands of both groups.

Other substantive issues raised by Reddy related to (1) alleged discriminatory hiring practices of the Alliance government in favour of Fijians and (2) lack of consultation with the Opposition. The Opposition Leader argued that 'It is pertinent to raise these issues while we are talking about a government of national unity' (Premdas, 1981 p.12). Referring to the Alliance's government policies, Reddy queried; 'Can you sow the seeds of strife and sue for peace? Is this how we build national unity?' (Ibid.). In a way, Reddy's reply seemed unduly provocative if not untimely, and easily raised the ire of Mara.

Mara's reply essentially amounted to a withdrawal of his proposal for a government of national unity. He blamed this action on the attitude of the Federation Party and the Opposition Leader. The Prime Minister argued that his proposals were sincere and that his party had already taken steps to prepare for such a government by reducing their demands. In effect, the Alliance said that the remarks of the Opposition Leader were offensive because they questioned the sincerity of the Alliance's motives in advocating a government of national unity. In setting forth its reply however, Mara specifically addressed issues which were vital to Fijians. Like Reddy, Mara could not enter any form of government without preserving these interests for his constituents.

Ratu Mara's interpretation of what Reddy said would be challenged by the Opposition Leader. However, in a mass audience, accuracy of interpretation was secondary to the psychological solidarity needs of the followers of the faith. This applied equally to Mara and Reddy. The choice of a public forum to sort out sensitive communal issues proved disastrous. Mara then proceeded to put forth the critical question which would shore up his own leadership in relation to challenges to it emanating from the Nationalists:

> We are not unmindful of the fact that the price for the establishment of dialogue on the government of national unity demanded by the Leader of Opposition - the undermining of the constitutional protection afforded to Fijian interests - is too much for any Fijian leader to entertain (*Fiji Times*, 1980 p.1).

Reddy would subsequently claim that Mara had misinterpreted him. However, the most significant point was that Mara could not appear too conciliatory to his communal antagonism when the Fijian Nationalists had charged that Mara had attended to Indian interests and neglected to promote Fijian demands as Prime Minister. Partisan survival as well as personal credibility was clearly at stake. The internal needs of the Alliance had to be met first; the Federation leader had to be firmly rebutted. In this way, the Alliance claim that it best represented Fijian vital interests could be affirmed. The larger interest of inter-communal amity in the state was being sacrificed at the stake of partisan claims and counter claims.

The other substantive issues raised by Reddy were partly answered. However, the main focus of the Alliance counter-attack was on the land issue which was magnified to symbolize the totality of Fijian vital interest. The blame for the torpedoing of the unity proposals was placed on Reddy's doorstep. Said Mara:

> The Leader of the Opposition has publicly discouraged our party to continue discussion on the government of national unity and finalize our

53

views on it. He has cleared the way and encouraged us to prepare for the next election, based on the present system of government (Premdas, 1981 p.12).

Reddy replied, placing the blame on the Alliance and in turn suggesting that the proposal for a government of national unity was possibly floated in public as 'a public relations gimmick.' Both Mara and Reddy agreed that discussions of the proposals between them had never gotten underway before they had been submitted to public perusal.

(ii) The quest for electoral victory

The breakdown of the 'negotiations' for a government of national unity would turn the clock back on inter-ethnic relations placing them into a crisis zone. What the Federation leader said in effect was that the practices of the Alliance government tended to undermine vital Indian interests in relation to land and employment opportunities. To the Federation Party, the governing Alliance was unprepared to treat Indians as equal citizens free from state discriminatory practices. The Alliance proposals for a government of national unity offered a solution that was tantamount to the dissolution of the Federation Party under the paramount control of the Alliance. Only one choice seemed open to the Federation Party, that was, to win the elections and control over the government so as to alter its policies. Put differently, the mode of ethnic conflict resolution had moved away from consociation and sharing towards victory and dominance. The sharing of power and privileges in the sectoral divisions of labour implied in the concept of balance was set aside.

In the 1982 elections, a bitter campaign was waged by both sides and until the last week prior to the elections, it appeared that the Alliance was likely to lose to the Federation Party acting in loose concert with a Fijian splinter party, the Western United Front. When this failed, in the next round of elections scheduled for 1987, the Federation joined forces with the newly formed Labour Party to oust the ruling Alliance Party from power. A new form of struggle marked by open and outright zero-sum contest for power was inaugurated. It will be useful to look briefly at these 1987 elections which led up to the first military coups.

IV The Elections of 1987 and Military Intervention

The main premise of our argument up to the stage of the coup is that the set of deals and compromises which the constitutional fathers struck in 1970 were eroded so thoroughly by the mid-1980s that only a bare constitutional skeleton devoid of its spirit continued to exist. Comity between the Fijian and Indian political elites had been destroyed. Balance in the distribution of power and privileges was superseded by a fierce zero-sum struggle for dominance of the state. The coup of 1987 merely made formal a constitutional funeral that was long overdue. Both the Fijian and Indian party leaders acted in a way that contributed to the undermining of the constitutional balance that was formalized in 1970. Fijian leaders succumbed to outbidders, such as the FNP's Butadroka, resorting to administrative practices that negated the Indian's equal access to state opportunities and resources. Access to land as was perceived by the Indians was diminishing; the government returned crown land to the Fijian domain instead of making it available to the land-hungry farmers. Indian access to scholarships and promotions was circumscribed, frustrating them and making them feel like second-class citizens. Budgetary allocations were consistently tilted in favour of projects benefitting Fijians. All of this was perceived to be true by Indians. They then questioned the value of their citizenship. The Bill of Rights failed to protect them against discrimination. The prospect of improvement was bleak within the context of balance and compromises. Indians then electorally realigned themselves to acquire political power so as to change their economic well-being.

Fijians construed Indian behaviour not only as greedy, in wanting more land and employment opportunities, but also as seemingly deliberate schemes to win power and overthrow the 'balance' in the distribution of spheres of pre-eminence. In March-April, 1977, the Alliance lost the elections. Fijians did not see Indian electoral behaviour as a defensive act made in reaction to discrimination against them. For Fijians, this was a surreptitious grab for power by Indians in defiance of the balancing principle. Fijians and Indians were both blind to their own self-serving behaviour. In the absence of third person adjudication, the acts of each section confirmed the fears of ethnic dominance imputed to each other. Again in the 1982 elections, the Alliance was nearly defeated. Accompanying each of these attempts at acquiring power by the Federation Party was the stark threat that Fijians would suffer complete economic and political domination from an economically ascendant Indian alien community. This flouted the 'paramountcy' doctrine. Should Indians assume power, it seemed to Fijians that they also faced the prospect of seeing their traditions eroded and their chiefly system discarded. The Fijians' land and values were equally threatened. The loss of power could then have far-reaching repercussions for the survival of the Fijians as a people. For this reason, the paramountcy doctrine seemed to safeguard their future. The reference to the Deed of Cession in the 1970 constitution legitimated their claims to authority. Vital interests were at stake for both the Indian and Fijian community. Neither was about to yield to the other.

Over a period of 10 years, both the Fijian and Indian communal leaderships violated the formal and informal terms of the compromises embodied in the 1970 constitution. The primary triggering instigators in this process of erosion came from the outbidders in both the Indian and Fijian sections. They initiated the process of destabilization of the delicate balance on which communal peace depended. In quest of their own political ambition, they damned the moderate communal leaders as 'sellouts' and 'traitors'. Against a backdrop of economic recession and deprivation, such an explanation had an appeal. Once the outbidders had succeeded in implanting doubt in the legitimacy of the balancing concept, it took only the rise of the appropriate historical circumstance to nurture doubt into destruction. Communal harmony itself became subject to questions. To battle against the outbidder, moderate leaders such as Mara and Koya were driven to co-opt the outbidder's programme, thereby destroying their own moderation and becoming more intolerant. Old compromises and comity relationships were quickly eroded. The balance was overturned. Instability became endemic in the plural society inviting military intervention. This pattern of reinforcing intransigence in self-justifying claims and its accompanying harm is found in many polyethnic societies of the Third World.

In Fiji, the elections of 1987 represented a major disjunction in resolving ethnic claims and counter-claims that had been left outstanding and festering. We turn first to the elections of 1987 in this chapter followed by the historic military intervention. The solution came in the coup. The upshot was Fijian ethnic dominance. Instead of balance and sharing, inequality and dominance reigned.

A. The 1987 general elections

The 1987 general elections were the fifth in Fiji's history since independence. In most respects, the basic features of these elections were similar to the antecedent ones. To begin with, the electoral system remained constituted of a combination of communal and national seats. The prescribed parliamentary ethnic ratios were 22 Indians, 22 Fijians, and 8 General Electors (Europeans, Chinese, Mixed Races etc.). The elections were for the 52 seats in the House of Assembly and were administered by a politically neutral Elections Commission.

The main actors in the elections were almost the same, dominated by the two old established parties, the Indian-based National Federation Party and the Fijian-based Alliance Party. However, there was one major addition among the party contestants, the Fiji Labour Party (FLP). The FLP grew out of a struggle between the Alliance-run government and the Fiji Trades Union Congress in 1985 (Robertson, 1985; B. Lal, 1986). Faced with demands for higher wages and salaries but also with a shrinking revenue base and increased deficits, the ruling regime imposed a prolonged freeze on workers' income. Public servants, both Fijians and Indians, were bitterly aggrieved. They were, however, among the most educated, highest paid, and best organized in the country's population. In effect, they were prepared to confront the Alliance Government. A strike was threatened by the Public Service Union which was constituted of civil servants who formed part of the apex Trade Union Congress. Faced with the crippling of the country's vital services, the Alliance government promised to retaliate by sending in the Fiji Royal Armed Forces to break the strike. Fiji workers would not forget this frustrating experience. The government won the standoff by the threat of military force. But in the next elections, it would be the workers' turn to wreak revenge on the ruling party.

The Fiji Labour Party was born from the confrontation between the government and the unions. Formed almost two years before the next scheduled elections, the FLP had ample time to build a grassroots organization to challenge the Alliance Party in electoral battle. Demonstrating its credibility, the FLP competed in local elections soon after it was formed and won most of the seats in the council elections in the ethnically mixed capital city of Suva. This victory stunned the Alliance regime. In a by-election for a vacant parliamentary seat, the FLP came within a whisker in winning what had traditionally been a stronghold electorate of the Alliance (Naidu, 1986). The warning, clearly, was that in the next general elections, the FLP would be a credible threat.

Electoral performance in local and by-elections is not necessarily a convincing indicator of how voters will respond to the intense mass communal appeals which tend to occur in country-wide general elections. The FLP faced the formidable task of confronting both the Indian-based Federation Party and Fijian-based Alliance Party. To win a majority, it would have to break the entrenched communal patterns of voter preference. Several fortuitous events transpired to aid the FLP in defying the odds and bringing home an astonishing victory. First, the Indian-based Federation Party was torn internally by fierce factional infighting to the point where several of its key members resigned and a few joined the Labour Party. A badly weakened Federation Party, faced with its own probable humiliation at the polls, was then persuaded to join the Labour Party in a coalition arrangement. The popular Indian leader, Jai Ram Reddy, although he had stepped down from the formal leadership of the NFP, played a pivotal backroom role among the Labour-Federation coalition strategists in swinging the Indian vote to the coalition parties.

The second critical event that eventuated in aiding the Labour-Federation coalition to victory pertained to the continuing internal fissures within the ranks of the Fijian community. In particular, the Western United Front (WUF), which represented the interests of disgruntled Fijians in the Western Division of Viti Levu, continued to mobilize its supporters in alliance with the Labour Party. Also, the Fijian Nationalist Party headed by Sakiasi Butadroka, although defeated and harassed in previous elections, commanded the loyalty of some 5 to 8 per cent of Fijians. It would be in a number of critical constituencies, where Indian/Fijian population ratios were roughly equivalent, that the small parties like the WUF and the Nationalists would upset the Fijian-based Alliance Party. The other major division in the Fijian community came from the Labour Party itself, whose leader was a Fijian commoner, Dr. Timoci Bavadra, and whose economic programme was critical of the government's treatment of the poor and disadvantaged, who were mainly Fijians. The 'Bavadra factor' would also elicit votes from Fijians who were critical of the political dominance of Fijians by their chiefs.

It was therefore from within the recesses and cracks in the established Fijian and community that Labour would squeeze out critical margins in certain electorates for victory. In a polity where communal loyalties still predominated, issues played an unusually important part in determining the outcome. Some credibility can be assigned to the claim that Labour's campaign around economic issues, such as the wage freeze, alleged government corruption, and the plight of the poor and unemployed, dampened the enthusiasm of the indigenous Fijian voter in turning out to vote. In an astounding election statistic, it was shown that only 70 per cent of the indigenous Fijians voted as compared with 85 per cent in the 1982 elections. Certainly, if these Fijians had turned out and had all voted for the Alliance Party, the Labour challenge would have been squashed. But no one knows for whom the absentee Fijian would have voted. It was quite probable that many of these voters were disenchanted with the Alliance Party and might have voted Labour.

There was an ideological issue which was periodically thrown into the campaign fray as an issue. Specifically, the Alliance charged that the Labour Party was socialist and would in victory, bring the Russians to Fiji and with it 'chaos, bloodshed, and instant instability' (Delaibatiki, 1987 p.1). Apart from strongly advocating a programme to redress the class inequalities in Fiji and making the government more accessible and accountable, the Labour-Federation coalition also promised to alter the country's foreign policy to one of non-alignment (Shrimpton, 1987). Under Prime Minister Mara, Fiji had been a faithful ally of Western hegemony in the South Pacific. Mara had banned Russian vessels from Fiji's territorial waters while permitting U.S. nuclear vessels to dock (Premdas and Howard, 1985). The Labour-Federation coalition firmly promised to follow New Zealand's lead in forbidding all nuclear vessels from its ports. It also announced that it would re-align Fiji's foreign policy to maximize benefits to Fiji. It would not, however, invite the Russians to establish an embassy in Suva (Shrimpton, 1987).

The ideological issue, particularly emphasized by the Alliance as the elections came closer, also raised the problem of Labour policy towards nationalization. The Labour coalition did not see anything wrong with nationalization *per se* and pointed to the successful case of the Alliance purchase of the foreign-owned sugar company, the Colonial Sugar Refinery, which had, at one time, dominated Fiji's economic life (Narsey, 1979). Labour, however, did not have an extensive programme for nationalization. In its election manifesto, it said it would nationalize the country's only gold mining company, (Emperor), and would seek partnerships in other businesses. This apart, the Labour coalition indicated that it would continue the country's reliance on foreign investment to promote Fiji's economic growth (Ibid.). Overall, Labour was careful not to devote much energy towards discussing the details of its economic reform apart from aiming at a more equalitarian and just order. Economic reform did not emerge as the main theme in the elections. Labour's promises were cast in pragmatic non-doctrinaire terms intended not to cause consternation.

The Alliance fought a defensive electoral battle as far as the issues were concerned. The Labour-Federation coalition had anchored its appeal on the catchy slogan 'For a clean and caring Government' for which the Alliance failed to find an adequate response. Apart from its half-hearted charge of socialist leanings of the Labour Party, the Alliance denied the charge of the

Fijian Nationalist Party that it had failed to give special advantages to poor Fijians. It enumerated the large number of cases where it offered special allocations, loans, scholarships, and subsidies to native Fijians. Further, it argued that it successfully kept down inflation to about 2 per cent annually while it expanded job opportunities to absorb the country's growing population keeping unemployment to 19 per cent (*Fiji Sun,* 1987). A total of 35,000 new jobs were promised for the next five years. It claimed, contrary to Labour's charges, that it had both improved the standard of living and maintained an equitable system. It denied, but not too convincingly, that it had become old and corrupt. To thwart the attractiveness of Labour's novelty, the Alliance advanced the claim that it was the most experienced and best suited party to run a government (Iyer, 1987). The Alliance underlined that running a government was not an amateur's avocation and that it was not the same as running a trade union. It appealed to Indian voters recapitulating its record of making Indian tenure more secure and making more land available to Indian farmers (*Fiji Sun,* 1987).

But the Alliance resorted to other standard electioneering artillery that it had used in the past. In particular, it sought to scare Fijians that they could lose their land with a change of government (*Fiji Sun,* 1987). The Labour-Federation coalition was described as the old Indian menace in disguise with popular Indian leader Jai Ram Reddy the real power behind the coalition scene (Iyer, 1987). This was a not too surreptitious use of the fear of ethnic domination by Indians to ensure the loyalty of the Fijian voter (*Fiji Sun,* 1987). An Alliance stalwart ominously warned that 'without the Alliance in power, this country could turn into another Uganda where Indians were made to leave' (Iyer, 1987 p.1). In addition, with regard to the issue of Fijian chiefs, the Alliance charged that the Labour-Federation coalition was intent on eliminating the traditional system of indigenous leadership (Delaibitiki, 1987). Also, it charged that Labour would fire the Fijian Governor-General (*Fiji Sun,* 1987). The Bavadra candidacy symbolized for some a challenge by Fijian commoners against the entrenched Fijian chiefly system that was loyal to the Alliance Party.

It remains to be answered what role the communal vote assumed in the election outcome. Apart from a small but significant percentage of votes, the evidence points unequivocally to the conclusion that the communal factor, as in past elections, dominated voter preference in the 1987 general elections. Several indicators uphold this conclusion. First, in an electoral system where there were separate communal and national constituencies, all the communal seats (Indian; Fijian; and General Electors) were won overwhelmingly by the Alliance and Labour-Federation parties. The coalition did not mount a credible challenge to any Alliance communal seat. In the Labour-Federation coalition, the Federation component under Jai Ram Reddy delivered the Indian communal votes to the coalition. Second, in those National seats, where either Indians or Fijians overwhelmingly predominated, the respective Labour-Federation or the Alliance candidates won easily. Third, in the four critical seats that the Labour-Federation coalition took away from the Alliance, the Fijian-Indian ratio was close but slightly in favour of the Alliance. In these cases, namely the South Eastern Fijian and Indian National seats and the Suva Fijian and Indian National seats, the victory for the Labour coalition came as a result of Fijians splitting their votes (Kumar, 1987). This was clearly so with regard to the role of the Fijian Nationalist Party in the case of the South Eastern Fijian and Indian National electorates. In effect, in these cases, the indigenous Fijians did not cast their ballots across the communal divide. In rejecting the Alliance, they switched to another Fijian Party. In the Suva Fijian National seats, the Fijians who cast their ballots for the Labour-Federation candidate, Dr. Tupeni Baba, seemed to have done so because of Baba's own rousing campaign style as well as the fact that the constituency contained a large number of disgruntled Fijian civil servants who were hurt by the Alliance wage freeze. This was the main area where pragmatic rationalism seemed to have influenced voter preference.

The aggregate data from the elections confirmed the conclusion that the pattern of voting was communally-bound. In previous elections, Indians tended to give about 15 per cent of their votes to the Alliance Party. In the 1987 elections, this remained unchanged. In Indian communal seats, the Labour-Federation coalition obtained 82 per cent of Indian votes whereas in 1982 the Federation Party obtained 83 per cent. In the Fijian communal seats, the Alliance obtained 78 per cent in 1987 but got 82 per cent in 1982. In the General Communal seats, the Alliance support fell from 89 per cent in 1982 to 82 per cent in 1987. Essentially, then, a sectional voting pattern persisted in the communal seats. Fijians in previous elections gave only 2 per cent of their votes to the Federation Party. In 1987, they gave 9 per cent to the Labour-Federation coalition. It was mainly in the national constituencies that the Alliance lost votes to the coalition. It was the split Fijian community, the absentee Fijian vote, and in particular, the role of splinter parties in four critical constituencies that led to the Labour-Federation victory. In the Fijian national constituencies, the overall Fijian vote for the Alliance fell from 84 per cent in 1982 to 49 per cent in 1987. At the same time, the coalition increased its share from 33 per cent (Federation Party alone) in 1982 to 46 per cent in 1987. It is safe and fair to conclude, therefore, that in the 1987 general elections, communal voting dominated the elections, especially in the communal seats and in the safe Indian and Fijian national seats which accounted for 48 out of the 52 seats in the House of Representatives. Even though in four critical electorates, a small swing of Fijians to the coalition occurred and accounted for the defeat of the Alliance Party, the overall results were certainly not about class realignment of voter preference (Premdas, 1989; Plange, 1992).

B. The Labour coalition's 33 days in office and acts of destabilization

The victory of the Labour-Federation coalition was a signal event in Fiji. For the first time in the seventeen years since independence, political succession from one regime to another occured by peaceful electoral means. To Prime Minister Mara, the proud but fallen Fijian High Chief, the loss was overtly taken with grace and statesmanship. He conceded victory to his political adversaries saying to the people of Fiji: 'Fellow citizens you have given your decision. The decision must be accepted. We must now ensure a peaceful transition to enable the new government to settle in and get on with the important task of further developing the nation. There is no room for rancour or bitterness, and I would urge you to display goodwill to each other in the interest of our nation. Democracy is alive and well in Fiji' (*Fiji Sun,* 1987 p.6). In an editorial, the *Fiji Times* echoed Mara's sentiments:

> There have always been those who doubted the people of Fiji, who said we would never live ' in harmony, never reconcile our differences. But yesterday the people spoke. Although coming from different religions, many backgrounds, we are yet one people. So the greater victory is for democracy (*Fiji Times,* 1987a p.6).

For the Alliance, its loss signalled a fundamental violation of its political eminence which it had believed embedded in the Deed of Cession and premised in the concept of balance. But one could argue it was the Alliance's own persistent violation of the Indian sphere of pre-eminence and the accompanying loss of Indian equality that led to the destruction of the 'balancing arrangement'. Regardless of who it was to be blamed, the 'balance' was long destroyed. The key problem was that the Fijian elites did not anticipate losing the government at anytime in the future despite its discriminatory anti-Indian and anti-labour policies. Holding pre-eminent power for close to two decades, they had become complacent and overconfident. Hence, after the elections were over, they conspired to regain power by openly challenging the Labour-Federation government.

Almost as soon as Dr. Bavadra and his government were sworn in, a grumble commenced about alleged Indian dominance in the government. Dr. Bavadra himself was Fijian and he took the sensitive portfolios of Fijian and Home Affairs which covered institutions close to native Fijian interests (Delaibitiki, 1987). In a cabinet of fourteen members, six went to Fijians, one to a General Elector, and seven to Indians. In those sensitive areas of Fijian concern such as Fijian Affairs, immigration, education, labour, land, rural development and forests, as well as the country's prime ministership, all the portfolios were assigned to Fijians. Bavadra, as a commoner, was very careful during his first days of office to pay homage to the Fijian chiefly hierarchy. He visited High Chief George Cakabau who greeted him effusively. Despite this, Bavadra had no way of gauging how traumatic a threat his leadership posed to the entrenched privileges and traditional powers of the Fijian chiefs. Fijian chiefs, for instance, kept for themselves over four fifths of all land rents which Indians paid to the Fijian landowners. Under Bavadra, they could lose this.

To the mass of native Fijians, also, there was initially a silent acceptance of the change of guard. The fact that a Fijian remained Prime Minister would temporarily assuage Fijian anxieties of the future of Fiji under an Indian-dominated government. It would take the deliberate and systematic instigation of latent Fijian fears by a small contingent of disaffected Alliance leaders to arouse Fijians to mass action. At meetings and demonstrations organized and led by Alliance parliamentarians and ex-cabinet ministers -Taniela Veitata, Apisai Tora, Filipe Bole, and Josaia Tavaiqia among others. Fijians were told that the Bavadra government was a front for Indian interests and that their immediate objective was to deprive Fijians of ownership and control of their land. Labelled the 'Taukei Movement', the meetings picked up momentum at first from small half-hearted gatherings, then included road blocks, fire-bombings (including that of the law offices of Jai Ram Reddy), and outright racist appeals to Fijians. *Fiji Sun,* 1987).

Fed by unexplained sources of abundant funds, the Fijian leaders of the street demonstrations brought in Fijian re-enforcements from the rural areas and outlying islands by the boat-load and truck-load (*Fiji Sun,* 1987). Soon the streets of Suva and Lautoka, Fiji's largest cities, were in control of the demonstrators. Less than three weeks after taking office, the Labour-Federation government was in grievous straits, jolted and steadily destabilized to the point where the regime was paralyzed. Calls by Mara and the Fijian Governor-General for the 'Taukei Movement' to restrain its actions came to naught. Mara, himself, left Fiji during the height of the crisis for a prolonged visit to Hawaii, while his party stalwarts persisted in turning the government into shambles. Some of the placards of the Fijian crowds expressed their demands and fears cryptically (Gaunder, 1987).

1. Fijians only to Lead Fiji.
2. Land is Sacred. Hands off.
3. Government by Fijian Chiefs Forever.
4. Fiji for the Taukeis.
5. We don't want to be like the Maoris.

6. Jai Ram Reddy, you don't belong here.
7. Fijian land and leadership to be guaranteed.
8. Cancel all ALTA land leases.

The placards articulated the fear of the loss of land as the centre-piece of the protests, despite the fact that the government did nothing and could do nothing constitutionally to infringe any aspect of Fijian land ownership. Some of the placards also expressed apprehensions that Fiji's indigenous people would be reduced to a permanent and impoverished minority in their own land as has been the fate of the Maoris and Aborigines in New Zealand and Australia. Finally, some placards threatened outright eviction of Indians from Fiji along Ugandan lines.

To the Bavadra government, the destabilization campaign was inspired by a conspiracy of both internal and external interests. Internally, it was felt that certain Alliance ex- cabinet ministers who were at the forefront of the demonstrations, could not face the deflation of status and financial reward that attended their standing as parliamentary backbenchers. This group, it seemed, harnessed its frustrations to the threat posed to the Fijian chiefs by Bavadra's band of commoners. The Fijian masses were then manipulated and mobilized by Alliance leadership elements (some say that Mara was himself implicitly involved although he was physically present in Hawaii) in complicity with the Fijian chiefs in the campaign to destabilize and bring down the government. In an additional aspect of this hypothesis, some of Bavadra's inner circle felt that the demonstrations were instigated by the fear of certain ex-Alliance ministers of revelations of their heavy involvement in corruption. Mara himself was accused of being implicated in the misuse of public funds.

The external actors in this conspiracy scenario pointed to certain individuals in local multinational corporations and to the role of the American Embassy in Suva, Fiji's capital. The Labour-Federation government which in their election campaign had promised to nationalize the Emperor Gold Mine Company had proof that one of the expatriate executive officers of the gold company was active among the leaders of the demonstrations. In one of its final meetings, the Bavadra cabinet actually discussed deporting the expatriate in question but failed to reach a decision. With regard to the alleged American connection, Bavadra summoned the American ambassador and complained about the alleged role of an embassy staff member in the demonstrations. Overall, the Labour-Federation government was sure that funding for the demonstrations came from the external sources which together represented the fear of nationalization and the fear of American loss of a faithful ally in the Pacific. Bavadra himself would subsequently make a direct charge that the C.I.A. was involved in his overthrow. One of the first acts that the Labour-Federation government did was to ban American nuclear vessels from visiting

Fiji ports. This was accompanied by a declaration in favour of a foreign policy of non-alignment. General Walters, President Reagan's ambassador to the U.N. visited Fiji two weeks before the coup warning that 'the United States had a duty to protect U.S. interests in the South Pacific' (*Fiji Sun*, 1987h).

C. The coup

It was in the shadow of the demonstrations and breakdown of order directly instigated by the 'Taukei Movement' that the military intervened. The coup maker, Lt. Col. Sitiveni Rabuka, third-in-command of the Fijian Armed Forces, declared that the military were assuming power to prevent communal conflagration and to pre-empt the government's call on the military to repress the Fijian people (Keith-Reid, 1987; Robie, 1987). The military forces, from the beginning, were almost completely dominated by ethnic Fijians. When the coup took place, the 5 per cent contingent of Indians in the armed forces, were placed under house arrest.

Soon the smooth, bloodless coup that had led to the hijacking of the government and the kidnapping of Bavadra and his coalition parliamentarians exhibited strong connections between the coup leader and the Taukei movement. Put differently, Lt. Col. Rabuka and his men were not irresistibly drawn into the overthrow of the government, but rather, there was direct collaboration and planning of the intervention between 'Taukei Movement' civilians and Fijian military officers. Rabuka himself admitted that he had been playing with a planned scenario to intervene if necessary, several months prior to the coup (Dean and Ritova, 1988). What was, however, most damning, was that Rabuka was seen playing golf with Ratu Mara just a few days before the coup.

Whatever the motivations, inspirations, and surreptitious maneuvering involved in the making of the coup were, the fact remained that Bavadra and the Labour coalition were unceremoniously evicted from office just 33 days after peacefully assuming power. The coup leader echoed the fears and demands of the Taukei demonstrators. The military junta proclaimed that 'Fiji was for Fijians', and that in their own land, Fijians would not be dominated by an alien race. Only a Fijian-run government could protect Fijian interests. To this end, the military announced that the old constitution was abrogated and a new one would be prepared to guarantee Fijian political paramountcy in perpetuity. The language and rationale of Rabuka and the Taukei leaders as they grabbed power and sought to justify their actions bore an uncanny resemblance to the demands and grievances that were first articulated by the Fijian nationalists a decade earlier.

After seizing power illegitimately, Lt. Col. Rabuka proceeded to call on the

Fijian Governor-General, High Chief Ratu Penaia Ganilau, to swear in a military council as the new government of Fiji. In what would transpire as a tangled set of exchanges between the Governor-General and the military, the Governor-General would emerge as the new chief executive of Fiji who was 'advised' by a council constituted of ex-Prime Minister Mara and a majority of Alliance ex-cabinet ministers. To be sure, this group, which also included Rabuka, invited Bavadra and the Indian leader of the Federation Party to join the new governing council, but they refused. In the end, the new government of Fiji after the coup was under the control of the Governor-General whose views broadly reflected that of the military and the Taukei movement. A new constitution was drafted to entrench Fijian paramountcy and institutionalize Indian, European, and Chinese political inferiority.

Fiji, at one time, represented a unique case history in the Third World where a system of ethnic conflict management had worked for over a decade and a half. So long as one of the two major groups, the Fijians, had won the elections, the regime was regarded as legitimate. When the other major ethnic group won, it caused consternation. It would not, however, be accurate to say that Fijians spontaneously mobilized to overthrow the Indian-dominated Labour-Federation coalition government. The evidence clearly shows that at least four interests combined to instigate Fijian mass mobilization against the government: (i) a minority of frustrated Alliance dissidents who were ex-ministers of the outgoing government assumed the instigator leadership role; (ii) the small number of Fijian chauvinists who generally tended to support the Fijian Nationalist Party and other Fijian extremist groups; (iii) representatives of multi-nationals who feared nationalization; and (iv) the United States government which was displeased with the potential loss of a reliable ally in the Pacific islands. How these interests conspired or combined to galvanize the Fijian masses for the destabilization of the Labour-Federation government is anyone's guess. What we know is that the oppositionist agitational actions sabotaged the coalition government and jolted Indian-Fijian peaceful co-existence that lasted for some seventeen years. In place of compromise, armed force had now become the pre-eminent method of obtaining a government. The military intervention had set in motion a train of events that led to overt acts of repression and the destruction of the social and economic fabric of the society.

V The Coup d'Etat, Racism and Abridgement of Human Rights

The restraints on the deteriorating inter-ethnic relations between Fijians and Indians were removed on May 14, 1987, when a small group of ski-masked soldiers stormed the Fiji Parliament while it was in session and kidnapped the Prime Minister and his cabinet. Led by Lt. Col. Sitiveni Rabuka, third in command of the Fiji Royal Military Forces (FRMF), the soldiers successfully staged the first military coup d'état since Fiji had become independent in 1970 (Premdas, 1989; Howard, 1991; Sanday, 1989; Prasad, 1988; Robertson and Tavanisua, 1987; V. Lal, 1990). In a sudden fell swoop, the many years of post-independence democratic rule were extinguished. With the ousting of the Labour-Federation government which had won the general elections barely thirty-three days earlier, representative, parliamentary democracy was crippled. The army then proceeded to infringe practically every civil liberty guaranteed by the constitution as they sought to neutralize all opposition forces and consolidate their control over the state.

In the demise of parliamentary democracy, there were now no restraints on human rights violations or accounting to the people. The army literally decapitated the democratic system by seizing and confining the Prime Minister and his cabinet colleagues. They were dragged out of Parliament at gunpoint, those resisting arrest were threatened with bodily injury, and all were taken to a place of confinement and held incommunicado. The governing cabinet that was seized was almost equally divided between Indians and Fijians. The military's coup motto, 'Fiji for Fijians', guided their action to separate the Fijian Ministers from the Indian as they were dragged out of Parliament. In what must have been a shock to the soldiers, the Fijian and Indian ministers held on steadfastly to each other refusing to be separated. The ethnic and communalist texture of this first of military acts in executing the coup would characterize the tenor of their subsequent behaviour as the coercive forces sought to divide the population and cement their control.

In this chapter, we shall look at the systematic infringement of the rights of citizens. Both Indians and Fijians associated with the Labour Party came in for intimidation and harassment. However, it was almost inevitable that supporters and opponents of the new government would divide into ethnic groupings, given the manner in which partisan politics evolved in Fiji. However, the new military regime and its successor had deliberately embarked upon a course of action that supplanted a multi-ethnic party with a polity that was deliberately designed around ethnic symbols and separatism. Ethnic repression became systematic imparting the defining feature of the new order. It was clear that the new governing powers were intent on preventing any breaches in the ranks of Fijians, this, in their view, being the main cause of the defeat of the Alliance Party in the 1987 elections. Dissident Fijians came in for special pressure to maintain the facade of Fijian solidarity. Indians as a whole were deemed the collective enemy. During the riots following the first coup, indiscriminate violence was directed against Indians especially in the capital city, Suva. Gangs of young Fijians prowled through the streets of Suva and broke into businesses and homes. Ironically, one of the reasons advanced by Lt. Col. Rabuka in carrying out the coup was his fear that the Taukei protestors were planning to attack Indian premises and it was necessary to intervene to prevent this. The ethnic discriminatory strain that was displayed in the failure to protect citizens came to dominate the behaviour of the army in identifying and terrorizing its enemies in the post-coup period. By using ethnic symbols to consolidate power, the coup makers sought to conceal their own private motivations as well as those of their covert backers in the seizure of power. Not all of these tactics succeeded.

Political and constitutional confusion followed the military takeover. While the coup itself was carried out with military precision, the political transfer of power to a set of new governors was not clear-cut but marked by protracted pandemonium. The Governor-General Ratu Penaia Ganilau, the paramount High Chief of Caukadrove, the same province from which Rabuka, a commoner came, seemed initially to resist the coup. He failed to offer unequivocal support to the coup makers. Rabuka called for a new constitution and a new political order under which Fijians would be accorded undisputed paramount control of the government. The Governor-General was sympathetic, but he was caught in a quandary since he wanted the Queen of Britain as head of state to acquiesce to the illegal seizure of power. Rabuka formally transferred power to the Governor-General who proceeded to appoint a Council of Advisers substantially constituted of members of the defeated Alliance party as well as representatives from the Taukei protestors to run the country until new elections were called. Rabuka would later confess in his memoirs on the coup that he had approached the Governor-General prior to the coup about the need for a forcible change of government. The Governor-General appeared ambivalent but did not actively discourage him, nor did he report the matter to the Prime Minister. Later, Ganilau would argue for Fijian pre-eminence to be entrenched in a new constitution. On May 23, about one week after the coup, the Governor-General signed an amnesty pardoning Rabuka and the coup makers. All this would cast a shadow of suspicion on the Governor-General's role in the coup. The Fiji Council of Chiefs assembled on May 19 and endorsed the military takeover.

Forces opposed to the coup mobilized to harass the new military controllers. Demonstrations and prayer vigils against the coup were mounted, mainly in Suva. These were multi-ethnic events. Pamphlets against the military takeover with a call for popular resistance were widely distributed. To meet this challenge, the military, constituted of only about 3,600 soldiers, decided to augment its numbers by inducting into its ranks large numbers of the pro-coup Taukei protestors, giving several of their leaders and other civilians high military rank. With their new official status, these Taukei 'soldiers' commenced a campaign of terror against all opposition activists, Indians and Fijians alike, everywhere. Throughout the capital city, on rooftops and strategic locations, army sentinels were deployed against an opposition that refused to use arms. In the atmosphere of high tension and extensive terror, citizens stayed in their homes as the coercive state apparatus proceeded to arbitrarily enter the premises of all its major adversaries, which included persons from the University of the South Pacific, the unions, churches, and media. At the University of the South Pacific, academics associated even only sympathetically with the ousted Labour-Federation Party were submitted to intimidation and arrests. A number of academic staff who had actively participated in aiding the Labour-Federation coalition in organizing the party and in acquiring office were forced to flee the country. The ethnic assertions of the coup-makers drove a wedge into the erstwhile amicable relations between Fijian and Indian staff at the university, government offices, and businesses.

The mass media was also seized. Both of the country's major independent dailies, *The Fiji Times* and *Fiji Sun,* were closed after having been allowed to operate freely for a couple of days immediately after the coup. Critical journalists, Fijians, Indians, and Europeans alike, were submitted to arrest and intimidation, and when the newspapers were again allowed to publish, they were severely muzzled. The editor of *The Fiji Times,* an Indian, was frequently harassed by the army. *The Fiji Times* offices were placed under surveillance and journalists were practically immobilized. As elsewhere, ethnic divisions among support staff surfaced at *The Fiji Times.* The *Fiji Sun,* which had published scorching stories and exposés of how the military enforced its will on its adversaries, was subjected to special repressive measures. A select set of

Fiji Sun journalists were inquisitorially harassed and intimidated. The radio stations, which were owned by the government but had, in the past, been autonomous in designing their programmes, broadcast only government announcements and music for several days. When the stations resumed broadcasting, the personnel had changed and programmes had been sanitized. The mass media therefore were brought into service of the military regime for years thereafter. When their formal autonomy was restored, they operated under stringent guidelines that became self-regulating. Many journalists, mainly Indians, migrated from Fiji for fear of their lives. Most complied silently. Moreover, what was also true and very significant was that the staff on the newspapers became, for the most part, ethnically divided in their loyalty to the new government. A few Fijian journalists refused to surrender their autonomy and were terrorized, but by and large, an atmosphere of ethnically structured inter-colleague distrust pervaded the staff of the mass media organizations. Dissident journalists who sought refuge overseas opened news magazines devoted to covering events in Fiji.

Trade union leaders came in for special intimidation and harassment (Leckie, 1991). The main leadership component of the ousted Bavadra Labour-Federation coalition government was the Fiji Labour Party. Ex-Prime Minister Timoci Bavadra was President of the Public Service Association, and several cabinet members and aides in the new government were drawn from the labour movement. To many leaders of the Alliance Party, their defeat at the polls was caused mainly by the role of the Fiji Labour Party. Hence, after the coup, trade union leaders came in for special targeting. However, they possessed enough residual power in their unions to mount boycotts, strikes and demonstrations against the new regime. To neutralize the power of the unions, the new government embarked on a tactic of divide and rule along ethnic lines (Ibid). While many unions were ethnically mixed, there were a few important unions which were preponderantly composed of Fijian members such as the Waterside Workers' Union and the Fijian Teachers' Association. The leader of the Waterside Workers' Union, Taniela Veitata, an ex-Alliance cabinet minister, actually participated openly in the organizing of the Taukei Movement which destabilized the government. After the coup, serving as a Minister in the new government, he was mainly responsible for the military's attack on hostile trade union elements. In a direct assault on the trade union movement, the new rulers refused to recognize the Trades Union Council as the legitimate bargaining agent of workers. This persisted for over five years. By banning strikes, prohibiting union meetings, arresting and intimidating union leaders, and appealing to indigenous Fijian loyalty within the unions, the military regime successfully coerced most workers and their leaders into relative quiet. The unions were revived and became the main pillar of opposition against the government in subsequent years. To combat union militancy, the new regime would attempt to form new ethnically-oriented unions which were parallel to the old so as to split workers' solidarity with the Labour Party. One such union was the Fijian-based Viti Civil Servants Association which was formed to offset the multi-ethnic Public Service Association which opposed the regime.

Opposition against the new government also came from the Western province, which was the home base of the deposed Prime Minister Bavadra. Western indigenous Fijians, possessing a distinctive sense of separateness from Fijians in the East, had long held grievances against the Alliance government which allegedly favoured the eastern chiefly establishment. The seventeen years of Alliance rule brought few benefits and patronage to the Western Fijians, who at various times had organized dissident movements against Alliance domination. It was, in part, because of this Western alienation that many Westerners chose to support their own home-grown son, Timoci Bavadra, in the 1987 elections. Hence, many Westerners were upset with Bavadra's overthrow, and joined demonstrations against the new rulers. At one point, many were ready to march *en masse* all the way from the Western region towards the capital city, Suva, to confront the army. It would be inaccurate to say however, that Western Fijians as a whole did not support Rabuka's takeover. Antipathy against Indians espoused by Fijians was universal in Fiji including the Western region. While many Westerners were unhappy with Bavadra's removal for regional reasons, most responded to the larger loyalty of Fijian togetherness in opposition to alleged Indian claims to political power.

From the Western region, another group began to boycott the government. These were the Indian sugar farmers. The ethnic marker generally defined the ranks of coup and anti-coup supporters. Most of Fiji's sugar production is located in the Western areas of Viti Levu, around the towns of Nadi, Lantoka and Ba. Sugar accounts for about 60 per cent export earnings and 15 per cent of the GNP. The Indian cane farmers had overwhelmingly supported the Labour-Federation Party, in part because of a primordial attachment, and more pragmatically because of their demand for security of their land leases. Indian cane farmers, boycotting the new military rulers, refused to harvest the cane in solidarity with other unions across Fiji. The ruling regime responded by issuing 'Public Emergency Regulations' by which the military was authorized to seize control of property, premises, equipment, land, and crops of cane farmers. Soldiers occupied cane factories and intimidated farmers and workers who had threatened to set cane fields on fire. In the end, little cane was cut and this frustrated the regime.

Together, the forces opposed to the coup mounted a credible drive against the coup-makers and the new semi-civilian government, but it was not enough to displace the military stranglehold. In part this was because of the ethnic

71

divisiveness and mobilization methods instigated by the military. Ethnic mobilization was essential to the military in upholding its claim that Fijian interests were endangered by surreptitious Indian attempts to grab power. The ethnic appeal elicited pervasive support among Fijians for the coup-makers. Many of the most prominent and effective opponents of the coup were, however, composed of both Indians and Fijians. Hence, the frontline of the counter-attack consisted of a visible cross-communal and multi-ethnic group derived from activists in the church, university, unions, and the media. Below this thin sliver of multi-ethnic attack lurked the larger force of ethnic solidarity, Fijians for the coup and Indians against. Inter-ethnic tolerance broke down. All civil liberties were suspended as military might became the law of the land. What eventuated during the first few weeks after the coup was a dual-headed governing apparatus in the form of an autonomous army and a semi-autonomous appended civilian government. This structure would prevail for years to come with Rabuka keeping the military under his control and serving as the arbiter of disputes and the most important political personality in Fiji. The semi-civilian government under Ratu Mara could not control Rabuka who acted arbitrarily whenever and wherever he wished to enforce his own version of internal security. The Governor-General continued to pretend that he had pre-eminent power and held discussions with the ousted politicians for a review of Fiji's constitution.

A. A new political compromise and a new military coup

Both domestic and international pressures prevented the military from assuming outright power after the coup. Britain, Australia, New Zealand, the USA, India and all major powers refused to recognize the new government and cut off aid, demanding restoration of Bavadra. The domestic sources that restrained the excesses of the military emanated from the Governor-General who, while not opposed to the coup, wanted a smoother transfer of power to a new regime while avoiding international ostracism, especially potential expulsion from the Commonwealth of Nations and the withdrawal of the Queen as Fiji's head of state. In indigenous Fijian life, the British royalty occupies a sacred place; many Fijian homes are adorned with a prominent display of a photograph of the Queen and members of the royal family. The other domestic sources included the trade unions, the Fiji Council of churches, and an assortment of political dissidents. The Australian and New Zealand trade unions, responding to a request by the Fiji Trades Union Congress for a boycott, implemented a firm cargo and passenger ban on ships and aircrafts bound for Fiji. This had an immense effect since Australia and New Zealand were the main sources of Fiji imports.

The intensity and persistence of the internal and external opposition to the first semi-military regime was completely unanticipated by Rabuka and his covert civilian backers. What followed became even more damaging when investors suspended all operations in Fiji and a dramatic run on the Fiji currency commenced. When the coup took place, foreign reserves stood at (F)$160m., but in a few weeks they were reduced to about (F)$113m. The currency was devalued and production levels fell. Indians, especially businessmen and professionals, began a panic exodus from Fiji taking capital and skills with them. To some extent the haemorrhage was permitted to persist since it entailed the elimination of Indians from Fiji and a source of continuing opposition and tension. Tourism was also struck a devastating blow. It had emerged as the second most significant pillar in Fiji's economy generating foreign exchange almost equal in significance to sugar exports. Most tourists came from New Zealand and Australia. Foreign airlines suspended operations into Fiji. The disruption of trade and shipping by overseas union boycotts was telling. As the months rolled by and the various sources of opposition did not let up, the revenues of the country decreased steeply. This led to a devaluation of the currency by 17.5 per cent, the first since independence. Another was soon to follow. Military expenditures had escalated and no foreign aid was forthcoming. The regime proceeded to trim its expenditures by arbitrarily cutting the salaries of public servants by 25 per cent and retrenching many workers. In the meanwhile, however, the size of the armed forces nearly doubled to over 7,000.

It was in the lengthening shadow of this decline that an attempt was made between August and September to restore a measure of legitimacy to the regime by incorporating the ousted Labour-Federation coalition leaders into the new interim political order. The opposition forces, organized around the Coalition, with its persistent domestic activists augmented by virile external support, developed much morale in peaceful resistance. They proceeded to launch a highly successful 'Back to Early May' petition that garnered over 100,000 signatures or about one third of the electorate, calling for a government of national unity. Although the signatures were mainly from Indians, the resistance movement persuaded the Governor-General to embark upon a rapproachment between the Alliance Party and the Labour-Federation Party. Negotiations for a Council of National Reconciliation were intensely pursued, sending trepidation through the ranks of most Taukei leaders whose cause of unqualified Fijian paramountcy seemed to flourish in conditions of instability and disunity. They, along with elements in the army, sought to disrupt the negotiations by mounting marches and protests. After about a month of negotiations, an agreement was struck called the 'Deuba Accord'. Under it, the Labour-Federation Party and the Alliance Party agreed to form a new government composed of equal numbers of cabinet members from each party. The Deuba Accord was only an interim arrangement, preparatory towards the convening of new elections and formulating of a new constitution. But by bringing back Labour-Federation elements which included such prominent Indian politicians as Jai Ram Reddy, Rabuka felt very uneasy and almost marginalized in the proposed power equation. His earlier "Fiji for Fijians" stance was severely compromised. Further, he feared that the Labour-Federation victory would be allowed to stand even in part as well as the defeat of the Alliance. The cause of launching the coup could be lost under the new compromises. As all of this was transpiring, Rabuka realised that he still had complete control of the military and for all practical purposes, any government that ruled did so at his pleasure. The Deuba Accord seemed to have returned the Labour-Federation politicians through the back door and threatened to dilute the claims of Fijians to paramount political control of Fiji.

The Deuba Accord however, contained many of the critical ingredients required to retrieve a badly torn country from self-destruction after the coup. In the optimistic atmosphere of an impending reconciliation in the accord between the ousted leaders and the Alliance, sugar workers had called off their boycott and harvested the cane. International airlines had re-commenced flights to Fiji. Some relaxation in the manner in which the ruling regime's adversaries was treated by the security forces also occurred. It was shocking, therefore, when on September 25, Lt. Col. Rabuka struck again, committing a second coup aimed at nullifying the Deuba Accord. For Rabuka, the compromises in the Accord were too difficult to reconcile with the inflated status that he now enjoyed. Rabuka's action was partly prompted by the influence of extremist elements in the Taukei Movement which had openly called for a military takeover to forestall the implementation of the Deuba Accord. Rabuka did not trust Mara and the old guard in the defeated Alliance government. He wanted to wash away once and for all, all traces of non-Fijian influence in government decision-making and to install a new parliamentary order with unequivocal Fijian paramountcy. Certainly, this was on the agenda of the Taukei group. Rabuka also saw in power-sharing as a potential threat which could lead to the paring of the wings of the Royal Fijian Military Forces and his sacking as military commander. In committing the second coup, it was clear that Rabuka exercized a clear option in preference for uni-ethnic rule rejecting multi-racialism in government. This must be emphasized, since it cannot be argued that Rabuka was forced by events into a compelling corner that dictated his decision. It was a clear, voluntary choice to torpedo the new effort of a government of national unity and reconciliation. He did not want nor seek a regime of sharing or balance but one of ethnic pre-eminence and Fijian paramountcy.

In committing the second coup, the armed forces incurred the wrath of the international community. Fiji was declared a Republic, no longer a part of the

Commonwealth of Nations from which it was expelled. An unqualified military government seized control of Fiji under Rabuka. The Governor-General as representative of the Queen was no longer needed. And Ratu Mara, the interim Prime Minister decided to return to his island home in order to give Rabuka a free hand to carry out his plan for Fiji's future. The cabinet of the Rabuka military government was in part constituted of the major Fijian extremists in the Taukei Movement among whom were persons such as Sakiasi Butadroka who, in his capacity as the new Minister of Land and Natural Resources, wanted to tightly restrict the availability of land for lease to Indians and non-Fijians and eventually to squeeze Indians off the land and then out of Fiji. In the ardour of anti-Indian and anti-foreign fanaticism that this new orientation inspired, arbitrary and violent seizures and evictions of legally leased land had commenced in a few areas, causing grave repercussions in the international community about the investment climate in Fiji and a possible new exodus of refugees. Under Decree No.10, which amended the Fiji Public Service Act, the military regime took further steps to reduce the size of the non-Fijian presence in the public sector by stipulating that fifty percent of posts were to be reserved for Fijians and that promotions, demotions, transfers and acts of discrimination were unappealable.

The naked military regime sent terror into the minds of its political and ethnic adversaries by the new provisions of Decree No.12, under which it suspended freedom of assembly, association and petition (demonstrations and marches included) aimed mainly at recalcitrant trade unions, and prescribed a new procedure to allow for arbitrary detention in such a way as to deny recourse to *habeas corpus* rights and other forms of appeal. Decree No.12 embodied a peculiar style of repression that the military regime adopted and that was carried over to subsequent regimes. This was to publicly proclaim, with much blandishment, a commitment to the familiar set of civil liberties and political freedoms found in democratic governments, but then to proceed, in the next breath and more quietly, to stipulate a wide assortment of conditions under which these rights were to be exercised so that they were abridged and for all practical purposes summarily nullified. The frequent arrests and detentions after the second coup eliminated the pretenses of the military government to democratic rule as a major clean up was undertaken to purify all areas of the government that detracted from Fijian pre-eminence. The judiciary was entirely re-shuffled consonant with the new concept of Taukei justice.

The terror of the Rabuka-led military government lasted for nearly four months. The economy was literally driven into the ground and an imminent collapse seemed inevitable (Cole and Hughes, 1987). The costs of intransigent, polarized, ethnic politics were being felt. Most of the international boycotts were resumed. During its short tenure of unrestrained control over the government, the armed forces penetrated all parts of the public service, placing its own personnel and policies. This translated into the implementation of an intimate interlocking relationship between the command structure of the military and the public service hierarchy. Military officers and public servants sympathetic to the Taukei Movement were deployed throughout all strategic areas of decision-making in all the ministries in the government. This feature of interlocking policy and personnel obedience would remain a fixed aspect of the public bureaucracy even after Rabuka surrendered power to a semi-civilian government. A system of control was put in place so that the claims of Fijian and military dominance would at all times find compliance. The ethnic politicization of the public service under military soon came closer to reality.

One aspect of the Rabuka military regime assumed remarkable insensitivity in the multi-cultural structure of Fiji society. As an avowed Born-again Christian, Rabuka decided to translate the demands of his brand of Christianity into the official policy of the government. For Rabuka, a self-professed, fundamentalist lay preacher in the Methodist Church, 'Indians are not Christians. They do not worship God and His Son Jesus Christ' (Dean and Ritova, 1988 p.37). He declared all of them 'heathens' and threatened to ban public celebration of their ceremonies. Rabuka proceeded to promulgate by decree the Sunday Observance law under which no commercial trading and work could be carried out on the day of Sabbath. All vehicular transport including the operations of public buses as well as sporting activities were banned. Sunday was the day of Sabbath in the Christian calendar and all were called upon to recognize it as a day of rest and prayer regardless of whether they were atheists, Hindus, Muslims, or Sikhs. Not all Christians adhered to the view that the day of Sabbath required a cessation of commercial and recreational activities, but they too were required to comply with Rabuka's edict of intolerance. The Fiji Council of Churches, in dissenting from the promulgation of the Decree, argued not only for Christian tolerance in love of neighbour but pointed out that the Sabbath was made for man and not man for the Sabbath. Many Indians saw the Sunday Observance Decree not only as an abridgement of their freedom of conscience, but as an attempt to constrain their economic activities and enterprise. For instance, during sugar harvest, when the cane must be cut immediately to prevent spoilage, to cease work was to court economic disaster for the cane farmers, most of whom were Indians. Muslims who celebrate their day of worship on Fridays, also took grave offence at the Sunday Observance Decree.

The judicial system came in for special assault under the military regime of Rabuka. When the military seized power, the judges of the Supreme Court constituted of both Fijians and Indians but headed by a Fijian Chief Justice declared that the coup was illegal. The Supreme Court judges emerged as a bulwark of civil liberties during the first few months after the coup as a counterpoint to Rabuka's arbitrary arrests of the new regime's adversaries. It was only after he had seized power a second time that Rabuka was able to assault the judicial system and comprehensively bring it under his edict. This he did by pressuring the Indian members of the Supreme Court and the magistracy in general to resign and migrate and then proceeded to Fijianize the judiciary. Like the public bureaucracy in the Executive arm of the government and the political leadership in the Cabinet, the judiciary was politicized and incorporated into the script by which the military ruled. Rabuka, for all practical purposes, had emerged as the chief legislator, executive head, and judge. Even when he had surrendered power, Rabuka had set in motion a level of ethnicized politicization in the judiciary that could not be easily reversed.

The international reception that Rabuka's regime received from its traditional allies such as Australia, New Zealand, and the United States (excepting Margaret Thatcher's Britain) was cool, marked by the suspension of diplomatic recognition and foreign aid. To compensate for this loss, the new military rulers sought allies in countries which it felt would be sympathetic to its policies. Malaysia, which also practised a militant policy in favour of its native Malay citizens, mainly against its resident Chinese 'alien' community, sent the first foreign mission to visit Fiji after the second coup. Malaysia expressed great sympathy with Fiji for its policies and offered credit, trade and investment opportunities. Indonesia, as a repressive military regime, was approached by Fiji's military rulers for the supply of arms as well as for a new source of aid, trade, and investment. Indonesia, long feared by Pacific Island countries because of its treatment of Irian Jaya residents on the other half of the New Guinea island (Premdas and Nyamekye, 1979) and East Timorese, was readily embraced by Fiji and reciprocal arrangements were initiated so that these two military-run governments entered into several cooperate deals that included credits for rice imports from Indonesia. France also entered the turmoil on behalf of Fiji's desperate new rulers seeking to exploit a magnificent opportunity to wean Fiji away from its old attachments to its regional rivals, Australia and New Zealand. France had its own interests in seeking support for its foreign policy in New Caledonia and French Polynesia. France then entered into a special set of unprecedented arrangements with Fiji's new rulers providing Rabuka with a source of aid and weapons that in part filled the breach caused by the suspension of relations with Australia and New Zealand. Finally, among Fiji's new international supporters was Israel, which offered vital services in the area of security and intelligence training in relation to Fiji's fears of terrorist attacks. The Israelis would soon add sophistication to Fiji's internal capabilities in dealing with dissidents. In the end, Fiji's new diplomatic ties did offer some badly needed external assistance that kept Rabuka's tottering, strife-torn, economically haemorrhaging regime afloat. But it would not be enough to save the regime from its own chauvinism and incompetence.

B. The new interim semi-civilian regime: the embedding of patterns of human rights violations

If, during the first six months following the coup of May 1987, Fiji's new rulers trampled on the rights of citizens to see how far they could go without penalty, in the subsequent four years following the installation of a semi-civilian government under Ratu Mara in December, 1987, the groundwork for a more permanent system of repression and human rights violations was laid. It would be in this period that the elements which later entered into the structure of the new constitution in a new political order germinated. In this part of the chapter, we shall see how a dual headed image of "democracy" was contrived on the anvil of acts of repression. Specific repressive acts which had an experimental antecedent in the first months after the coup were selected and were consolidated into a pattern of behaviour with boundaries of permissiveness and prohibition drawn from case to case. It was a learning process for both government and citizenry in adapting to 'a new reality'. In each significant area of civil liberties, the new interim government, headed again by Ratu Mara after Rabuka had terminated his military regime, enunciated and defined the new relationships between citizen and state. We shall examine these specific cases of human rights violations to show what the new limits that were imposed on human rights were (Ghai, 1990). In particular, the new regime had to craft its repression in a manner aimed at its communal adversary without inordinately inconveniencing its own sectional support. The new latitudes of liberty were still tentative largely determined by restraints and costs imposed by domestic opposition activists and international actors.

Two months after assuming full control of the Fiji government following his second coup of September 25, 1987, Rabuka decided to surrender his rule. Rabuka had placed his military regime under the influence of a number of extremist Taukei cabinet ministers over whom he had little control. In the Taukei-oriented military government, chaos and mismanagement of the economy occurred with many ministers acting unilaterally in consultation with no one else in the cabinet so that Rabuka claimed in dismissing the cabinet that 'they were an embarrassment more than anything else' (Howard, 1991 p.343). Rabuka, burying his pride, recalled Ratu Mara and Ratu Penaia Ganilau to assume control of the government. In transferring power to a more moderate all-Fijian set of rulers to restore economic viability and international respectability to the country, Rabuka was forced to concede to Mara and

Ganilau the return of the soldiers to the barracks, the dismissal of the entire Taukei-oriented cabinet, and partial re-staffing of the judiciary. Four military officers however were permitted to remain in the new Mara-led cabinet while Rabuka retained control of the armed forces.

In the transfer of power on December 11, 1987 to Ratu Mara as Prime Minister and Ratu Penaia Ganilau as President of the Republic, a new all-Fijian semi-civilian administration, exclusive of elements from the Coalition parties, was installed. In retaining control of the military, Rabuka hovered over the activities of the new regime. He, in fact, was left almost totally free to stamp out any threats to the security of the state that he perceived by any measure he chose. His popularity had remained undiminished amoung Fijians while that of Prime Minister Mara was sullied and secondary. This allowed Rabuka virtually to run a separate government with impunity. He would frequently interfere directly in political affairs especially in going after and harassing opposition activists while the civilian sector of the government, often times helplessly embarrassed by Rabuka's actions, administered policies to restore health to the economy. Bavadra referred to the new Mara government as a military regime concealed in civilian cloak. This is not to suggest that Rabuka ran the government from behind the scenes but rather to point to the existence of a dual-headed structure of government with two seemingly contradictory, but in fact complementary sectors, one open and tolerant in the semi-civilian part and the other concealed and repressive in the military part. In some ways, each was autonomous and together they appeared to be uncoordinated and conflictual. From time to time, Mara and Rabuka clashed publicly suggesting the existence of two centers of power but in practice they expounded the same set of goals and views but differed on modalities of implementation.

What became clear in this seemingly schizophrenic order was that both parties supported Fijian political paramountcy, which severely restricted the basic freedoms of all citizens, but aimed especially at emasculating the political and economic rights of Europeans, Chinese, and Indians, who together constituted over half of the population. Hence, whenever Rabuka capriciously descended with his military forces to harass, intimidate, or arrest journalists, university students, church workers, and political opposition activists, these actions generally fitted within the trajectory of change towards a new political order which the semi-civilian government was constructing. In effect, while Rabuka periodically overtly overstepped the civilian regime's moderation, his acts served to discourage and contain levels of disruption from opposition forces to the larger effort of forging an inequalitarian order for the new Fiji. Apologists for the new interim government often used the term 'new reality' to encourage dissidents to adapt to the new order so as to confirm the ruling regime's claims to legitimacy. The opposition forces refused to accept the 'new reality' and persisted in challenging the terms and conditions under the new emergent dispensation. It will be useful to examine how this 'new reality' was being put together from ongoing challenges; it was the stuff from which a future was studiously forged.

The interim government deliberately embarked on a policy of discrimination to deny equality to all citizens. Both Mara and Ganilau were firmly committed to a constitution that conferred political pre-eminence to indigenous Fijians. They were not interested in returning to the old formula of power- sharing embodied in the 1970 constitution even though it was tilted in favour of Fijian political control. The old formula was not secure enough, as evinced by the victory of the Labour-Federation Coalition in 1987, in guaranteeing Fijian paramountcy. While they were willing to entertain some non-Fijian participation in government, they felt that the political sphere must be reserved for indigenous Fijian control. Until the military intervention of May 1987, neither Mara nor Ganilau had openly articulated their sentiments on Fijian paramountcy but it was implicit in their adherence to the concept of balance in the sharing of spheres of influence amoung the three main ethnic communities in Fiji. It will be useful therefore to describe their ideas on Fijian claims to political paramountcy and then proceed to examine how this outlook structured their policies towards enacting 'the new reality' in Fiji.

Mara couched his position under the general claims of indigenous peoples for special rights, saying that 'special rights for indigenous peoples are not something new and are provided for under international law. One such law is the 1957 Convention on Indigenous and Tribal Populations' (*Fiji Times*, 1989c p.1; Premdas, 1993c p.310). Mara cited the preamble to this convention to justify the need for special rights:

Recognizing the aspirations and rights of the indigenous peoples to jurisdiction over their own destiny and institutions, to exist as distinct societies and peoples, to maintain and develop their identity, language, religious and philosophies of life, to determine their cultural, society, economic, spiritual, and material development without the adverse imposition of foreign life styles (Ibid.).

Mara argued that it was precisely this interest that Fijians espoused and warned that the 'Fijian people have learned from history and wish to make history in their own country and not become history' (Ibid.). Mara reminded detractors to his argument of the fate of other indigenous peoples saying that 'the Fijian people are all too aware of the destiny of the indigenous Aztecs of Mexico, the Incas of Peru, the Mayas of Central America, the Caribs of Trinidad, the Amerindians of Guyana, the Maoris of New Zealand, and the Aborigines of Australia' (Ibid.). From these arguments, Mara concluded that Fijians must be awarded majority representation in Parliament and control of the government as 'an affirmative action to guarantee and protect the rights and aspirations of the Fijian people against other communities' (Ibid.). He reminded critics of his position that Fijians had settled in the islands over 3,500 years ago and this fact entitled them to paramount control of Fiji" (Ibid.). Further, he felt that affirmative action in favour of Fijians was not discriminatory against other communities in Fiji (Ibid.). Ganilau had also supported a radical reform of the old constitution to entrench Fijian dominance. Ganilau said that 'Fijians' representation in parliament was such that it did not allow them to fulfil their aspirations' (*Fiji Times,* 1989b p.9). He argued that under the 1920 constitution indigenous Fijians got only 22 seats as compared with 30 seats for other ethnic communities, and that this was a 'gross mistake' that led to the coup in 1987 (Ibid.). He also underscored that only a small minority of Fijians had voted for the Labour-Federation Party and that was an unacceptable to Fijians as a basis for forming a government.

The positions taken by Mara and Ganilau elicited a strong dissent from deposed Fijian Prime Minister Bavadra. He felt that the policy of affirmative action was, in the context of Fiji, a misapplication of the principle (Glaser, 1977). Argued Bavadra:

> The 1957 Convention was designed to safeguard the interests of the indigenous peoples who had become minorities in their own land and who continued to suffer the effects of dispossession, discrimination, and political marginalization. The Fijian people do not, by any stretch of the imagination, fall into such a category. Far from being politically marginalized, traditional Fijian leaders have enjoyed sustained political control of the country since independence. It is therefore totally absurd to liken the position of Fijians today to that of the Aztecs, the Incas, the Maoris, the Aborigines, etc. all of whom suffered the territorial fate of genocide or systematic oppression as a result of settler colonialism. Ratu Mara also attempts to legitimize the discriminatory provisions for majority Fijian representation by claiming that it constituted affirmative action and that it is not intended as an act of discrimination. Politics of affirmative action is aimed at rectifying inequality or discrimination suffered by disadvantaged groups. Nowhere in the world are they aimed at establishing paramountcy of a particular group at the expense of others (*Fiji Times,* 1989c p.7).

Bavadra proceeded to contend that the notion of affirmative action was, in reality, a cover to permit the retention of power in the hands of the Fijian chiefs who had controlled the government since independence. Fijians in the western province had long protested against their unequal representation in the councils of power because of the dominant role of the eastern chiefly establishment.

The views on Fijian pre-eminence expressed by Mara and Ganilau fostered an atmosphere of discrimination and intimidation that compelled citizens, mainly from one ethnic group, to relinquish their homeland and seek refuge in another country by legal and illegal means. By 1990, over 30,000 Indian citizens of Fiji had emigrated from Fiji, selling their properties cheaply and abandoning generations of labour and industry invested in building their homes and homesteads. Non-Fijians as a whole became nervous about their continued residence in Fiji. A small trickle of Fijians also left Fiji. The exodus persisted as thousands of Indians sought refugee status in host countries especially in Australia and in Canada. The interim government placed no hindrance against mass Indian emigration and actually extended low cost government loans to Fijians who wanted to purchase low-priced Indian homes and properties so that Indians could leave immediately. The intimidatory and repressive acts of the coercive forces seemed to bear the character of a premeditated tactic designed to drive Indians out of Fiji. Because most loans granted to indigenous Fijians in the past tended to lapse into default and were forgotten or forgiven, these new loans which were granted, in particular, to a select set of well-placed Fijian middle class civil servants, appeared to be gifts and payoffs for political loyalty to a strategic stratum of Fijians.

Rabuka actively promoted the exodus of Indians, arguing that they were only 'guests' in the country of their birth even though they were third and fourth generation citizens. Insisting that he was not a racist, and 'not an Idi Amin' and that in fact he wanted Indians and other non-Fijians to stay in Fiji, he nonetheless viewed them as 'guests in this country' (Dean and Ritova, 1988 p.119). He took a negative position on Indian business activities arguing that 'they already have a more than fair share of Fiji's bounty through their very substantial control of business and the economy' (Ibid.). He feared that this economic might was not likely to be confined to the economic sphere but would expand into the political arena, threatening to infringe on the Fijian sphere of influence and violating the unwritten rule regarding the 'balance' in the distribution of power and privilege among the three main ethnic groups in Fiji. But Rabuka's attacks were not merely aimed at containing Indian expansion but in reducing them to a politically impotent group. Hence, in regarding them as guests he fully intended to strip them of their citizenship retaining some as essential workers in service of the regime. A minority of Indians, Europeans, Chinese, and other non-Fijians was always tolerable.

The systematic harassment of Indians, the discrimination against their entry into the public service after the coup, and an array of policies and practices aimed against the Indian community had the ultimate impact of levelling the ratio of Indians to Fijians in the population by 1990. The Fijian population, which had been surpassed by Indians since 1946, was now almost equal. To reduce or eliminate an entire population group marked by distinctive racial and ethnic identity, even if not done through physical extermination but by intimidation and discrimination, it could be argued, borders on a variant of genocide. It is paradoxical since an indigenous group, accustomed in other places such as Australia and North America to being victims of indirect forms of genocide, was committing the very acts that it had condemned. At various conferences the policies of the Fiji government under Rabuka and Mara had been endorsed by indigenous Pacific island groups as well as those in North America and Oceania. It seemed to be a case of displaced aggression against a vulnerable group, as compensation for inability to attack the powerful settler communities that have usurped indigenous lands elsewhere.

The illegal seizure of power, the repression and intimidation, and the establishment of an inequalitarian order was bound to stir sufficient dissatisfaction which threatened the security of the new regime. The new ruler turned out to be very alert and fearful of real and imagined enemies. Months went by and no armed movement organized a resistance. To be sure, there were several marches, demonstrations, and prayer vigils. Yet, the military and security forces doubled in size and persisted in their surveillance of perceived opponents. A psychology of siege prevailed, accompanied by a fantasy of drummed up enemies, all of which, in turn, provided an excuse to maintain the security system. With the Labour-Federation opposition forces along with the unions totally excluded from power in a deteriorating economic situation, but with their opposition persistently pestering the ruling regime, bringing international embarrassment, the new government needed a formal legal mechanism to arbitrarily round up, enter the homes, and arrest anyone who dared to defy it. By passing such a law, it was hoped that naked repression could be legitimized (Ghai, 1990). The international community could not be alienated again lest the boycotts resumed in the loss of tourists, markets, and investment. In order then for the interim government and Rabuka to contain internal criticisms and deter the opposition, it needed a suitable instrument of justifiable arrest. This it concocted by claiming that terrorists had shipped arms into Fiji and were preparing a campaign to remove the interim government (Harder, 1988). Hence, when two years after the coup it was announced in Sydney Australia in June 1988 that customs officials had intercepted a cache of arms bound for Fiji, this provided a trigger for a massive round-up of regime opponents and the promulgation of a draconian Internal Security Decree. This claim of subversion was backed up by a theatrical display of soldiers 'discovering' guns and ammunitions on the farms and premises of a number of Labour Party members, regime opponents, and Indians. Whenever these arms were 'discovered' on several raids conducted across the country, government photographers and invited journalists were coincidentally in ready attendance to record the event. These were splashed in the press with pictures of an assortment of AK-47 rifles, boxes of grenades etc. as proof of the existence of the terrorists. The 'discoveries' were repeated several times and twenty-one persons were arrested and held without bail.

In the wake of the 'arms find', the government announced that it was promulgating a National Security Act fashioned on the Singaporean model permitting it to arrest, enter the homes, and detain anyone without the right of *habeas corpus*. From June to September 1988 the National Security Act was in force; it drew widespread international condemnation. Dissidents and opposition elements were arbitrarily detained, homes searched, and an atmosphere of unprecedented terror prevailed among persons likely to be perceived as enemies to the government. Apart from a number of Fijians including a notable Fijian chief from the western province who had identified with the Labour Party, the impact of the National Security Act was ethnicized and felt most keenly in the Indian community. The Fijian community was called upon to put non-Fijians under surveillance and consequently strained if not destroyed all residual signs of intercommunal amicability. This the ruling regime deliberately sought to do as a means of justifying its authority and its claims to Fijian rule.

While the semi-civilian government under Mara worked to revive the economy, Rabuka's army operated freely, especially under the period of the National Security Act. As part of its security exercise, a tremendous amount of new eavesdropping and surveillance equipment was purchased (Dalton, 1990). The Israeli Mossad was contracted to provide assistance to Fiji and a comprehensive apparatus of surveillance abridging all rights to privacy was established. In September 1990, all of this matured into the formal creation of a Fiji Intelligence Service (FIS) after the system was actually in place and had operated for the previous two years. In contemporary Fiji, the FIS does not seek guidance under the judiciary, its budget is unpublished, and it falls under the direction of the National Security Council chaired by the Prime Minister.

To install a veritable control system under which all dissent was monitored and discouraged (Premdas and Hintzen, 1982), the military apparatus itself had to be expanded. Following the first coup, Rabuka dismissed the Commissioner of Police who was an Indian and brought the entire police force under the direction of the military as Dr. John Dalton pointed out: 'There is no doubt that the Police Force is now under the ultimate if not directional control of the Army, a development which represents the politicization of the process of law and order and internal security' (Dalton, 1990 p.6). This did not change until about five years later when a British-born Commissioner of Police was appointed. The budget of the armed forces was dramatically expanded so that expenditures for it multiplied nearly five-fold from (F)$8 million prior to the coup to (F)$38.3 million in 1990 (*FINS*, 1991). In fact, the military budget is still the largest component in the entire Fiji budget even today. Much of this expansion of the army's budget came from the demands of Rabuka for more internal security even as all semblance of opposition disappeared. Rabuka publicly warned that politicians should not 'tinker with the Army's proper role as final guarantor of national security' (*FINS*, 1990a).

In all of this, it is clear that a *de facto* authoritarian state with a distinctive ethnic slant was engrafted onto Fiji's erstwhile open society. Even while the civilian interim government used the rhetoric of constitutional review and the need to restore democracy, the Fiji Military forces were busily engaged in establishing a pervasive repressive apparatus. One scholar described this process as the horizontal integration of the army into the civilian polity:

A certain degree of horizontal integration has already occurred between the political and military elites with the granting of commissions to political figures. After the coup, two former Alliance Ministers and two former Alliance Senators were granted commissioned rank in the military. Army officers have filled political, diplomatic, and administrative positions and the Army is having young officers trained for positions as judges and magistrates to make the legal system more reflective of Fijian values and social moves. (Dalton, 1990 p.9).

The growth and sophistication of the security apparatus under Rabuka gave him enormous power, in addition to the near universal adulation that he received from indigenous Fijians. No one could restrain Rabuka. He soon openly and boldly extended his oversight over the trade union movement, continuing into the period of the civilian government a practice he had initiated immediately after the coup. The main trade union leader he had singled out for harassment was Mahendra Chaudry, the popular Indian secretary-general of the Fiji Trade Union Council (FTUC). In one more recent example, Chaudry's home was physically attacked by five persons who made no attempt to disguise their military gear. Damage done amounted to over (U.S.)$6,700 (IBI, 1990). On this notable occasion which drew international attention, Chaudry had coordinated a series of protests by the National Farmers' Union (NFU) which represented the country's 23,000 sugar cane farmers. The confrontation between the government and the NFU arose as a consequence of a major revision in the award of workers' benefits in the sugar industry. The ensuing strike assumed a crisis of national proportions in which the Taukei Movement was re-mobilized to confront the strikers who were mainly Indians. The Taukeis called for the expulsion from Fiji of twelve of the strikers (Ibid.). To combat NFU, which was an ethnically-integrated union of farmers, although composed of a majority of Indians, the pro-coup forces had splintered away the Fijian membership from the union and formed an all-Fijian sugar union. It was this splintering tactic of unions that were hostile to the government, carried out not only among sugar farmers but also civil servants, that the interim government used and exploited in confronting Chaudry and the Fiji Trade Union Congress. In harassing Chaudry, the message intended to deter all trade union protests and strikes with the penalty of harassment and terrorism on the person and property of transgressors. All of this flew in the face of the claims of the civilian government that it had restored the rights of citizens to associate freely and to petition.

The coercive apparatus went beyond the trade union movement into the academic area of the regional University of the South Pacific. From the university, some of the first efforts at opposing the military intervention emanated. Indeed, several academics had served as advisors to the Fiji Labour Party. The military had entered the university and then infiltrated it with its agents, touching off an atmosphere unconducive to open inquiry and dissemination of knowledge. Nevertheless, many students and staff continued their protests, thereby making the university and the trade unions the two most visible points from which opposition to the civilian government emanated. On occasion, the more surreptitious methods of surveillance and terror gave way to open physical assaults by the security forces on the university campus. One recent example in October 1990 involved the abduction of a physics lecturer by soldiers. The lecturer was severely beaten and had to be sent to Australia for medical rehabilitation (Singh, 1991). The lecturer in question was chairman of the Group Against Racial Discrimination (GARD), an association formed to protest discrimination and repression by the government. Several GARD members had burnt a copy of the new constitution at prayer meetings at a Hindu temple and were arrested and charged with sedition. At the end of the prayer meeting which was held at a temple, a copy of the proposed new constitution of Fiji was burnt (*FINS*, 1990b). When the journalists who covered the event reported the story to the press, they in turn were arrested under the Public Order Act of 1976. Amnesty International took up this case and in its report said that those arrested 'have been charged for the non-violent exercise of their constitutionally-guaranteed rights of freedom of expression and freedom of assembly and association under sections 4, 13, and 14 of the constitution' (Amnesty, 1990). Amnesty found that the arrests were not for ordinary crimes but were politically-inspired and advised the Fiji government that 'if they were found guilty and imprisoned on these charges, Amnesty International would consider them prisoners of conscience' (Ibid.).

As a result of the international outcry over the abduction and the arrests of the journalists, the civilian government said that it had apprehended five soldiers for the illegal kidnapping of the university lecturer. These soldiers appeared before a magistrate, given a brief trial in which no evidence was taken, pleaded guilty, and were fined (F)$340 and a suspended sentence for twelve months. The university physicist who was abducted was beaten with an iron bar, tortured, burnt, spent three weeks in hospital, and suffered several permanent injuries including partial loss of sight (Singh, 1991). Witnesses said that the five soldiers convicted were not the ones who partook in the event. No questions were asked about whose orders they were following. The lenient sentence itself served to underscore that the judiciary had become part of the system of control and repression.

The repercussions of the incident regarding the physics lecturer reverberated throughout the academic community. While the kidnapping was not the first case of direct military intervention on the University of South Pacific Campus, this particular event was accompanied by open threats by the government that its 60 per cent annual subsidy to the university budget was likely to be trimmed if academics did not cease using the campus as a haven for their political activism (FINS, 1990b). In response, the Vice-Chancellor of the university issued a memorandum to all staff prohibiting them from accepting official positions in political parties and if they did "they will be deemed to have resigned"(Ibid.). The Vice-Chancellor was acting under direct pressure from the Minister of Education, Philipe Bole. Dr. T. Baba, who was Minister of Education under the ousted Labour-Federation Government and a Vice-President of the Fiji Labour Party, resigned his position as Head of the School of Humanities in protest. Academics were further warned not to use university phones, word processors, and stationery for political purposes. Further, academic staff who wrote on political affairs were threatened with misconduct should they publish views 'that were not balanced.' Along with these new guidelines, the government accelerated its programme of Fijianization of the academic and administrative staff at the university providing ample subsidies for scholarships to its supporters in order to politicize the university with its own sympathizers. Academic staff generally concurred that a comprehensive system of surveillance had been put in place at the university to report on 'political irregularities.'

As the case of the journalists reporting on the burning of the constitution at the prayer meeting illustrated, the press in Fiji remained muzzled for some time. After the semi-civilian government came to power in January 1988, in an attempt to refurbish the tattered image of the military government of Rabuka, a new law was issued on the mass media called 'The Fundamental Rights and Freedoms of the Individual Decree, 1985.' The decree claimed to provide for 'total freedom', but limited this by the words that 'no person shall with reasonable justification or excuse cause any expression to be made that would tend to lower the respect, dignity and esteem of institutions and values of the indigenous Fijians or show disrespect for the Great Council of Chiefs and the traditional Fijian system and titles.' Since the new interim government under two of Fiji's highest chiefs, Mara as Prime Minister and Ganilau as President, who were operating a regime in the name of protecting indigenous Fijian rights, this limitation on the freedom of expression and the press was diffuse and daunting. Immediately after the first coup, two major daily newspapers had remained in Fiji: *The Fiji Times,* owned by international press magnate Rupert Murdock, and *The Fiji Post,* owned by indigenous Fijians with partial financing by Australian businessman John Beater. *The Fiji Sun,* which was closed by the military after the second coup, refused to abide by the loaded military directive that stories published not 'incite racial strife' and 'encourage public disorder'. This provision allowed the coup makers to define and judge the content of the news media to which the *Sun* refused to abide and decided to close down permanently (Herman, 1990). Two main newspapers, *The Fiji Times* and *The Post,* subsequently continued to operate a system of self-censorship but their journalists lived under the fear of transgressing the unwritten limits of offending the ruling regime by reporting critically on unsavory events.

When the journalists who had reported on the constitution burning incident were charged under the Public Order Act, this brought a strong reaction from U.S. Congressman Stephen Solarz, who was chairman of a sub-committee on the Pacific region. Solarz, along with twelve other U.S. Congressmen who were part of the 'Congressional Human Rights Causus', wrote to the President of Fiji saying that 'they were deeply disturbed by events in Fiji', and argued that 'the journalists had a right to report and should not be restricted in a democratic society' (*FINS,* 1991 p.4). In May 1990, to underscore the limits of its tolerance for criticism and unfavourable reporting which were often labelled as 'inaccurate' or 'biased', the West German- financed *PAC News* agency, located in Fiji and well-known regionally for its autonomy and comprehensive coverage of the South Pacific region, was expelled from Fiji. *PAC News* had carried stories critical of Ratu Inoke Kubuabola, the then Fiji Minister of Information who had gained widespread notoriety for his censure of the press and had successfully alienated foreign journalists operating in the region. Ratu Kubuabola was part of the inner circle of power close to both Mara and Rabuka, and known for his militant defence of the military intervention and Fijian political paramountcy. Censorship in Fiji had become equated with Kubuabola and journalists universally expressed fear on the very invoking of his name.

Today, unwritten rules of censorship also operate in the radio services and book distribution system. The government radio stations have returned to providing programmes in English, Fijian, and Hindi. Most citizens of Fiji depend on the national radio run by the Fiji Broadcasting Corporation (FBC) for daily news. Under the Broadcasting Act, the FBC is required under sections 12 and 13 to respond to the Minister of Information in prohibiting or broadcasting any programme. The biased broadcasts by the FMC since the coup brought protests from opposition, politicians, trade unionists, and others. One neutral Australian observer attached to the FBC noted that "in the case of the FBC, there have been instances in which the organization has been requested to broadcast replies to original stories not run by the FBC, even in cases where the national radio station would not handle the story in the first place for fear of courting the displeasure of the powers that be" (Herman, 1990 p.31). A private radio station, FM 96, also operates on condition of voluntary compliance to regime rules, and television services with international cable connections have been introduced. Like the press, these media carry on without engaging political controversy in a system of self-censorship by desisting from commentary critical of the government. Two regional monthly magazines, *Pacific Islands Monthly* and *Islands Business,* also are published in Fiji and especially *Islands Business* has tended to break the bounds of self-censorship in carrying bold articles critical of the interim government. For this, the editor of *Islands Business* has been harassed and made to report to the Minister of Information and security forces. *Islands Business*, however, has grown to sufficient regional and international reputation that the regime is forced to permit it to operate. Even so, the editors admit to fear and operate in an aura of self-censorship. A new Fiji-based monthly has appeared, *The Review*, and has grown in influence but also operates in the atmosphere of self-censorship. In the sphere of book distribution, a number of books on the military coups have disappeared form book shelves. Distributors express fear of victimization. While some titles have disappeared such as *Coup and Crisis: Fiji a Year Later,* edited by S. Prasad, and *The Political Economy of Independent Fiji,* by J. Narayan, a number of new ones have appeared in plentiful supply, including *The Facade of Democracy* by Asesela Ravuvu. *The Facade of Democracy,* written by one of the keenest defenders of the military intervention, is an uninhibited attack on Indians and opposition elements in Fiji and a stout defense of Rabuka and Fijian paramountcy (Ravuvu, 1990). The book, which has a congratulatory introduction by President Ratu Penaia Ganilau, was found displayed in most bookstores and at the international airport. Overall, on the issue of the right of the citizen to freedom of expression in Fiji, an observer argued that 'in the current Fiji, censorship comes in subtle ways through different forms of pressure' (Herman, 1990 p.31). In the area of freedom of religion and conscience, certain practices which emerged during Rabuka's military regime between September and December 1987, were consolidated in the period of the new interim government and thereafter. In particular, the official declaration that Fiji was a Christian country and the decree that Sunday was a day of sabbath to be observed by all were noteworthy cases. Both of these points were reported by the Manueli CIAC Committee [discussed at length in the next chapter] as being overwhelmingly endorsed by indigenous Fijians. In the constitution that was proposed therefore, the preamble commenced with the declaration that Fiji was a Christian country although it proceeded to provide for the free expression of conscience by other faiths. To Hindus, Muslims, Sikhs, and many Christians, this constitutional provision conferred symbolic superiority on the Christian faith and was seen as discriminatory. The Pacific Conference of Churches and the Fiji Council of Churches condemned the idea of religious intolerance that was implicit in the elevation of Christianity for special mention in the constitution as well as the passage of the Sunday Observance Decree. Initially, the cessation of all work and commerce imposed by the Decree was waived for the many tourists and tourist-operated places. However, when the decree threatened to destroy the sugar crop which had to be harvested immediately, it was waived also for sugar harvesting on Sundays. Rabuka reluctantly acceded to these concessions requested by Ratu Mara who was brought back to restore health to the economy. However, the Methodist conference to which over 85 per cent of Fijians belong, with its new pro-coup leadership under Rev. Lasaro, condemned the exceptions that were conceded. On one occasion, an Indian in the sugar cane town of Labasa was beaten by Fijians for harvesting cane on a Sunday (FINS, 1990a). In October 1989, a number of Methodist youths burnt a Hindu temple in Lautoka. In addition, many Indian-run curry restaurants which were ostensibly opened for tourists on Sundays were closed. Together, a sense of religious siege pervaded Fiji. Rabuka, who at one stage immediately after the coup referred to all Indians as 'heathens' and had threatened to ban all Hindu, Moslem, and Sikh festivals, seemed to have mellowed and accepted these faiths as part of Fiji's multi-cultural fabric. Yet, an atmosphere of intolerance persists as the Sunday Observance Decree continues as the law of the land.

VI The Grievances and Demands of Fijians and Non-Fijians

The military coup provided the opportunity for the full vetting of Fijian grievances, as well as the concerns of other interest groups. In this chapter we shall examine the claims and counter-claims coming from representatives of the major groups (Keith-Reid, 1988; FTL, 1988). For the purpose of presentation, we shall divide the competing interests into two broad categories, those espousing the aspirations of indigenous Fijians, and those advancing claims to the contrary, as well as other claims. These claims and counter-claims contended for incorporation in the new constitution of Fiji. The mechanisms for doing so in any kind of balance or fair way were not available. The interim government of Ratu Mara, which succeeded in the wake of the withdrawal of Rabuka's military regime on December 5, 1987, at once sought to display an image of democratic accommodation, as well as to assert and institutionalize Fijian political paramountcy. Hence, the invitation that was extended to the diverse interests in Fiji to express their demands assumed the air of a charade, a perfunctory ritual intended to court the international community about the openness of the government. Even so, the very fact of allowing different interests to ventilate their positions, despite the premeditated unresponsiveness of the ruling regime, served to highlight the main actors in the conflict, their bases of support and the issues which defined the nature of the struggle. For this reason, it is important to survey the divergent claims and counter-claims that had crystalized, since this indicated the seams along which the polity was likely to be challenged and possibly ruptured in the future. It would be in the accommodation of the articulated grievances of all parties, if reconciled at all, that the new constitutional order would win or lose legitimacy. Put differently, if a satisfactory balance was not struck in the distribution of power and privileges, then the constitution would be invalidated from the moment of its promulgation.

To begin with, however, we must present the claims and counter-claims of the rival interests in some sort of systematic way. From the different actors, these were articulated in the context of an ongoing sequence of events which was precipitated by the military intervention of May 1987, and followed by the appointment of a Constitutional Review Committee (CRC) on July 11, 1987 by the Governor-General. The CRC terms of reference expressed the triumphal mood of the moment for the pre-eminence of Fijian interests: 'To review the constitution of Fiji with the view of proposing to the Governor General amendments which will guarantee native Fijian political interests and in so doing bear in mind the best interests of other people in Fiji' (Government of Fiji, 1989a p.13).

Four groups were invited to express their interests to the CRC, including delegations chosen by the Fijian Council of Chiefs, the Alliance Party, the Coalition Labour-Federation Party, and the Governor-General himself. It was mainly at this forum afforded by the CRC that the positions of the different groups were crystalized, remaining fairly durable in all subsequent debates. It was also the manner in which the CRC arrived at its final recommendations, in the almost total exclusion of the demands of the ousted Labour-Federation Party and the full accommodation of the interests of the Fijian Council of Chiefs, that the nature of the constitutional game became defined.

The CRC recommendations were announced in mid-August 1987, but were pre-empted by the second military coup of Rabuka on September 25, 1987, when it seemed that a rapproachement between the Mara and Bavadra-led coalition was about to be implemented under the Deuba Accord and a Council of National Reconciliation in order to launch a new government of national unity. It was not until February 23, 1988, nearly three months after Ratu Mara's semi-civilian government had replaced Rabuka's military regime on December 5, 1987, that a new attempt in the form of a Cabinet committee was appointed to make recommendations for a new constitution. Prime Minister Mara envisaged two major tasks confronting his administration - to restore confidence in the economy and to design a new constitution for Fiji 'acceptable to a majority of people' (Mara, 1988 pp.35-37). His new cabinet committee, however, lacked all the formal trappings of a consultation as found in the antecedent CRC. It produced a 'Draft Constitution' which was made public on September 15, 1988. The 'Draft Constitution', even though it took six months to produce, merely re-affirmed acceptance of the essential interests which the Fijian Council of Chiefs expressed to the CRC (Government of Fiji, 1988).

The 'Draft Constitution' evoked a storm of affirmations and denunciations from the main actors in the constitutional debate, which led the Mara interim government to appoint yet another Committee on October 5, 1988 called the Constitutional Inquiry and Advisory Committee (CIAC) 'to recommend amendments or additions to the Draft Constitution for its general acceptability' (Government of Fiji, 1989). In effect, the CIAC's mission was essentially to ensure that Fijian authority would be unambiguously entrenched in the constitution. The CIAC held many hearings and received submissions from the public before making its recommendations, which were submitted to the Governor-General on August 30, 1989. The CIAC report contained the gist of the new constitution of Fiji, but before its recommendations were accepted, the report was screened by the Fijian Council of Chiefs and the Cabinet. In the end, in July 1980, a new constitution of Fiji which largely reflected the recommendations of the CIAC was promulgated.

This three year-long sequence of constitutional committees and inquiries (starting on June 11, 1987 with the appointment of the CRC and culminating in July 1990 with the promulgation of the constitution) succeeded in clearly identifying the main actors, interests, and issues which underlaid the struggle over the control of the state in Fiji. In the following section, which is divided into two parts, the interests of Fijian paramountcy are presented, first as represented in the views and demands of Rabuka, the Royal Fijian Military Forces, the Taukei Movement, CIAC Report, the Alliance Party, and the Fijian Council of Chiefs. The views opposed to the claims of Fijian Constitutional pre-eminence are represented by the Churches in Fiji and the Coalition parties.

In the section that follows, an elaboration is offered into the general views of Sitiveni Rabuka since he dominated the political arena. His own views and general outlook shaped the demands that were made by others on behalf of the Fiji community. It is therefore pertinent to enter into a short discussion on Rabuka's general views. These would later be translated into specific demands by the Taukeis and others.

A. Fijian demands and interests

(i) Grievances of Lt. Col. Sitiveni Rabuka

Indian domination For Lt. Col. Rabuka, the Fijian coup-maker, the most powerful motive underlining the May 14, 1987 coup had been the fear of Indian domination. For him, it was God's intent that Fiji was for Fijians, that Fijians be governed by Fijians, and that Fiji be a Christian country. Rabuka had no doubt that it was his mission to dismiss the recently elected civilian government, even though it was led by an indigenous Fijian Prime Minister in a cabinet that had about 50 per cent Fijians and 50 per cent Indians. Rabuka's biographers reported that :

Rabuka is emphatic that the Bible makes clear that God chose Fiji for Fijians. It is 'the land that God has given them.' Rabuka asserts. When the missionaries came to Fiji in 1835, they brought Christianity and turned Fiji 'from cannibal land to Paradise' (Dean and Ritova, 1988 p.11).

The British brought Christianity but in order to preserve the Fijian way of life which, at the time of Cession in 1874, was already severely eroded (Thompson, 1968). They confined most Fijians to their villages while they imported Indians and Pacific Islanders to toil on the European plantations. Hence, British colonial policy at once ushered in Christianity and protected the Fijian way of life, on the one hand, but on the other, imported large numbers of alien Indian labourers who, ironically, would be deemed a threat to Fijian paramountcy in the islands.

Rabuka gave the Indian role in Fiji's history a radically different interpretation from that held by most Indians. Indians regarded their coming as an act of deliverance of the Fijians from virtual slavery on the European plantations, a fate which other indigenous peoples in the Pacific Islands were not spared. Indian indenture promised to arrest the decay of the Fijian way of life. Rabuka had chosen to describe the role of the Indians in quite a different light, however. Insisting that he was not a racist, that he was 'not an Idi Amin' and that, in fact, he wanted the Indians to stay in Fiji, he nonetheless viewed Indians regardless of whether they were born in Fiji or not as 'guests in the country' and declared that 'they already have more than their fair share of Fiji's bounty through their very substantial control of business and the economy according to Fijian assessment' (Dean and Ritova, 1988 p.19). Rabuka saw continued Indian presence in Fiji after independence as illegitimate. He felt that with Britain's departure in 1970, all Indians should have returned to India, a position advanced by Sakiasi Butadroka over a decade earlier. Said Rabuka:

In London, the Fijian people and their chiefs were brushed aside. The matter was out of their hands. It was in the hands of the politicians. The Fijians felt that their land should have been handed back to their chiefs who in good faith ceded the islands to Queen Victoria. So far as the Fijian is concerned, this is the missing link - the handing back of their beloved country to them and not to strangers, who, in the course of time, would decide Fiji's destiny in their own country (Ibid.).

From a negative, stereotypical view of the Indians, Rabuka proceeded to evaluate them culturally and religiously:

The problem is fundamental. With a handful of exceptions, the Indians are not Christians. They do not worship God and His Son Jesus Christ. They are...heathens (Ibid.).

Rabuka's negative perspective on Indians was shared by Fijians in general (Premdas, 1978). The fact of the matter was that Fijian-Indian antipathy was deeply embedded in the society. The two communities had a long history of mutual hate and suspicion. Indians and Fijians perceived each other through the prism of long-established communal prejudice (Norton, 1978). In particular, Fijians feared the possibility of 'Indian domination'. After World War II, the Indian population for the first time surpassed the Fijian, a fact which caused much consternation among Fijian leaders. In Rabuka's mind, Indian numerical superiority loomed large as an ominous threat so that he, by his own admission, 'had virtually made up his mind before the Fijian election of April 11, 1987, that a coup would be necessary to protect the interest of indigenous Fijians' (Dean and Ritova, 1988 p.33). Continued Rabuka:

In the simplest terms, the May coup had been staged to restore control of the country to the indigenous Fijians. Everyone is welcomed to come and live here as our guest, as long as Fijians run the nation (Ibid.).

(ii) The decline of the Fijian Chiefly System and the erosion of traditional values

One of the startling features of the Labour-Federation electoral victory in May, 1987 had been the rise of a Fijian commoner to the Prime Ministership. Since 1968, when a fully operative cabinet system was introduced in the colony and a competitive two-party system had emerged, the Alliance Party headed by a Fijian high chief, Ratu Mara, had won all the elections and governed the country. A Fijian-dominated government ran Fiji from 1968 to 1986. Not only was Fijian political paramountcy seemingly ratified by the electoral process, but the idea of the government run by a Fijian high chief was equally entrenched.

When the British assumed control of Fiji in 1874, they recognized a number of persons as chiefs and established a separate 'Fijian Administration' through which the Fijians were governed. British indirect rule sanctified and solidified the Fijian chiefly system extending it to regions where these chiefs had previously had no traditional powers (France, 1969; Durutalo, 1986). When an element of popular representation was first introduced in a colonial council in 1904, Fijian interests were represented by nominated Fijian chiefs. In subsequent colonial assemblies, this practice continued until 1963 when universal adult suffrage was introduced. But by this time, a Fijian Great

95

Council of Chiefs had also been established by the British as the apex organization to reflect Fijian interests. Since independence, Fijian chiefs had occupied the position of Prime Minister and Governor-General.

The ascendancy of Dr. Timoci Bavadra, a Fijian commoner from the western region to the Prime Ministership after the March 1987 elections disturbed certain elements in the Fijian chiefly system. However, this was not the first time that Fijian chiefs and commoners had met on a collision course. In 1974, when Sakiasi Butadroka launched his Fijian Nationalist Party, one of his platforms called for the removal of Fijian chiefs from secular leadership positions. The Fijian social system was studded with a large number of small and large chiefs; Butadroka aimed his criticisms mainly at the more prominent and powerful chiefs. He charged that these chiefs had been abusing their positions in politics by collaborating with rich financial interests, to the detriment and neglect of lower income Fijians (Premdas, 1980b). From time to time, similar criticisms were made, not only of Fijian chiefs generally, but specifically of the Fijian chiefs belonging to the eastern Lauan group from where Ratu Mara hailed. A major regional division among Fijians emerged around this chiefly issue. Western Fijians had long resented being ruled by eastern chiefs (Durutalo, 1986). Dr. Bavadra came from the Western Fijian group. During the 1987 general elections, Bavadra's Labour Party made the chiefs and their arrogation of leadership of all Fijians a major issue in the campaign. Chiefly privileges were to be removed and the chiefs themselves limited to social and cultural functions. Most Fijians still blindly followed and revered their chiefs. To them, the Federation-Labour Party's attacks on the chiefs sounded like sacrilege. The criticisms were particularly harsh on Ratu Mara who was portrayed as old, authoritarian and inefficient.

Rabuka shared the sentiment that the Fijian chiefs were beyond public criticism. He saw such open criticism as part of a wider erosion of Fijian customs. Said Rabuka :

There was a growing materialism which deeply worried the Fijian traditionalists - young Fijians were ignoring or defying the old values, their chiefs and elders. The Labour-Federation coalition appealed specifically to this factor in Fiji's domestic politics by challenging the continuing power and influences of the chiefly system (Ibid., p.43).

Rabuka's concern for the erosion of Fijian traditional values was sufficiently strong to constitute a basis for the military intervention. He, in fact, saw the Labour-Federation Party as a major instigator of the erosion. He regarded the criticisms of the chiefly system as an insult to Fijians, impelling him to use rectifying military force. Said Rabuka:

The chiefly system was ridiculed as being out of date and out of touch. We Fijians cannot stand by and listen to our chiefs being ridiculed and called names (Ibid.).

(iii) Communism and preference for Western democracy

As a high-ranking military man, Rabuka was aware of the role of Fiji in Western security interests in the Pacific Islands. He had a definite anti-Soviet and anti-communist bias, as was to be reasonably expected from an officer in a pro-western military force, and from his affiliation with the Methodist Church. Rabuka was convinced that the Russians and their surrogate, Libya, had connections with the Bavadra government. He inferred this in part from the use of the term 'comrade' among a few of the Labour Party officials. He saw this as 'indicative of a trend towards socialism' signalling 'an alarming change of direction in Fiji's national and international policies' (Ibid.). This drove him to act against the Bavadra government. Said Rabuka :

> Beyond the Coalition's apparent plans to join New Zealand's nuclear non-aligned policy which prevented U.S. warships from porting in that country, there was the association of Labour politicians and coalition politicians with Libya and Russia (Ibid., p.34).

Rabuka was convinced that the Labour Party had connections with Russia and Libya. He alleged Libyan financial support for Labour's election campaign (Ibid., p.38) and also pointed to philosophical influences. In particular, he concluded that because the Labour Party had trade union support, this betrayed its socialist credentials.

Another indirect method that Rabuka utilized to associate the Labour-Federation government with the Soviet Union was the alleged 'India Link'. During the 1982 general elections in Fiji, a beleaguered Alliance Party, seemingly on the verge of defeat, publicly alleged that its adversary, the Indian-based Federation Party, had received funds from the USSR and India (Ibid.). This allegation may have swung the vote in favour of the Alliance, which won by a very narrow margin. A post-election Royal commission of Inquiry exonerated the Federation Party of all charges, and in a defamation counter-suit, the leader of the Federation Party won an out-of-court financial settlement against the Alliance, which apologized. Regardless of this outcome, the Indian factor as well as alleged Soviet interference had become embedded in the consciousness of Fiji citizens. For Rabuka, India's foreign policy, which tilted in favour of the Soviets, provided the evidence of the Indian-Russian connection with internal Fiji politics. Rabuka openly charged that one of India's diplomats, Mrs Kochar, interfered in Fiji politics. It must also be recalled that Rabuka had personal experience with India, having lived for a year there and having done his M.A thesis in an Indian Military College. Said Rabuka's authorized biographers:

> This particular sojourn (1979-80) in India painted into his experience attitudes that were later to play a significant part in the motivations of the May 14 coup... he was indelibly impressed by the depth of India's relations with the Soviet Union(which) raised the question of what might come from an upgraded Delhi-Suva connection (Ibid., p. 24).

(iv) Loss of Fijian jobs

Rabuka alleged that once the Bavadra government had assumed power, several indigenous Fijians were 'pushed sideways' or fired through its Indian component. He argued that this went beyond the prerogative of a new government in shifting certain civil service personnel around, suggesting that they were executed in retaliation for certain Fijians giving Indians a hard time in the past. Further, he charged that the new government had planned action against senior Fijian public servants and that it was necessary to protect them from victimization.

(v) Interference in the Royal Fijian Military Force (RFMF)

Another reason advanced by Rabuka to justify the coup referred to the anticipated interference by the Labour-Federation government in the affairs of the Royal Fijian Military Force (RFMF). Like most military officers, Rabuka abhorred the prospect of civilian interference in the military establishment. The RFMF was almost an exclusive preserve of the indigenous Fijians. Few Indians were recruited into the military. Ex-Prime Minister Mara's son-in-law served as the head of the RFMF, and in many other ways the officer corps served as a source of placement and privilege for the sons of influential Fijian chiefs. Hence, apart from its ethnic predominance, there were irregularities such as nepotism in the recruitment and promotion of members of the RFMF.

Rabuka feared that the Bavadra government with its predominant Indian ethnic support base and lower-income labour programme would interfere in the structure and general affairs of the military. Rabuka further surmised that the left-wing ideological orientation of the new government might lead it 'to introduce specific policies aimed at curbing the influence of the RFMF in Fiji and the indigenous Fijians in the Army' (Ibid.). In his diary, Rabuka further recorded:

Party members do not trust the RFMF and doubted our loyalty, therefore they are likely to introduce measures to gain political control over RFMF e.g. introduction of racial parity principles into the RFMF. This will erode the standard of the RFMF and destroy the government's reputation built over the years. This we cannot and should not accept (Ibid., p.49).

(vi) Fijian split caused by the Labour-Federation Government

Finally, Rabuka felt that the Bavadra government was dividing the Fijian people and destroying their solidarity. In one example, Bavadra personally prevailed on an old Alliance stalwart, Milton Leweniquila, to serve as Speaker of the House. This enraged Rabuka who said it made him more determined to execute the coup (Ibid.). Rabuka also had in mind the role of a critical cause that led to the electoral loss by the Alliance Party: the splitting of the Fijian electors. Prior to the 1987 elections, with the exception of the March-April elections of 1977, Fijians had generally voted with a 97 per cent solidarity for the Alliance Party. Indians had generally given up to 15 per cent of their votes for the Alliance Party. In the 1987 elections, however, some 30 per cent of the indigenous Fijians stayed at home, and of those who voted, only 68 per cent cast their ballot for the Alliance. In a few constituencies where this split occurred, this was all that was necessary to give the Federation-Labour Party the margin of votes to win a majority of seats in parliament. To Rabuka, the split in Fijian society was heresy. He wanted a new mode of political organization which would not lead to the division of loyalties amoung Fijians. In this regard, Rabuka had conveniently forgotten that income, region, and status had already divided Fijians into distinct groupings with different interests. A common Indian enemy was being invoked to unify them.

The Taukei's, Butadroka, and the Fijian Council of Chiefs The 'Taukei Movement' was a spontaneous organization of the like-minded Fijians who sought to remove the Coalition government from office and to institute reforms that constitutionally guaranteed Fijian paramountcy. As a loose grouping, lacking formal organizational trappings such as a charter, officers, headquarters, and fixed membership, the Taukeis consisted of a diversity of characters and sub-groupings difficult to pin down (Howard, 1991). Fijians who identified with it were for Fijian pre-eminence but this concealed a range of sentiments from total intolerance for Indians and non-Fijians to minor concessions to non-Fijians. The ranks of the Taukeis included Lauans and Westerners alike, as well as the educated and uneducated. As a sentiment, the Taukei Movement was clearly defined in an antagonistic relationship with Indians in particular, and bound by a fear of domination and a sense that the Alliance Party had betrayed them in its dealings with Britain, businessmen, and non-Fijians in general. Taukeis were bound together by a powerful 'we-they' solidarity sentiment that concealed their own internal contradictions. After a while, a number of leaders emerged among the Taukeis and served as spokespersons for the movement. Yet this did not demarcate Taukeis easily, since some floated freely without affiliation, some were found in the Alliance Party, and some in Butadroka's Fijian Nationalist Party. Rival factions also emerged within the Taukei movement, each claiming the mantle of authenticity. In one sense, a Taukei referred to any Fijian who espoused a stringent assertion of Fijian paramountcy to the militant exclusion of non-Fijian, and in particular, Indian participation in power and political office in Fiji. The Taukeis also wanted to utilize the state to extend Fijian participation in the private sector of the economy. Hence, the Taukeis as a whole did not believe in the 'balance' in the distribution of spheres of influence limiting Fijian paramountcy mainly to the political arena. They were ethnic supremacists. Some were outright opportunists who saw in the coup the chance to reap personal gain. Generally, they all empathized with the views of Rabuka whom they idolized. One of its more prominent proponents, Dr. Asesela Ravuvu, argued that it 'is therefore imperative that positive discrimination be practiced in favour of Fijians in education, politics, business development, and other areas in which they are lagging' (Ravuvu, 1988 p.188). His intention, shared by many Taukeis, was not merely to be a participant in those areas on par with other groups but, as he argued, 'unless Fijians again predominate socially, economically and politically in their own country, the future looks bleak and racial strife and unhappiness will be exacerbated' (Ibid.). Taukeis like Ravuvu followed the old claim by Sakiasi Butadroka made in 1975 renouncing democracy and equality as alien imports.

The Taukeis were not assigned a separate delegation before the CRC. Instead, the views of the Taukeis, the Alliance Party, Rabuka and the Fijian Council of Chiefs were aggregated and set forth as a collective demand of the Fijian Council of Chiefs before the CRC. These included :

1. Retention of Fiji within the Commonwealth.
2. A unicameral parliament of seventy one members elected on a communal roll distributing the seats in proportions of 41 for Fijians, 22 for Indians, and 8 for General electors (Europeans, Part-Europeans, Chinese, Pacific Islanders, etc.).
3. 50 per cent of public service jobs to be reserved for Fijians.
4. All major political positions such as President, PrimeMinister and key cabinet posts exclusively reserved for Fijians.

Submissions by Fijians to the Fiji Constitution Inquiry and Advisory Committee (CIAC) Fijian interests were articulated to the Fiji Inquiry and

Advisory Committee (CIAC), which gathered oral and written submissions from Fijians throughout Fiji. The CIAC was under the chairmanship of retired army officer, Colonel Paul Manueli, a firm supporter of the Alliance Party. It was composed of a safe set of Fijians, Indians and part-Europeans whose task was to fortify the popular basis of Fijian authority. Essentially, Fijians expressed preferences for six subjects: membership in parliament; employment in the public bureaucracy; political control; Christianity; religious tolerance; and Sunday Observance.

The vast majority of Fijians argued that on the basis of their indigenous status, they should have political and administrative dominance in the executive and bureaucratic structures of government. In effect, Fijians sought political as well as administrative paramountcy. Reported the CIAC :

> ... the majority of the submissions from the Fijian community were conclusive in their view that they were the indigenous people of the country, and as such, their aspirations, and special status should formally be recognized in the country's political and administrative structures ... the Fijian community was adamant in this wish not to subjugate their political position to that of any other community. The change in government in favour of the non-Fijian NFP-Labour Coalition in 1987, in their view, was politically unacceptable and was seen as a forerunner of the future political powerlessness and economic ineffectiveness of their community. It was evident from their submissions that the coup d'état 'nipped in the bud' that potential threat (Government of Fiji, 1989a p.13).

Furthermore, Fijians, recognizing that they were economically not as prosperous as Indians, Europeans, and Chinese, decided to depend on lucrative employment in the civil service to rectify this imbalance. Hence, the CIAC reported that most Fijians wanted 'affirmative action' in public service employment to redress the disparities in income distribution in their favour (Ibid.).

On religion, although most Fijians were tolerant of other communal sections practising their own faiths, they wanted the great contribution which Christianity had played in their social development and in their way of life to be recognized. More specifically, they argued that 'Christianity should be made a religion of the state' (Ibid). Further, Fijians demanded that 'the observance of Christianity should be supported by total restrictions on Sunday activities other than religious worship' (Ibid.). Fijians did not care to make concessions to the claim that such a practice was an imposition on other religions, especially where Sunday observance hampered their economic activities. In fact, most Fijians expressed a desire as a mark of respect to Christian practices, to compel other communities not to engage in any form of distractive behaviour on Sundays. To be sure, these ardent Christian Fijians were willing to relax the stringency of the Sunday Observance rule to allow for the provision of essential services, such as the operation of the public transport system. Arguments by other more liberal Christians such as the Fiji Council of Churches that 'the Sabbath was made for man and not man for the Sabbath', had no effect on the tenacity with which most Fijians defended Sunday observance. In fact, they concurred with an earlier proposal for a new constitution (The Draft Constitution) in which references to Christian scripture were frequently made in the constitutional text.

A special submission to the CIAC was made in the name of the 'Commander and senior Officers of the Fiji Armed Forces'. We shall look briefly at this even though we have already examined the view of Lt. Col. Rabuka at length.

First, the Military Forces argued for the political paramountcy for the Fijian people. Reported the CIAC:

(The Fiji Military Forces) asserted that the present crisis has its roots in the prevailing unsatisfactory social, economic, and political situation as a result of which the indigenous people of Fiji were being deprived of their rights. They were firm in their view that the indigenous people should be given dominant political control in their country (Ibid., p.43).

In the economic sphere, the soldiers displayed special sensitivity to the plight of the poor in Fiji, without specifying their ethnic identity. They argued that Fiji should safeguard economic interests in the poorer sections of the community. They believed that political stability would be guaranteed by such an economic policy. On leadership, the Military Forces stressed the need to recognize the importance of Fijian chiefs in the running of the country.

Finally, the soldiers spoke repeatedly of the need for political stability in relation to what they perceived as external and internal threats of security. To facilitate this end, they called for inter-communal cooperation in finding a solution to Fiji's political dilemma and for a constitution which had been generally accepted 'to unite Fiji's communities as well as various sections of each community' (Ibid.).

B. Demands and interests of the coalition and the churches

The claims and demands of other groups opposed to those who advocated the rescinding of the 1970 constitution and the strengthening of Fiji pre-eminence span a wide spectrum, from communal groupings such as the National

Federation Party to multi-ethnic groupings such as the Fiji Labour Party, the Coalition or Labour-Federation Parties, and the Fiji Council of Churches. The views of the Federation Party and the Labour party did not coincide. When they came together as the Coalition Labour-Federation Party, they agreed to a body of common platforms to fight the general elections in 1987. Hence there was a combined coalition viewpoint separate from an exclusive Federation and Labour Parties viewpoint. The Labour and Federation viewpoints were more or less similar. We shall note the differences and similarities among them as we go along. Apart from these groupings, a salient force that emerged to contest and qualify the position of the Taukeis and other Fijian chauvinists and their views as embodied in the Draft Constitution consisted of the various ecclesiastical bodies in Fiji, especially the Fiji Council of Churches and the Pacific Conference of Churches. Their viewpoint will also be discussed in this section.

(i) The views of the Coalition, Federation and Labour Parties

Dr Bavadra, speaking on behalf of the Coalition, began by challenging the very terms of reference of the CRC with regard to the strengthening of Fijian rights. Bavadra felt that Fijian rights were adequately protected in the 1970 constitution and that, in a multi-ethnic society, giving more to one group at the expense of another was unnecessary and wrong. Argued Bavadra in a letter to Governor-General Ganilau:

> I believe it is fundamentally wrong to assume that the strengthening of indigenous Fijian political rights goes hand in hand with strengthening Fijian political representation. I have stated to you my belief that the rights of the indigenous Fijian people are adequately protected in the present constitution. To effectively disenfranchise people born in Fiji, for no other reason than their ethnicity will not make for long term peace and stability of Fiji. On the contrary, it will be sowing the seed of resentment, disharmony, and even confrontation (*Fiji Times*, 1987c p.3).

Bavadra and the Coalition parties targeted their demands and responses around the issue of discrimination and inequality. They demanded that the 1970 constitution be retained in its entirety (Howard, 1991). The critical issue turned on the problem of Fijian paramountcy as the appropriate mode of recognizing and protecting the claims of indigenous citizens. The President of the Indian-based NFP was vehemently opposed to the proposal for Fijian political over-representation and Indian under-representation denouncing it as 'naked racism'. He ominously warned against the proposed unequal status of Indians saying:

Fiji cannot continue to sustain its present level of greatness unless each of its parts is given due recognition - this consists of all groups of people who live here. There can be no lasting peace unless each of us is recognised as equals before the law, particularly before the supreme law which is the constitution (*Fiji Times,* 1989e p.2).

The President of the NFP observed that, when the coup was carried out, the new government had since then established a 'Ministry of Indian Affairs' similar to bodies which were established in New Zealand, and Australia called respectively, 'The department of Maori Affairs' and 'The Department of Aborigines Affairs'. In each of these cases, these departments oversaw the affairs of an oppressed people. Indian leaders condemned this practice in Fiji accusing the government of hypocrisy and 'splitting the country into racial compartments' (Ibid.). The NFP called on the government to scrap the Ministry of Fijian Affairs.

The position of the main Fijian leaders, as was to be expected, was diametrically different from those of the NFP. Ratu Penaia Ganilau, the then President of Fiji and formerGovernor-General, said that the 1970 independence constitution was flawed because it gave Fijians only 22 seats in parliament as compared to 30 seats to non-Fijians and therefore denied Fijians their right to govern Fiji. Ganilau proceeded to argue that 'only 11,000 Fijians had supported the Coalition Party during the 1987 elections as compared with 100,000 Indians' showing 'that the majority of Fijians did not consider the Coalition Party could safeguard their aspirations, traditions and heritage' (*Fiji Times,* 1989b p.9). He endorsed the proposals of the CRC 'as the best safeguard for the Fijians ... guaranteeing the Fijians a stronger say on how the country is run' (Ibid.). Prime Minister Ratu Mara supported superior Fijian representation in Parliament also by calling attention to the fate of other indigenous peoples in the world :

The Fijian people have learned from history and wish to make history in their own country and not become history. 'Fijians are aware of the destiny of the indigenous Aztecs of Mexico, the Incas of Peru, the Mayas of Central America, the Caribs of Trinidad and Tobago, the Amerindians of Guyana, Inuits of Canada, the Maoris of New Zealand and the Aborigines of Australia (*Fiji Times,* 1989c; *Contact,*1989 p.2).

From this premise, Mara concluded that Fijians had the right of political dominance over other groups:

I also wish to submit that the majority representation provision in the draft constitution is an affirmative action by the internal government to guarantee and protect the rights and aspirations of the Fijian people against other communities and is not intended as an act of discrimination (Ibid.).

The arguments in favour of special rights for indigenous persons received equally strong counter positions from the ousted NFP-Labour Coalition, which felt that it was still the only group that had a legitimate right to speak on behalf of all Fiji citizens. It began its counter-offensive by rejecting outright the CRC Draft proposals calling them 'more immoral, undemocratic and authoritarian than even that of South Africa' (*Fiji Times*, 1989e p.6). As mentioned in the previous chapter, Dr Timoci Bavadra, an indigenous Fijian, noted that the 1957 U.N. Convention to which Ratu Mara referred was designed only to protect the interests of indigenous peoples who had become oppressed minorities in their own land. For Dr. Bavadra, indigenous Fijians were neither a minority, nor marginalized, dispossessed, or discriminated against.

Representatives of the Indian community had generally approached the 'indigenous rights' argument by conceding that only in areas such as land protection, indigenous peoples should be offered entrenched and inalienable safeguards. But that area apart, they argued for general political equality. Harish C. Sharma, the official head of the Indian-based NFP at the time articulated this argument thus:

The reality of the situation is that most Indians today are third or fourth generations of *Girmitiyas* (indentured labourers) and rightly regard themselves as equal citizens with equal rights in the country of their birth. Citizens of Indian origin in Fiji have always recognized the rights and aspirations of our Fijian brothers and for that reason our leaders agreed to the entrenched (land) provision in the 1970 constitution safeguarding those very rights (Sharma, 1989 p.6).

Opposition against the doctrine of special indigenous rights came also from another indigenous group of Fijians. As mentioned earlier, Fijians were not traditionally a homogeneous people, but were divided by dialect, region and social organization (France, 1969; Routelege, 1985). Western Fijians, from where Dr Bavadra hailed, had a different dialect and social organization from Easterners who had hierarchical chiefly structures similar to those of the Polynesians. Western Fijians had more of an equalitarian social structure than Easterners who, at various times in history, were colonized by and intermarried with Polynesians, especially the nearby Tongans. When the British colonized Fiji and recognized the chiefly system as the appropriate governors of the Fijians, they recognized the Eastern Chiefly system as rightful rulers over all Fijians including the Westerners (*Fiji Times*, 1989d p.22). It

105

was from this background that Westerners came to resent Easterners, who constituted a minority among Fijians, referring to their rule as 'internal colonialism' (Ibid.). To the Westerners, the constitutional proposals were unacceptable. A number of them forming themselves into a 12-person Committee representing the 'Western Confederacy' claimed that the draft constitution 'not just discriminate purely along racial lines' but it 'will permit an aggressive minority to use the power of government to colonize these people (the non-Eastern Fijians) for their own benefit' (Ibid.). By favouring the minority East and by giving many new powers to the Fiji Council of Chiefs, the Westerners anticipated a situation in which a class of Fijians would exploit another class of indigenous Fijians making a mockery of the proposals for special indigenous rights. Said the Westerners:

> Sadly, the Draft Constitution sanctions and implements discrimination against indigenous Fijians. The so-called racial and indigenous rights issues provide a convenient smoke screen to obscure what is really being attempted. By reciting the litany of indigenous rights and offering up what the President has called the migrant races as scapegoats and culprits, the interim government has effectively diverted attention from the genuine universal human rights issues involved. The interim government's draft constitution not only partially disenfranchises Fiji's Indians, it also, and in some cases more seriously disenfranchises almost three-fourths of the Fijian population (*Fiji Times,* 1989d p.22).

Submissions by the Labour-Federation Party, as well as by Westerners, proceeded to adduce evidence, by using detailed population and voting figures, showing how the proposals of the Draft Constitution discriminated against not only Westerners but also against indigenous Fijians who were urban dwellers (Dean and Ritova, 1988).

(ii) The position of the churches

Religious factors featured as a critical component in the coup. Rabuka was convinced that the coup d'état was 'a mission that God had given me,' (Ibid., p. 10) and 'that the Bible makes clear that God chose Fiji for the Fijians' (Ibid.). Under the Deed of Cession of 1874, Rabuka claimed that the Fijian signatories 'were desirous of securing the promotion of civilization and Christianity' (Ibid.). For Rabuka, who was a lay preacher in the Methodist Church, it was pre-determined that Fiji became Christian. Thus, when the Labour-Federation Party won the 1987 elections by virtue of its electoral base being preponderantly Indian, this posed a threat to Fiji's destiny as a Christian country. To the Christian Rabuka, all Indians were 'heathens' who belonged to an 'immigrant race' that threatened to dominate Fiji (Ibid.). Rabuka, although acting according to God's command, did not execute the coup in isolation. He confessed in his memoirs that he had a few confidantes, which included Inoke Kubuabola, the President of the Fiji Bible Society. On the night prior to the coup, Rabuka, in a state of nervous doubt about his mission, sought the advice of Kubuabola who assured him that the coup was spiritually sanctioned. Finally, Rabuka said that prior to the coup he had 'accidentally stumbled' on a meeting of the Taukei Movement where an inspirational prayer was made by Rev. Tomasi Raiviki, a close childhood friend: 'God, save us and save our land. You saved the Israelites when the land was taken from them by foreigners. Dear God, please answer our prayer and do the same for us' (Ibid.). Rabuka prayed the night before the coup for rain to fall in the early morning as a sign of God's consent. It was the dry season but in the morning it did miraculously rain. Rabuka decided that he had the final green light.

All of this is important primarily because the Christian Churches would offer their own interpretation of the military intervention and make their own demands for constitutional change. Most Fijians were Christians; the overwhelming majority belonged to the Methodist Church. The opinion of church leaders tended to bear heavily on the political views of Fijians. The Methodist Church was first implanted in Fiji on October 12, 1845 and under the dour discipline of the Protestant ethic, converted Fijians *en masse* and penetrated the Fijian cultural system so that 'the Wesleyan Church became the Church of the Fijian nation and this is true to this day' (Froman, 1986 p.11, 1962). In contemporary Fiji, over 80 per cent of all Fijians are Methodists. Of the 5 per cent Indians who converted to Christianity, a small group espoused Methodism. They were organized separately from indigenous Fijians as an autonomous presbytery but as a part of the Methodist Conference as a whole (Thornley, 1974).

The coup d'état of May 14, 1987, created an immense split in the Christian churches in Fiji, especially in the Methodist Church. For the non-Christian faiths (mainly the Hindu, Sikh and Moslem churches which served the Indian community) there was no dissension in their midst in condemning the coup, because their religious interests coincided with their ethnic identity. For the Christian churches, however, which drew their congregation overwhelmingly from the indigenous Fijian community, the coup was a cause of dissonance. While Fijians enthusiastically celebrated the restoration of unequivocal Fijian paramountcy in government, many of the clergy agonized about the 'rightness' of the coup. The issue of the morality of the coup and its consistency with Christian doctrine was brought to the surface for vigorous discussion by various Christian ministers. The Christian churches reacted separately and collectively just three hours after the coup witha statement:

107

We the heads of Christian Churches have been informed of the military takeover of our Government this day. We call on the Royal Fiji Military Forces to release the hostages immediately and to surrender to the sovereign authority of the land. We call on the people of Fiji of all religions to join us in prayer for an end to this most grievous situation and for the restoration of our duly-elected Government immediately (*PJT*,1989 p.39).

The leadership of these churches, which accounted for over 90 per cent of all Christians in Fiji, unequivocally called for the restoration of the duly-elected Labour-Federation government. Simultaneously, they called on the Fiji Military Forces to surrender control over the government. It was noteworthy that apart from the appeal to moral suasion, these churches had no practical way of compelling the military to return to the barracks. What was certain, however, was that the prompt declaration by the churches made clear that the coup maker's claim to divine guidance was not shared by all of the Christian community. In the week following the coup, demonstrations, protests and prayer meetings, some sponsored by a few Christian denominations, were held against the coup. Several clergy from the Christian denominations organized collective prayer vigils in protest against the coup, and were arrested and jailed. Among these persons was Father Rouse, a prominent Catholic priest whose work among the urban poor had made him famous in Fiji. Some time thereafter, Fr. Rouse was forced to leave Fiji when his work permit was not renewed (*Contact,* 1989).

The major Christian churches in Fiji appeared to be nearly unanimous against the coup. The apparent unity, however, was soon shattered when the Methodist church divided with most Methodists supporting the coup and Rabuka's call, 'Fiji for Fijians'. The Methodist church was for all practical purposes a Fijian Church and the ultra-nationalist Taukei Movement had its base in the Methodist membership. The President of the Methodist Conference in Fiji, the Rev. Koroi, did not consult his fellow Methodist clergymen in condemning the coup. He discovered afterwards that he had espoused a minority position in the church. A movement was initiated to depose Rev. Koroi before his term of office was over.

The person around whom the opposition against Rev. Koroi in the Methodist Church was organized was the Rev. Manasa Lasaro, the charismatic secretary of the Methodist Conference. The Rev. Lasaro was an open supporter of the coup and a close friend of Lt. Col. Rabuka. He viewed the coup in larger terms in which the Methodist Church was portrayed as an integral institutional pillar of Fijian culture. Said Lasaro:

The issues and events involving the church now are part of the national crisis that we have been facing over the past two years. The crisis has got to do with Fijians as a people who are trying to keep their own identity, who are trying to see what their future is in their own country. And when you are talking about the Fijian people you are really talking about the Methodist Church (*PJT,* 1989 pp.46-47).

The views of Lasaro closely approximated those of Lt. Col. Rabuka who, upon seizing the government for the second time on September 25 and making himself President of Fiji, issued 'the Sunday Observance Decree' which made Sunday a day of rest for everyone regardless of religious affiliation. 'The Sunday Observance Decree' would further plunge the Methodist Church into controversy and deepen the cleavage between the two schismatic parts, one headed by the moderate President Koroi and the other by Lasaro. The Koroi faction opposed the decree stressing the limits of imposing such a decree on other religious communities in a culturally plural society. 'The Sabbath is for people and not people for the Sabbath', argued the Koroi position. In concert with the Fiji Council of Churches, Rev. Koroi condemned the decree:

The Sunday Observance Decree crosses over the limits of state authority. It decrees that 'Sunday shall be observed in the Republic of Fiji as a sacred day and a day of worship and thanksgiving to Christ the Lord ...' To legislate for the worship of Christ the Lord is to go against the whole spirit of the Gospel which sets people free from the bondage of the law. Worship cannot be enforced by threat of punishment and force or arms (Ibid., p.43).

To this argument, Lasaro would counter that Sunday observance was vital for the preservation of the Fijian way of life, and that permitting other non-Christian groups to work and play during Sunday distracted and interfered with Fijians from exercizing their freedom of worship. While this debate ensued for several months, the Fiji government once again changed in December 1987, when Rabuka relinquished power to Ratu Mara, who modified the Sunday Observance Decree which had come up for critical scrutiny. Apart from religious objections, the Sunday Observance Decree, it was argued, was a hindrance to the restoration of the economy and a cause of civil unrest.

When the coup occurred in May, 1987, two institutions representing Christians both within Fiji, (the Fiji Council of Churches (FCC)) and throughout the Pacific Islands region, (the Pacific Conference of Churches (PCC)) were already established bodies with influence on public opinion. In particular, the PCC had grown, since its inception nearly three decades earlier, into a widely known and fairly powerful opinion maker, not only on traditional church issues, but also on secular and political matters. The FCC was a more recent body but its voice in Fiji was beginning to gather strength. Together, these two bodies became drawn into a discourse on the implications of the coup, in particular offering interpretation and guidance from a Christian perspective.

The Fiji coup fell into a category of problems unprecedented in the political experience of the PCC. It involved new issues, the forcible removal from office of a legally elected democratic government. There was one complication that made what would ordinarily have been a straight-forward issue into a complex one involving choice of conflicting fundamental values: More specifically, while the PCC advocated democracy and equality symbolically represented by free and fair elections, it was also committed to protecting indigenous peoples in the Pacific from domination and genocide. The PCC had expressed strong pro-indigenous positions with regard to the plight of the first peoples of Australia (the Aborigines), of New Zealand (the Maoris), of New Caledonia (the Kanaks) and of Irian Jaya and East Timor in Indonesia. The coup makers had invoked the slogan 'Fiji for Fijians', clearly arguing that the justification of the coup was the protection of indigenous rights in Fiji. They spoke the familiar language of indigenous rights. But the crux of the problem included not only indigenous rights, but revolved equally around the status of the Indians, Europeans, Chinese, and other non-indigenous Fijians in Fiji, nearly all of whom had been born and raised in Fiji and had lived in no other country and possessed no other citizenship. In a way, the choice of values was between collective indigenous rights and individual human rights. In its first declaration on the coup, the PCC joined its members who had already expressed condemnation of the coup and proceeded to say 'that we admire the courageous way we know some of you spoke out against the violations of human rights by the military regime' (Ibid.).

The PCC chose to focus its argument against the coup on the basis of the violation of human rights. It took, however, cognizance of the collective indigenous claims of the coup-makers' arguments but clearly suggested that to invoke the word 'indigenous' was not to make a morally wrong act right. Said the PCC:

> ... we are all mindful of the mistaken tendency to consider that all that is indigenous, all that is traditional or cultural and even the chiefly systems are right. All these have their good points but all are in need of purification or redemption in Christ (Ibid.).

The PCC was aware that certain aspects of indigenous Fijian culture which the coup makers had extolled were, in fact, structures of domination within the

Fijian community, pointing to the means by which the higher status Fijians exploited the poorer sections. In this respect, the PCC found itself on a collision course with Rabuka. Rabuka had declared that one of the reasons for the military intervention was 'a growing materialism which deeply worried the Fijian traditionalists - young Fijians were ignoring or defying old values, their chiefs and their elders' (Dean and Ritova, 1988 p.33). For some Fijians, the traditions of the Fijian chiefly system were worthy of unmodified retention. But many others saw in the system a picture of corruption and unjust practices. Hence, during the 1986 election campaign, the Labour-Federation coalition levelled strong criticisms against the alleged malpractices of the chiefly system including the failure of chiefs to distribute the monies paid annually in land rents by Indian tenants to ordinary Fijians.

The PCC was aware that the question of indigenous tradition, and especially chiefly rights, had become part of the election debate. It was also aware that the issue was less a debate between Indians and Fijians than it was a debate among indigenous Fijians themselves. More specifically, the more educated and the more liberal to left-wing indigenous Fijians tended to oppose the chiefly system. These persons often cite the record of colonial rule to show that the chiefly system as bequeathed by Britain to Fiji at independence was substantially a colonial creation (France, 1969). The British made 'chiefs' where there were none and froze a changing situation of ongoing competition among warring Fijian tribes in favour those groups and chiefs who supported British colonial control (Ibid.).

Hence, 'the indigenous issue' was caught in deep historical controversy. The PCC was, however, very committed to a position of equality and in its declaration on the coup underscored this point: 'Please allow us to share with you our hopes and expectations that the Churches in Fiji will have a special concern for the weak and poor' (*PJT*, 1989 p.43). Turning more specifically to the indigenous justification of the coup, the PCC argued that ' as followers of Jesus, his ways as expressed in the Gospels now become our measure of what is right and what is wrong' (Ibid., p. 44). The PCC was unwilling to buy the indigenous argument advanced by Rabuka and his supporters and underscored the point that the slogan 'Fiji for Fijians' was emotionally manipulative and unchristian and lent itself to racism and intolerance in a multi-cultural and multi-religious society. Said the PCC:

... we deplore not only the military coup in Fiji but also the violations of human rights, the violence, the tendency to racism and subtle persecution of peoples who do not share with us the same Christian faith (Ibid.).

To the PCC, the military coup was communally divisive. Its claims tended to destroy whatever amity existed between Fijians and Indians. The PCC sought to restore an environment of equality in dignity for social harmony. During the post-coup period, nearly all of the violence committed by the military was aimed at the Indian community. Many were hauled out of their homes by Rabuka's soldiers, detained and beaten. The PCC could not see how the claim of indigenous rights could justify such actions. On the issue of the Sunday Observance Day, the PCC was equally forthright in its point of view. Rabuka's fundamentalist understanding of the Christian message required him to observe the Sabbath as a day of prayer and rest. In a multi-religious society, he did not see anything contradictory between forcibly imposing Sunday Observances on other faiths on one hand and Christian tolerance and love on the other. The PCC articulated its own understanding of what the Sabbath meant, arguing that 'we are now in the New Testament, and Jesus tells us that man was not made for the Sabbath' (Ibid.). The PCC then proceeded to point out that Sunday Observance must be voluntary and in a multi-cultural plural society 'our respect for the Christian Sunday makes us also respect the belief of other religions. We do not enforce our belief on them; they are free to follow their conscience' (Ibid.).

The Fiji Council of Churches was a more recently formed body, less than five years old before the coup. It was an ecumenical body that envisaged inter-religious dialogue among the faiths in Fiji.

> We believe that under God, governments have the responsibility of seeking the welfare of all their people in their individual, family and community lives. This includes the responsibility of ensuring freedom and personal morality. This implies freedom from having the tenets of a religion forcibly imposed on any section of the population (Ibid., p.45).

The FCC pointed to the destructive effects that had in the past smeared Christian history when the faith became bonded with state power warning that 'some of the darkest moments in Christian history are associated with times when the state enforced a particular religious tradition' (Ibid., pp. 46-47). Accordingly it declared that:

> The Sunday Observance Decree crosses over the limits of state authority. To legislate for the worship of Christ, the Lord, is to go against the whole spirit of the Gospel which sets people free from the bondage of the law (Ibid.).

The FCC appointed an internal 'Think Group' to examine the theological issues related to the new constitution of the country. In fact, the 'Think Group' did not get into full swing until after the Mara-led interim government's own cabinet committee on constitutional change had issued its views publicly in September 1988, in the form of 'A Draft Constitution for the Republic of Fiji'. The FCC views, then, were in part a reaction to specific parts of the interim governments constitutional proposals. The first issue that the FCC took up concerned the relationship between Church and State. In the draft Constitution the 'Preamble' said that: 'Fiji shall be a sovereign Republic and shall uphold the teachings of the Lord Jesus Christ'. This affirmation was not viewed as requiring others to believe in the Christian faith, but served instead as a symbolic statement of spiritual orientation and commitment of the Government. Hence, the preamble also asserted the right of everyone to religious freedom and human rights. Taken together then, the interim government's provisions on religious freedom could be seen as as liberal as they were extensive. Apart from the initial declaratory statements saying that 'Fiji shall uphold the teachings of the Lord Jesus Christ', the freedom of conscience rights appeared quite standard fare for open liberal democracies. However, in a multi-religious community, especially where the majority of citizens were non-Christians, it appeared offensive to omit the teachings of the other faiths as the guide to the nation. The singling out of one faith for symbolic recognition was clearly discriminatory. It was the stuff out of which unnecessary social fraction was likely to be generated. Equality in citizenship would clearly be compromised where the faith of one group was extolled as the only set of teachings by which loyalty to the Republic of Fiji was to be upheld.

The FCC began its rebuttal of the proposals on church-state relations by noting that 'deep divisions have surfaced in the context of the current time of crisis' and saw 'that healing and reconciliation are necessary' (*PJT*, 1989b). It saw in the ethnic and religious diversity of Fiji 'gift which can be used to build a rich national identity'. It warned that constitutional proposals should be advanced to promote unity and 'not used instead to divide people' (Ibid.). The FCC saw lasting solutions to Fiji's constitutional crisis coming from 'the Pacific way of resolving differences through dialogue and a search for true consensus' (Ibid.).

The FCC disagreed with the religious proposals that called for the upholding of Christian doctrine. It saw in this a violation of the principle of separation of church and state. The FCC was emphatic in pointing out that 'the government had no authority to uphold one religion or to legislate the teachings of Christ in the new constitution' (*Fiji Times*, 1989a p.2). For the FCC, it was perfectly acceptable for the constitution to acknowledge a divine Creator, but 'the state would be overstepping its jurisdiction in legislating the teachings of Christ' (Ibid.).

The FCC also took aim at other discriminatory and divisive parts of the draft proposals. Two areas need to be pinpointed. First, the proposals made a distinction between indigenous peoples and other residents in Fiji, prescribing benefits and rights unequally between these two groups. Hence, in Chapter III, Section 20, special powers were assigned to the government to discriminate in favour of indigenous Fijians in the allocation of jobs, scholarship, training, etc:

> In its exercise of its responsibility under the preceding section, the Government, through the Cabinet, may give directions to any department of Government, Commission or authority, for the reservation of such proportions as it may deem reasonable of scholarships to educational institutions, training privileges or other special facilities provided by Government; and to assist Fijians and Rotumans to venture into business, when any permit or license for the operation of any trade or business is required by law, may give such directions as may be required for this purpose, and the department or the Commission or authority shall duly comply with such directions (Government of Fiji, 1988 p.24).

The discrimination extended to the composition of the parliament and to the offices of President and Prime Minister. In the parliament, the proposals offered a disproportionately large number of seats to Fijians. With regard to the Presidency and Prime Ministership, only indigenous Fijians could hold these positions. The Parliament would be controlled by Fijians who would be elected separately in a separate poll from other ethnic groups. This meant unequal representation would be institutionalized in the political system.

To the FCC, the issue of special rights for indigenous Fijians and respect for Fijian and Rotuman cultures required careful analysis. It felt that not only Fijian and Rotuman cultures ought to be respected, but all religions and cultures equally. And on the issue of representation, it noted that 'the grievances which led to the upheaval of the coup cannot be resolved by the simple process of allocating the majority of seats for one race' (*PJT*, 1989b p.8). The FCC urged that 'alternative models of allocating parliamentary seats be studied and evaluated so that social groups are represented fairly' (FCC, 1989 p.1).

The FCC had the opportunity to examine the various arguments and counter-arguments on aspects of the proposed constitution. But in the end, it had to work out its own positions consistent with its theological principles. The FCC had great difficulty in deciding where to stand on the indigenous rights issue. It took as its point of departure that it was part of its 'Christian mission and responsibility to affirm certain basic Christian values and to see that they are upheld in all institutions designed to promote the welfare of the people of Fiji' (Ibid.). Among the basic values and principles that the FCC enumerated as recognized by all major religious and international organizations for the protection of human rights were 'the respect for the

114

values and traditions of the indigenous people' (Ibid.). But it also subscribed to a seemingly contradictory principle: 'belief in the dignity of the human person and the rights of everyone to be treated with equal respect' (Ibid.).

The crux of the conundrum was the contest between 'special indigenous rights' and 'equal rights'. The FCC had to take a principled stand which it did by calling for a negotiated compromise in the form of a National Covenant (Ibid.). The FCC called for 'healing and reconciliation' to bring the two major communities together. It wanted them 'to exchange and discuss their views, fears and hopes' so as 'to create a shared vision for the country' (Ibid.). Above all, it wanted to avoid a situation of stalemate resulting in an internally divided society where 'these divisions ... become the basis on which its future is established' (Ibid.). Having said this, the FCC did not avoid giving a more specific view to the constitutional proposal that provided for 'positive discrimination' for disadvantaged Fijians. The FCC did not agree with the crude association between 'disadvantaged' and 'Fijian', noting that all disadvantaged persons were not Fijians. Rather, it argued for special treatment to be offered to all of the poor and disadvantaged 'of whatever ethnic, religious or other social background' (Ibid.). In this way, 'positive discrimination' and 'affirmative action programmes' were de-linked from communal membership. Poor Indians, poor Fijians and others who were poor, should be offered special opportunities.

The FCC offered views on another area of discrimination which was unrelated to communal membership. In the constitutional proposals, women were discriminated against in the sphere of citizenship. Whereas the foreign spouses of Fijian men were eligible for citizenship in Fiji, those of Fijian women were not. The FCC called for the alteration of this proposal. Further, throughout the draft of the constitutional proposals, sexist language referring only to 'men', 'brethren' etc. was used. These were also to be removed. The FCC offered opinions in areas unrelated to Fijian-Indian communal conflict. The important ones among these included: recommendations to provide for a leadership code against corruption, an Ombudsman with a strengthened role to receive and vet citizen complaints against government agencies; a system of checks and balances to moderate the use of power; and a better distribution of powers between the executive and parliament so as to limit the concentration of power in any one institution. Finally, the FCC took the military to task demanding that they be returned to the barracks in the establishment of a government of unambiguous civilian control. In expressing the positions of its individual members, the FCC initially had little challenge to its unity. This, however, was broken by dissension within the Methodist Church. We discussed the background to this event earlier. It should, however, be re-iterated that the Methodist Church under Rev. Koroi was a leader in the FCC in expressing viewpoints against the coup and against the policy of 'Fiji for

Fijians'. When the Methodist Conference altered its leadership in September 1989, the FCC lost one of its strongest pillars of support. The views of the new Methodist leadership representing the vast majority of indigenous Fijians espoused the constitutional proposals of the interim government.

VII Ethnonationalist Supremacy under a New Constitutional Order

On July 25, 1990, the President of Fiji, Ratu Penaia Ganilau, promulgated a new constitution for Fiji and with this single act, established Fiji as the only state in the international community with a political system based on outright communalist discrimination. Ethnic inequality became the defining cornerstone of the new order. The constitution was not based on majority rule; it was a document forged in the service of ethnic supremacy. The ramification was manifested pervasively in the institutions that were established. In every area of political and economic life, explicit priority was assigned to Fijian interests above others. The evidence however, suggested that the new dispensation dealt harm not only to non-Fijians, but also to most lower stratum Fijians. A class and status dimension seemed to be built into the new constitutional order so that those lower income and lower status Fijians, who had so enthusiastically supported the military intervention of Lt. Col Rabuka in the expectation of obtaining a just deal, were about to be systematically excluded and frustrated. Overall then, two types of exclusion were incorporated in the constitution, the first being ethnic, which dealt with the alleged Indian menace, and the second which dealt with the aspiration of indigenous Fijians for equality and justice in their own community. The justification for this ethnically separatist authoritarian order was the claim to paramount rights of Fijians as the indigenous peoples of Fiji. To many, this claim not only licensed a new system of oppression, but was also clearly designed to preserve the privileges of a Fijian elite, acting in conjunction with other privileged non-Fijian sections in the population. In examining the new constitution, we shall focus on these general themes pertaining to the protection of Fijian interests in relation to the problems of ethnic and class exclusion.

The point of departure, however, must necessarily be concerned about the manner in which the constitution came into effect. Most critically, it was promulgated by decree. It was never submitted for consent by the electorate through a referendum. The interim government argued that the population was consulted through the Constitutional Review Committee and the Constitutional Investigatory and Advisory Committee (CIAC), and further examined by the Council of Chiefs and the Cabinet. The Coalition Labour-Federation Party, however, regarded the constitution as illegitimate and literally imposed on the people, without their consent and by persons they had not elected:

> It (the Constitution) was promulgated by a President who was installed by the person who overthrew an elected government; he did so on the advice of a cabinet headed by a person rejected by the people at the last general elections. The shadow of the armed forces and their commander has been cast over the whole process, ensuring that no solution unacceptable to them would go forward (FLP, 1984 p.195).

Hence, a dark shadow of illegitimacy hovered over the constitution. It evoked an image of sheer power imposing its will on a populace. Yet, it would be incorrect to suggest that the interim government lacked support. It was fully capable of garnering up to 50 per cent of the votes if Rabuka consented to the constitution. It would, however, find it difficult to obtain more than a few Indian votes. In effect, the constitution lacked cross-communal consent and legitimacy.

We shall begin by looking at the system of representation incorporated in the legislature. Thereafter, the other organs of the governmental system will be examined, as well as the problems of a Bill of Rights and human rights generally. In doing this analysis, the social, economic and political issues which underlie the constitutional provisions will also be brought to the fore for analysis.

A. The Legislature

As we noted earlier, political representation has been a perennial problem in modern Fiji politics. Prior to independence, Fijians had expressed fear of Indian domination in an electoral system based on the principle of one-person-one-vote. The British administrators responded to this explosive issue of ethnic domination in the polyethnic society by imposing a system of communal representation. This served British interests in the colonial period (1874-1970) and was later to serve Fijian interests against Indian claims for political equality. In the independence constitution of 1970, the rival claims of communal versus individual representation were resolved by Fijian and Indian representatives. Essentially, Indians, despite their numerical superiority, acceded to a system of communal representation which resulted in Fijian control of the legislature and the political realm as a whole. This was part of a formula of balance in sharing of spheres of influence. The *modus vivendi* at that time attested to inter-elite trust and cooperation between the leaders of the Indian and Fijian sections. The issue of representation was muted within this aura of inter-communal amity. However, once this co-existence was ruptured through the instigation of outbidders, the representation issue became inflamed again, and the charge of ethnic domination became persistent and problematic.

When the first coup occurred in May 1987, the aura of inter-ethnic amity had almost completely broken down and each of the two major ethnic communities was attempting to assert dominance. The formula for power sharing had been destroyed. The seizure of power by the military settled the score in favour of Fijian political pre-eminence. Since the time of the first coup to the promulgation of the new constitution, the central pre-occupation of constitutional engineering was focused on guaranteeing Fijian pre-eminence. The main institution in which this was to be embodied was the national legislature. It was this forum that the Coalition parties had captured in the April 1987 election, overturning nearly two decades of Alliance party and chiefly rule. It was the loss of the legislature that symbolized to the Fijian military that Indian domination was at hand. The legislature was deemed the cockpit of power. When it was retaken by military intervention, it had, therefore, to be re-designed so as to ensure that it never again fell into 'alien' hands.

Hence, when the new constitution was formally promulgated it distributed seats unequally in the House of Representatives as shown in Table 7.1:

Table 7.1
The House of Representatives

		Seats	%	Population (1986)
Fijians	[46.83%]	37	53.00	329,305
Indians	[48.74%]	27	38.57	348,704
Gen.E/tors	[5.22%]	5	7.01	37,366
Rotumans	[1.43%]	1		
Total		70		

119

In the House of Representatives, for seventy seats Fijians were given a clear majority of 53 per cent. This did not consist of seats that could be contested by any other ethnic group, since the system of voting was segregated into communal compartments. Fijians, Indians and General Electors could only vote in their respective communal constituencies. Indians, whose population numbers had dropped in part because of migration, were still the largest ethnic cluster in Fiji at the time of the promulgation of the constitution and were assigned 38.57 per cent of the seats for a population percentage of about 48 per cent. Indian under-representation was not new in the history of Fiji legislatures. Even in the 1970 constitution, to which Indian leaders consented, they obtained only 42.5 per cent of the seats at a time when they constituted about 50 per cent of the population. The CIAC, whose recommendations largely determined the terms of the new constitution, had used an 'anticipatory argument' to justify Indian under-representation, pointing out that the depletion of the Indian population was so rapid and the increase of Fijian population so steady, that it was just a matter of time until the percentages of seats assigned to Fijians and Indians would be equivalent to their population numbers. Some evidence existed that Indian and Fijian numbers had drawn increasingly together, but it was not conceivable that Indian population numbers would fall as far as 38 per cent to match the seats assigned to them. In the new arithmetic of representation, it was the Fijians who gained the most, moving from 42.5 per cent of the seats in 1970 to 53 per cent in 1990. Proportionately, the largest losers were the General Electors, whose percentage of seats from 1970 was halved in 1990.

The most critical feature of the new House of Representatives was its inequality of representation built on ethnic criteria. The discriminating ethnic dimension was further reinforced by the prescription that voters cast their franchise communally. To add to this ethnic selectivity, the House of Representatives, which chose the Prime Minister, could only select a Fijian for that office. This was, in part, ameliorated by the practice that all members of the House of Representatives, regardless of ethnic affiliation, would vote together in selecting the Prime Minister. While on the one hand, these constitutional provisions guaranteed that the Prime Minister was Fijian, it did not prevent Indians from influencing the choice of the Prime Minister. This was a rather odd, if not contradictory, aspect of the constitution since Rabuka and the coup makers had overthrown the Coalition government, not because it was headed by an Indian Prime Minister, for Bavadra was Fijian, but because of Indian influence in the Labour-Federation Coalition. Rabuka had argued that the Indian voters brought the Coalition to power and in order to 'nip it (the Indian power quest) in the bud', he pre-emptively overthrew the government lest Indian influence become entrenched. Even though a Fijian such as Bavadra was Prime Minister, this was not enough to guarantee Fijian paramountcy. It would seem that, not only must the Prime Minister be Fijian, but one acceptable to the military. It was the extreme Taukei leaders as well as Butadroka's Fijian National Party which wanted an all-Fijian parliament. They made no pretense of any sort to a system of representation that made few concessions to non-Fijians. Yet, they too seemed to want not just any Fijian as Prime Minister, but one sympathetic to their interests. The new constitution-makers, however, wanted to have a Fijian as Prime Minister but did not overtly express an interest in his ideological identity. They sought to impart some semblance of legitimacy by partial inclusion of non- Fijians in the legislature. At one stage, the CIAC had actually recommended that the office of Prime Minister be left open so that whoever the House of Representatives selected, be it Indian or Fijian, could become the chief executive. In any case, the restricting of the Prime Ministership to a Fijian seemed to have solved only the more obvious aspect of preserving Fijian paramountcy; it still left in the area of ambiguity and potential strife the problem of non-Fijian influence behind the throne, and equally important, it did not resolve the issue of class or status of the Prime Minister.

In the new constitution, the legislature was bi-cameral. The other house was the Senate [Bose Levu Vakaturaga] and was composed as follows (Table 7.2):

Table 7.2
The Senate

1. Chiefs appointed by the Bose Levu Vakaturaga (BLV)	24
2. Chiefs appointed by the Rotuman Island Council	1
3. Prominent Citizens	9
Total	34

In the Senate, Fijians numbered at least 24 out of 34 or 70.58 per cent. This, in effect, meant that Fijian representation in the Senate was much more overwhelming than in the House of Representatives. Theoretically, if no prominent Indian citizen were nominated, no Indian could be in the Senate. If the President of Fiji appointed nine Fijians to fill the category of 'prominent citizens', Fijian representation could be 34 out of 34 seats. The significance of this, in relation to representation, is that Indians would be only marginally present in the Senate. Symbolically, this further institutionalized Fijian pre-eminence in a significant way. The powers of the Senate are limited to vetoing unacceptable bills originating from the House of Representatives and dealing with matters of Fijian and Rotuman land and customs. In effect, practically all legislative powers reside in the House of Representatives.

In both the House of Representatives and the Senate then, powerful inequalitarian motifs dominated the system of representation, aimed primarily at disempowering and excluding non-Fijians and especially Indians. This was the ethnic feature of the representation system. There was also an intra-Fijian regional discriminatory feature built into the legislature, aimed at urban and educated Fijians who had sympathized with the Coalition parties in the 1987 general elections. In the House of Representatives, this devaluation of the urban Fijian franchise occurred in a particular way. Specifically, 5 of the 37 seats or 13.5 per cent went to urban Fijians who constitute 33 per cent of the Fijian population, while 32 seats or 86.5 per cent went to rural Fijians who were about 66 per cent of the Fijian population. This meant that urban Fijians were valued by less than half electorally than the rural Fijians. The Fijians in the rural provincial areas were not equally valued either. The 32 rural Fijian seats were distributed unequally so that large provinces, such as Ba with 55,000 Fijians and Rewa/Naitasiri with 98,000, were assigned 3 and 4 seats respectively, while very small provinces like Lau (where Ratu Mara lived) with 14,000 Fijians, and Namosi with 4,000 Fijians, were assigned 3 and 2 seats respectively. It was no accident that this skewed distribution of seats occurred; it followed a stark political calculation in which the small provinces had tended to be more supportive of the Alliance party while the larger ones including Rewa/Naitasiri, from which Bavadra came, tended to favour the Labour Party. The more rural and traditional the Fijian, the more likely he/she was to support the old chiefly system and the Alliance party. The allocation of seats in the House of Representatives was gerrymandered, not merely to return Fijians as a majority, but to return Fijian members of Parliament who were more likely to support the status quo. All of this maximized the chances that future Prime Ministers would come from a particular stratum of Fijians. There were, additionally, registration procedures and residential requirements which further weakened the capacity of the urban Fijian to be registered on the *Vola Ni Kawa Bula* to vote.

Apart from the arbitrary and unequal manner in which seats were distributed to Fijians in urban and rural areas for the House of Representatives, the Fijian voter was also divided and emasculated by the role assigned to the *Bose Levu Vakaturaga* (BLV), or Fijian Council of Chiefs. The BLV was taken to be a representative institution on behalf of Fijian traditional interests. In the new constitution, it stood at once as a separate representative body bound by its own rules, but simultaneously it was linked to the Senate in a manner that rendered the Senate an extension of it. The BLV had the distinction of being the institution in which Rabuka placed the greatest authority and trust to speak on behalf of Fijians. When Rabuka returned power to a civilian body after the first coup in May 1987, he gave it to Ratu Penaia Ganilau and Ratu Mara, two of Fiji's paramount chiefs. It would appear from this fact that the BLV was a hoary institution anointed by ancient Fijian customs, and that its authority was political as well as theocratic. The BLV however, was nothing of the sort. Called the Great Council of Chiefs, it was invented by the colonial authorities to facilitate inexpensive indirect rule over Fijians. As part of the apparatus governing Fiji, a separate 'Fijian Administration' was erected to administer the fourteen provinces. Using their own criteria and interests, the British decided which set of chiefs to recognize and to appoint in running the Fijian administration. The Fijian Administration and the Great Council of Chiefs therefore, became the tools of colonial administration and, over time, emerged as a system of rule, ostensibly based on the proper recognition of the hierarchy of status and power that prevailed in Fiji. Traditional Fijian society was modified in a manner which reflected colonial interests. In the end, the artificially introduced Great Council of Chiefs, pretentiously serving as the legislative pinnacle of Fijian interests, was engrafted onto Fijian traditional practices as if it had always been there. It assumed a life unto itself but reflected the biases of the British administrators, preferentially for the rule of certain regional chiefs such as those in the eastern provinces. Three Fijian confederacies were arbitrarily recognized as the constituent elements into which all Fijians were assigned. Into this scheme of things involving 14 provinces, each with its own council, and Roko Tui (governor), every Fijian was fitted. Fijians as a whole were hierarchically classified in this system, generally respected their chiefs, and were expected to conform to the edicts of this colonially invented administrative order under the Fijian Administration.

Prior to the first military coup, the Great Council of Chiefs (GCC) was constituted of all elected Fijian representatives in Parliament, eight chiefs appointed by the Minister of Fijian Affairs, seven others appointed by the minister of Fijian Affairs, and two or three representatives from each province. The GCC was linked to the old Senate in the pre-coup Parliament, providing it with most of its membership and conferring on it veto powers on issues of land and customs. After the coup, the GCC, becoming the BLV, was constituted differently by the president of Fiji. Essentially, in the new 54 member council, all Fijian representatives from the previously elected Parliament which would have involved Bavadra and other elected Fijians from the Coalition were eliminated from participation in the BLV. The BLV was now constituted of safe and conservative elements in Fijian society as follows :

1. 42 representatives from the 14 provincial councils (3 each).
2. 3 nominees of the President.
3. 3 nominees of the minister of Fijian Affairs.
4. 1 nominee of the Rotuman Council.
5. 5 ex-officio members (including the President of Fiji, the Prime Minister,

the Minister of Fijian Affairs, the Permanent Secretary of the ministry of Fijian Affairs, and the Commander of Fiji's Armed Forces).

The importance of this belaboured discussion on the BLV pertains to the powers that were assigned to the BLV in the new constitution. The new constitution confers on chiefs a role in the making of the Presidency, in protecting Fijian land and customs, and in influencing appointments to the Public and Police Service commission. Institutionally, the new constitution recognizes the central role of Fijian chiefs in the collective form of the BLV. The constitution went so far as to call the Upper House of the national legislature, 'The Senate of Chiefs', even though as many as 9 out of 34 members could conceivably be non-chiefs. Perhaps the most crucial role of the BLV concerns its power to appoint the President of Fiji, as well as to remove him/her. The President, in turn, makes a number of appointments in consultation with the BLV. These powers apart, under the power of the Senate, they control and safeguard Fijian land and customs. On balance, compared with the 1970 constitution, the chiefs have more symbolic power and more conspicuous prestige, but substantively their powers do not greatly exceed those they had in 1970 unless they actually become embroiled divisively in the politics of naming the President.

The BLV was conferred with enormous powers in the constitution-making process and could not be held accountable for its actions. In a ritual that made a mockery of the deliberative process, the interim government placed the recommendations of the handpicked CIAC before the BLV for its approval. It approved. The BLV in the constitution had the unique power of naming the President of Fiji and provided 24 members out of the 34 persons sitting in the Senate. Despite its pivotal place in the constitution, the BLV had its own internal difficulties in relation to its representation of all Fijians. This was connected to the issue of the 'Fourth Confederacy.' Traditionally, the Fiji islands had been divided into three political provinces, each with its own chiefly structure, namely: Kubuna, Burebasaga and Tovata. Fijians in the western region were not recognized as a separate political entity and so fell under the dominance of eastern chiefs. Western Fijians demanded their own confederacy ('Vasayasa-Vakara'). They wanted to be governed by their own people and chiefs. Because of the refusal of the other three confederacies to admit them, Western Fijians had broken with overall Fijian solidarity vis-a-vis Indians. In the 1982 and 1987 elections, a Western United Front Party emerged to challenge the Fijian-based Alliance Party. Dr. Bavadra himself was a Westerner. In the new constitution, once again western chiefs and a western confederacy had not been recognized.

The legislature of the new government in the constitution can then, be properly conceived as consisting not of two chambers, but of three: The House of Representatives, the Senate, and the BLV. In each, Fijians are either in the majority and in executive control, or they are overwhelmingly, if not completely, in control. In a sense, the non-Fijian, and particularly the Indian population, have not only been marginalized by the unequal provisions of the constitution, but they have been substantially taken out of the equation of power in Fiji. This means that the new contest for power and privileges has devolved to Fijians themselves. This is likely to unleash grave internal rivalry among Fijians for the values of the system. Internal Fijian struggles have already emerged and to the extent that non-Fijian resources are enlisted in this struggle, non-Fijians can re-enter the equation of power politics. Being excluded, they will always threaten the stability of the system.

B. The Executive: Prime Minister, President, public bureaucracy and the military forces

(i) Prime Minister and President

In the new Executive created by the constitution, a number of signal changes alter the nature of the Fiji political system in important, if not ominous, ways. Both the Prime Minister and President must be indigenous Fijians. Under the Republic, the President no longer represents the Queen of England but, as in the prototypical parliamentary form of government, plays mainly a figure-head symbolic role with some crucial exceptions. Most importantly, the President (or Governor-General in a parliamentary arrangement) is often regarded as a person who expresses the larger unity and harmony of the state. This suggests that such a position should be filled by some one who is above the divisive political struggles of partisan politics and expresses the ideals of justice in the state. In a multi-ethnic and multi-cultural state, the position of President embodies immense symbolic significance in promoting inter-sectional harmony. Hence, in places such as Canada, India and other multi-ethnic countries, a special effort is made to appoint a person who symbolizes tolerance and unity. In the case of Fiji however, the President is prescribed as a Fijian so that the idea of ethnic political pre-eminence is asserted over other communities. From the outset, therefore, the Presidency imparts alienation and divisiveness. A distinguished Chinese, European, Part-European or Indian citizen of Fiji cannot aspire to the post of President. Such a person from another community could symbolically offer popular satisfaction in the commitment to multi-culturalism and ethnic diversity. This however was not the claim and justification of Rabuka and the coup-makers who proclaimed 'Fiji for Fijians.' Even among Fijians, the appointment of the President by the BLV virtually excludes a Fijian commoner from the post.

The main executive role of running the government resides in the role of Prime Minister. However, unlike the 1970 constitution and other prototypical parliamentary systems, the Prime Minister of Fiji under the new constitution has become almost imperial. A massive shift of powers was prescribed to the Prime Minister so that a highly centralized executive system was put in place. When attached to the idea that the Prime Minister like the President must be an indigenous Fijian, the power to repress disliked ethnic communities is made easily available. Put differently, by itself an authoritarian order can be deemed dangerous and undesirable, but when central powers are linked antagonistically to the ethnic identity of nearly half the population, a fascistization process is potentially embedded in the order of things.

The centralization of accumulated powers is evidenced by several constitutional provisions which render a number of critical institutions dependent on the Prime Minister. The judiciary for instance, which should be independent, is substantially staffed from the level of the Chief Justice to magistrates by a crucial role of the Prime Minister in appointments. Similarly, the removal of judges is initiated by the executive under the Prime Minister's control. While there is a provision for a Judicial and Legal Services Commission, it defers to the Prime Minister the appointment of many magistrates and registrars. The great dependence of the judiciary on the executive for its critical staff not only enfeebles the judiciary, but also emasculates the concept of separation of powers necessary to make governments moderate and accountable for their actions. The centralization of powers of the Prime Minister also extends into the Public Service Commission whose activities are intended to ensure impartiality and efficiency in the behaviour of the civil service. The Prime Minister advises the president on the appointment of members of the Public Service Commission, the Police Service Commission, the Constituency Boundaries Commission and a majority of members of the Electoral Commission. Apart from the standard power of the Prime Minister to dismiss Cabinet ministers and dissolve parliament, the Prime Minister of Fiji also possesses astounding powers to penetrate other institutions, undermine their independence, and bring them to the service of the regime in power. Under a moderate and trusting Prime Minister, no harm may be done to democratic practices. But under an extremist Taukei, or someone similar, the constitution confers a latitude of power and influence to the Prime Minister that can establish a constitutionally permitted repressive order marked by both ethnic and other antipathies. Finally, the Prime Minister can initiate action to dismiss the President, whose responsibility includes oversight over the compliance of the government with constitutional requirements. While under the dual rule of Mara and Ganilau, these roles were reconciled because of unanimity over the purpose of the government. In the future when these two incumbents disagree, an opportunity exists for Prime

Minister-Presidential strife. The more likely scenario consists of complicity between Prime Minister and President especially where each belongs to the chiefly establishment in utilizing the new executive order to install a veritable unaccountable authoritarian system.

(ii) The public bureaucracy

From a practical day-to-day standpoint, a substantial part of the struggle among the different ethnic communities pertains to access to employment, especially in the public service. As related in previous chapters, one of the major areas of contention and conflict between Fijians and Indians was employment in the public service and state enterprises. Under the 'balance' in the distribution of the spheres of influence, the governmental apparatus was regarded as the predominant preserve of Fijians. However, as Indians found the availability of land constricted and their numbers grew, they sought employment in the public sector and elsewhere. As recounted earlier, this triggered a contest over a public resource that in theory was allocated according to the principle of merit. Indians tended to outperform Fijians in academic achievements and this tilted competition for public service posts in their favour. The impact was to threaten Fijian predominance and control of the public service. This Fijians saw as a threat to the principle of 'balance', which allowed only for a certain tolerable amount of Indian presence in the public service and governmental system. In certain parts of the governmental apparatus such as the military forces, the Fijian Administration, and the National Land Tenure Board (NLTB), overwhelming Fijian presence has been jealously safeguarded. What complicated Indian entry into the public service was the fact that many of the senior posts were informally regarded as the preserve of the children of the chiefly establishment. Hence, Indian 'intrusion' was not merely impacting on the prospects of ordinary Fijians gaining privileged access to the public service, but on a critical stratum of Fijian society. The struggle for public posts and privileges including the award of government scholarships and access to loans was therefore locked into competition over class and status claims as well as ordinary employment opportunities.

When the first military coup occurred, one of the main grievances articulated related to employment in the public service. Fijians demanded that governmental apparatus not be overrun by non-Fijians, but be made a place where they could gain access to most of the jobs and benefits of the public service. It was therefore not unexpected that this claim to privileged access be enshrined in the constitution. Under Section 127(11), it was stipulated that 50 per cent of the posts at each level of the governmental service be staffed by Fijians and Rotumans, and this principle was extended to the Judicial and legal services division of the government under Section 124(4). Non-Fijians, even though they constituted over 50 per cent of the population, were allocated at least 40 per cent of the posts. The rationale for this system of inequality was the doctrine of 'affirmative action', which was invoked to rectify imbalance in group representation in the public arena. Implicitly, the use of affirmative or positive discrimination entailed the suspension of merit as the criteria of recruitment to the public service. In order to ensure that the public bureaucracy was responding to the demands for Fijian preponderance in the public service, the Public Service Commission was brought under the control of Fijian direction. The chairman of the Public Service Commission and at least one other member must be Fijian.

For Fijians, it was more than reasonable that 50 per cent or more of civil service positions be assigned to them since Chinese, Europeans and Indians find employment much more easily than Fijians in the private sector. Hence, Fijian over-representation in the public sector was offset by Indian over-representation in the private sector. For Indians, this constituted a spurious argument that would likely discourage Fijians from improving their qualifications and competing on merit with non-Fijians for jobs. Indians champion the case for appointment on the basis of merit. They favour the market as the determinant of the allocation of employment positions. They feel that their investment in educating their children is frustrated by the limitation on the number of jobs assigned to them in the public service. If Indians with the same or better qualifications than Fijian civil servants are turned down for public jobs, then they feel that new lands ought to be made available to them to enter agriculture. However, the land policy of the NLTB under the Fijian-run government had led to less rather than more land being made available to Indians every year. As a result of all of this, many Indians argue that they have had to migrate seeking job opportunities overseas.

The affirmative action provisions of the constitution set off a storm of protest, especially by the excluded communities. Not only were a minimum of 50 per cent of public service jobs to Fijians involved, but similar discrimination was also permitted in the award of schemes established by parliament for the allocation of government scholarships, the award of trade and commercial licenses, loans and the distribution of other state services. Taken together then, the 'affirmative action' programme institutionalizes the practice of ethnic discrimination. It both confirms Fijian economic inferiority and frustrates non-Fijian economic efforts. Fijians, however, feel that they desperately need this sort of compensatory assistance so as to participate meaningfully in the patrimony of the state where non-Fijians do disproportionately well. Statistically, the concessions made to Fijians in these areas are very large. The larger problem consists of the dual economic citizenship that has been created so that the effort and industry of one section is seen to be made to pay for the under-achievement of another group. At least, this is how many non-Fijians saw the matter. It was the Coalition parties that most vehemently condemned the programme of discrimination arguing that such discrimination should not be practised in relation to one ethnic community but in favour of those in need regardless of ethnic affiliation. Further, the Coalition saw the discriminatory provisions as intended not necessarily to bring preferential advantage to deserving Fijians, but to a particular stratum of privileged Fijians. The Coalition argued that while there should be a system of positive discrimination in specific cases, this should be extended only to 'those who are genuinely disadvantaged' (Ibid.).

It underscored this point, pointing out that 'some of the poorest and most wretched people in Fiji are Indo-Fijians with little education, low incomes, without security of land which provides the basis of their livelihood, and now also without an effective political voice' (Ibid.). It emphasized that 'they are as deserving of special assistance as the poor amoung the indigenous Fijians' (Ibid.). In part, the Coalition arguments were intended to destroy the myth that Indians as a whole were well off and Fijians poor. World Bank estimates showed that the income gap between Indians and Fijians was 'relatively moderate' with the average income of the Indian family at (F)$4,003 and the Fijian (F)$3,398 (Chand, 1990 pp.167-193). Among the employed, 62 per cent were Indians. The wealth often associated with Indians was owned mainly by a small community of businessmen; most Indians were not rich. In contrast, nearly all Fijians have access to an ample supply of land in their villages to which they can go if they choose. Most Indians have no such access. Among Fijians, a large middle class has emerged with privileged access to education and jobs. They constitute a minority of Fijians however. Hence, both among Fijians and Indians, underprivileged persons predominate. It was to these persons that a system of affirmative action should be addressed, it was argued. The Coalition levelled the charge that the problem of access as provided for by the constitution would serve only to re-enforce the privileged positions of some Fijians and perpetuate 'corruption, nepotism, and incompetence' (Government of Fiji, 1990).

It was important to the critics of the affirmative action programme that they not seem to favour some sort of device by the government on behalf of the poor and underprivileged either as individuals or groups. In fact, this is provided for by Article 4 of the *International Convention on the Elimination of all Forms of Racial Discrimination* but only under carefully circumscribed circumstances. Among these circumstances are (i) compatibility with democratic practices so that all communities are treated equally and fairly; (ii) avoidance of practices that maintain and perpetuate separate and unequal communities and instead the promotion of inter-community integration and harmony; (iii) the allocation of aid proportional to need; and (iv) such aid should be only temporary. Together then all these qualifiers had been violated in principle and practice by the new Fiji constitution.

(iii) The Judiciary and Ombudsman

For dominance to be complete, it was necessary that not only the legislature and the executive be preponderantly Fijian-staffed, but also the judiciary. Immediately after the coup, it was the Supreme Court judges led by Fijian Chief Justice and his Indian associates who declared that the coup was illegal and advised the Governor General accordingly. During the crisis over the transfer of power from the ousted Coalition parties to the new rulers the Supreme Court, which was ethnically-mixed, steadfastly refused to cooperate in giving legal sanction for the removal of the government by force. The courts had proven to be an embarrassment to the military so that when Rabuka seized the government in the second coup of September 25, 1987, he proceeded to reorganize the judiciary to suit his own needs. This he was able to do only in part and the Supreme Court continued to operate with some autonomy. Several of the judges of mainly non-Fijian descent, as well as magistrates were intimidated, and like many lawyers in the country, decided to leave Fiji. The incontrovertible fact was that the coup caused the creation of an ethnic divide in nearly all institutions so that in the judiciary, nearly all Fijians and Indians were for the coup and against, respectively. The opposition of Indian lawyers and judges therefore was tainted with ethnic interests. The insertion of the military into the government threw the entire legal system into confusion. It was not clear what laws still applied since the military ruled whimsically by decree and the old parliament and courts were sidelined.

A reconstruction of the judiciary was necessary to render it, in its laws and personnel, more compliant to the new ethnically-slanted system of justice administered by the military and interim civilian governments. In the new constitution, several changes were instituted to effect this end. To begin with, the Chief Justice must be a Fijian; this was an odd provision in the sense that the Chief Justice who gave Rabuka so much trouble was a Fijian. However, since he was close to retirement, once he was removed, it was hoped that his replacement would be more obedient to the ruling regime. The signal changes in the judiciary made in the constitution point to the greater direct and indirect involvement of the Prime Minister and President in the appointment and dismissal of judges and magistrates. More specifically, while section 101(3) states that '(E)very court shall, in the exercise of its judicial functions, be independent of the executive or any other authority', the Prime Minister appoints the Chief Justice, and the President and other judges after consulting the Judicial and Legal Services Commission. There is nothing to compel the Prime Minister or President to accept the advice of the Judicial and Legal

Services Commission. A Fijian-stacked appointment committee is likely to comply with the Prime Minister. Once appointed, judges need to enjoy the sort of tenure that can insulate them from the external influences. Under the new Fiji constitution, however, such insulation is very tenuous. The executive branch has the power to initiate charges for the removal of a judge and to appoint the tribunal to decide the merit of the allegations. This provision serves to ensure that uncooperative judges and magistrates can be easily reined in.

The formal structures in the judiciary need not necessarily lead to interference with the administration of justice. Many aspects in fact appear to be quite innocuous. However, the Fiji political situation became very unsettled after the military intervention and the authoritarian order needed to maximize compliance from all institutions to survive and redefine the new order. Inevitably, this meant that the judiciary, especially because of its initial recalcitrance, became a prime candidate for political manipulation. After the large exodus of lawyers, Rabuka's military regime had already started to recruit Fijians to constitute the bulk of the magistracy and to offer incentives for Fijians to enter the legal profession to replace the many non-Fijians who had migrated after the coup. The Fijianization of the judiciary permits the use of Fijian extra-legal pressures, through customary norms, to be invoked by Fijians chiefs and rulers ensuring compliance with the special political needs of those who govern. The recent spate of court cases where soldiers were implicated in assaults against a university lecturer and union leaders and the sudden lapse in the severity of justice administered on the self-confessing culprits suggest the shape of things to come in the administration of justice.

Another institution outside the judiciary, but which administers judgements on matters related to complaints in the public service, is the Ombudsman. Ordinarily, the Ombudsman, where free and independent, can constitute a salutary force in the administration of justice, especially in a country where the public bureaucracy is very large and plays an extensive and intimate role in the lives of the citizens. Under the new constitution, an Ombudsman is provided for, but many of its investigatory teeth have been removed. Specifically, a number of important institutions have been removed from its purview including the NLTB. The NLTB administers the leasing of land from Fijians to Indians; this has become an explosive area and many charges both by Fijians and Indians have been laid against irregularities in the NLTB. If, in the areas where the Ombudsman is permitted to operate, the investigation proves to be embarrassing, the Prime Minister can stop an investigation. The pretext under which this can be done is by invoking the interests of national security.

There are other areas of the judicial system and supporting structures which have been deliberately structured to effect a sectional bias. The chairman of the Police Service Commission as well as the Police Commissioner must be Fijian. The police force was, at the time of the first coup, almost evenly divided between Indians and Fijians, and the then Police Commissioner was an Indian. At least half of the staff in the judicial and legal services are now required to be Fijian. The judiciary cannot review the legislation that relates to Fijian and Rotuman customary institutions and practices. And finally, the constitution allows for the setting up of a separate set of Fijian courts in the Fijian Administration. Magistrates of these courts will be appointed directly by the Prime Minister.

C. Civil liberties and human rights

One of the most controversial areas of the new constitution relates to civil liberties and human rights. In promulgating the new constitution, the President pointed to the Bill of Rights, which was meant to entrench and guarantee the availability and protection of human rights and civil liberties for all citizens: 'Among rights specifically guaranteed are the right to life, liberty, security of person, freedom of conscience, etc.' One observer, a former President of the Fiji Law Society, noted the President's repeated and obsessive insistence that these rights were guaranteed: 'In his speech at the ceremony on July 25 when he proclaimed the constitution, Ratu Sir Penaia Ganilau dwelt at length on these freedoms, reassuring everyone yet again that they are 'guaranteed'' (M. Johnson, 1990 p.23). These rights are labouriously catalogued in Chapter II of the constitution. They are all swept away, however, by section 162(1) of the constitution, which is tucked away towards the end of the constitution almost in fine print. Section 162(1) evokes immense controversy for it provides for the easy suspension of all the basic rights by a simple majority act of parliament for dubious reasons. Says Section 162(1):

If an Act of Parliament recites that action has been taken or threatened by an substantial body of persons, whether inside or outside Fiji a) to cause a substantial number of citizens to fear organized violence against persons or property; b) to excite disaffection against the President of the Government; c) to promote feelings of ill-will and hostility between different races or other classes of the population likely to cause violence; d) to procure the alteration, otherwise than by lawful means, of anything by law established; or e) which is prejudicial to the security of Fiji, any provision of that law designed to stop or prevent that action shall be valid notwithstanding that it is inconsistent with any of the provisions of Chapter II, or would, apart from this section, be outside the legislative power of Parliament....(Government of Fiji, 1990).

132

Under section 162(1), the special legislation that empowered the suspension of basic rights allows not only for this to be done by a simple majority in Parliament, already controlled by more than a majority of Fijians, but also provides that 'emergency' circumstances which are deemed prejudicial to the security of the state can be entirely imaginary and concocted for political ends. The threat to Fiji's security needs not be submitted to any form of validation and can be perceived to come from 'any substantial body of persons, whether inside or outside of Fiji.' The opportunity to challenge the basis of invoking section 162(1) is taken away by the constitution. Under section 19 of Chapter II of the Bill of Rights, a citizen can challenge the infringement of his/her rights by appealing to the judiciary. Under section 162(1), this recourse is eliminated. Commented Queen's Counsel George Newman who served as legal advisor to the Commonwealth Office in London:

I have been referred to Section 162. According to this, the act of Parliament simply has to recite that action has been taken by any substantial body of persons inside or outside of Fiji, and it has to be one or other or of A to E, and that is sufficient for the law to remain valid, notwithstanding the provisions of Chapter II. As it stands, I have seen nothing here which would enable such an act to be challenged or reviewable because the constitutional means for redress would not be applying since they are in Chapter II (Johnson, 1990 p.23).

Established substantially to entrench and protect minority rights, the Bill of Rights in democratic systems typically cannot be set aside without at least two-thirds support by Parliament and a national referendum in addition. Under Fiji's new constitution, all the 'guaranteed' rights can be easily swept away, leaving minorities vulnerable to persecution. George Newman remarked that 'I have never seen anything that has taken this shape in other constitutions. It runs into a number of fairly elementary constitutional problems, it offends quite a number of elementary constitutional rules' (Ibid.).

The diametrical contradictions between Chapter II and Section 162 of the constitution underline the dual-headed structure of pressures that confront any new Fijian-dominated regime. On the one hand, the need for international recognition has to be met; without it, Fiji could face boycotts and lose aid and markets for its products. At the same time, the ruling regime must protect itself from challenges to its hold to power; this, in an unjust order is bound to be recurrent and therefore demands a repressive system of government aimed at eliminating opposition. To some extent, this duality in the conflict of demands can be explained away by invoking claims to indigenous rights. Indigenous rights had become a broad category under which unusual self-serving and repressive acts were justified. It allowed for room to institute an order based on inequality however controversial it was. However, the establishment of a system of rights that is easily abridgable and that can be used against any opponent of the ruling regime, regardless of ethnic identity, suggests ulterior motives. It seems, whether it was justified or not, that the objective was to institute a form of authoritarian government by those who initially seized power on the pretext of protecting indigenous rights.

Even if it is conceded that the emergency powers under Section 162 will be used sparingly, there are still numerous offensive features put into the Bill of Rights in the new Fiji Constitution. To begin with, freedom of speech and expression is limited 'for the purpose of protecting the reputation, dignity, and esteem of institutions and values of the Fijian people, in particular the *Bose Levu Vakaturaga* and the traditional Fijian system and titles.' Clearly, this provision provides for a sweep of constraints, much of it within the sphere of ambiguity that can cripple legitimate criticism against structures such as the BLV and Fijian chiefs, which are deeply enmeshed in politics. If it is true that the underlying structure of power that is erected upholds the claims of a particular regional group of Fijian chiefs to power, then it will be very dangerous to aim critical commentary on how public decisions are made, and why. It is noteworthy that the Coalition parties, which won the elections in 1987 criticized the alleged corruption that existed in the chiefly system and had promised to alter this state of affairs. Rabuka gave as one of his reasons for executing the coup the 'disrespect' that was shown to the chiefs by the Coalition parties during the election campaign. Bavadra had charged that certain paramount chiefs were involved in business deals for their own gain and that chiefs should be confined to traditional ceremonial roles. The leader of the Fijian Nationalist Party Sakiasi Butadroka, who was politically on the opposite political pole from Bavadra, had also condemned the role of chiefs in politics and business. The chiefly hierarchy in power would now be able to silence both the Fijian Nationalists and the Coalition.

To curtail other aspects of freedom of expression, after the constitution was promulgated the interim government under Mara threatened to initiate a controversial system of annual registration under which newspapers were in effect required to obtain a license to operate. Prime Minister Mara argued that such registration was necessary 'to ensure responsibility, accuracy and cultural sensitivity' (*Fiji Times,* 1990a p.2). Mara denied that he had ever issued oral or written instructions to the mass media to practice self-censorship. However, under a system of licensing, this would become a reality. The very threat of the licensing system was sufficient to cause self-censoring compliance in the mass media.

A major area where basic rights have been abridged outright relates to equality in relation to the franchise. The fact that a non-Fijian is permanently consigned to a minority offends international law and specific conventions to

134

which Fiji is a signatory. *The Universal Declaration of Human Rights* states that all persons are 'equal in dignity and rights' and that this should not be abridged on the basis of 'race, colour, sex, language, religion, political or other opinion, national or social origin, property, birth, or other status' (article 2). These prohibitions are repeated in several other conventions including Articles 2, 3 and 26 of the *International Covenant on Civil and Political Rights*; Article 3 of the *International Covenant on Economic, Social and Cultural Rights*, and Article 5 of the *International Convention on the Elimination of All Forms of Racial Discrimination*.

These international covenants to which Fiji is a signatory provide for equal franchise under governments based on equal citizen participation in free and fair elections. The constitution-makers in Fiji sought to get around these requirements by invoking various conventions on indigenous peoples, especially the International Labour Organization's *Convention on Indigenous and Tribal Peoples of 1989*. However, the problem with invoking this particular convention is that it sought, in the case of Fiji's new constitution, to enable indigenous peoples to enjoy more rights than others and to institute a new system of domination and inequality. The context in which these rights were originally adumbrated in various international conventions occurred where indigenous peoples were in a minority and were treated inhumanely and unjustly. The central idea of the ILO's *Convention on Indigenous and Tribal Peoples in Independent Countries* was to institute an order that guaranteed equally fundamental rights including equality of franchise.

Another area where the Fiji constitution has infringed basic rights pertains to the compulsory allocation of at least fifty percent of public service jobs to one ethnic community. Article 21(2) of the *Universal Declaration of Human Rights* and Article 25(c) of the *International Covenant on Civil and Political Rights* confer equal access to employment and the ILO's 1958 *Convention on Discrimination (Employment and Occupation)* required that signatories provide equality of opportunity with respect to employment and occupation. Further, under Article 3 under UNESCO's *Convention Against Discrimination in Education (1962)* quotas in education for scholarships and admissions are prohibited 'based solely on the grounds that pupils belong to a particular group'. Together, all these provisions are qualified by the right to affirmative action only when it is temporary, aimed at the genuinely disadvantaged regardless of race, sex, religion, etc., and hedged in by other qualifiers which render the Fiji constitution guilty of gross infringement. As discussed earlier, the affirmative action programme of Fiji, embedded in the constitution, fails to accommodate the disadvantaged needs of all persons regardless of ethnic identity and seems calculated to cater to the demands of maintaining political power of a particular group of Fijians. Affirmative action then, has emerged as a system of patronage and seems to be permanent.

There are other difficulties found within the constitution such as the unequal treatment of women with regard to access to citizenship, and of indirect difficulties associated with the appointive powers of the Prime Minister vis-à-vis the judiciary. These apart, the final major problem that should be mentioned relates to the role assigned to the Fiji Military Forces. Specifically, under Section 94(3) the Armed Forces 'shall have the overall responsibility ... to ensure at all times the security, defence, and well-being of Fiji and its peoples.' Clearly, this is an open recipe for military intervention. No test of criteria is offered to authenticate the judgement of the military in carrying out this duty. Above all the institutions of democracy which are embedded in the new constitution is the superimposition of the unelected military as the final arbiter of the well-being of the people.

Looking at the constitution as a whole, the reception that it received from the international community was one of universal condemnation. Australia, Fiji's most significant regional ally and power, through Senator G. Evans, its then Minister of Foreign Affairs said that 'it was not terribly impressed by the constitution' which was 'racially-based' (FINS, 1990a p.4). The Australian sector of the International Commission of Jurist released a nine-page response to the constitution giving a detailed critique based on both ethnic and class grounds. It said:

(the constitution) is a means by which Fiji may be ruled in perpetuity by an oligarchy of Fijian chiefs and their associates. ...the government will not be answerable to the governed, racial and geographical divisions against citizens are enshrined in the constitution which the majority is powerless to alter (It) denies a large majority of the people, particularly a proportion of indigenous Fijians and the overwhelming majority of Indo-Fijians an effective and equal voice in the choice of those who should govern them and the laws by which they should be bound (Ibid.).

A group of prominent Australian lawyers and judges joined in arguing that the constitution was 'as bad as the apartheid laws of South Africa for discriminating against Indians and Indigenous Fijians' (Ibid.). A group of Fiji emigrants in Leicester, England engaged in a round of constitution burnings. The United States State Department expressed its own disappointment suggesting that 'a lasting solution can only result from a political solution acceptable to the majority of the country's people' (Ibid.). The Government of India, as was expected, vehemently condemned the constitution calling it 'racist', 'evil', 'undemocratic' and 'similar in character to the humiliating system of apartheid, and sets the clock back on human civilization' (Ibid.).

The universal condemnation is focused mainly on the ethnically unequal and discriminatory provisions of the constitution, but also aimed at the authoritarian features generally, which also discriminate against lower-income and commoner Fijians. The power holders are not only ethnic supremacists, but have also cordoned themselves apart from lower-income Fijian commoners, whose name they invoked to execute the coup and on whose backs they expect to maintain power. While these objectionable features of the constitution were boldly espoused, an attempt was nevertheless made to offer another face of democracy in the new political order by enshrining a comprehensive Bill of rights in the constitution. The new rulers believed that they could thereby persuade the international community of their good intentions. But underscoring the deception of it all, they cleverly inserted a sly provision under which all basic human rights and civil liberties can be swept away on the skimpiest of grounds by a simple majority, which they also arrogated to themselves by constitutional prescription. But what is more sinister than the formal constitutional abridgements and inequalities is the spirit of the new elite and rulers, backed up by an enlarged arsenal of terror. They seem intent on preserving their power against both the Indian 'menace' and other socially and economically disadvantaged Fijians using whatever means available. Military might parades everywhere, maintaining an atmosphere of awe and intimidation. The element of terror is supplemented by the role of the Fiji Intelligence Service (FIS) with its unchallengeable arbitrary powers to intercept mail, faxes, and phone calls; to enter private premises, seize documents, plant listening devices and make arrests. This element of terror adds an intrinsic element to the authoritarian nature of the regime. The military not only stands behind the new constitution but, in its officer corps recruitment practices, it incorporates elements from the privileged stratum of Fijian chiefs. Hence, an interlocking system of socially circumscribed power exists between the civilian system of government and the coercive apparatus of the state, the former to persuade, the latter to compel. The ruling Fijian oligarchy sees nothing wrong about its ascent to and exercise of power. Rather, they feel entitled to it by birth and rank traditionally prescribed in the Fijian cultural system. Privilege is based on ascription and serviced by discrimination.

Apart from external sources of potential destabilization, there is one internal salient force that is capable of upsetting the 'new reality' in Fiji. This refers to the problem of relative disparity in standards of living between Fijians and non-Fijians. More than likely, this will become worse for a simple reason. Fundamentally, the Fijian communal social structure which gives priority to collective endeavours and sharing is inconsistent with the individualistic and more materially-oriented social structure of Europeans, Indians and Chinese. Apart from this factor, most Fijian children live in environments which are sparse in educational supports so that they tend to underperform relative to other ethnic groups. From these causes has emerged

137

the condition of relative deprivation among Fijians in the modern sector. Hence, the Fijian community displays less conspicuous signs of prosperity than the Indian, European and Chinese communities. In turn, this has thrown up comparisons reflecting badly on the social status of Fijians relative to other groups in Fiji. But more importantly, over the years the relative wealth of Indians, Europeans and Chinese has accumulated and visibly outstripped that of the Fijian community. To Fijians, the latter factor may have significance in the political arena where the greater wealth of the immigrant groups will eventually yield *de facto* greater influence on government decision-making. In effect, the perception of greater economic wealth among non-Fijians, even if this is not quite accurate in its size, can undermine and make a travesty of the substance of Fijian political paramountcy. Under the programme of 'affirmative action' only a small rectification of the disparities is likely to occur. The perceived disparities featured as a prime cause that underlaid Fijian support for the military intervention. The persistence of the preferential treatment of some Fijians is also likely to add fuel to this simmering fire that can engender new acts of instability. Nothing in the new constitution can arrest the increasing disparities between Fijians and non-Fijians, and at another level, between a small elite of Fijians and other Fijians.

Inherent then in the new political order are the incendiary materials for internal insurrection and external interference. In a democratic world of individual human rights, the Fiji constitutional system stands isolated, constantly inviting opprobrium and condemnation at all international fora. The claims of indigenous peoples to special protection from oppression offer a moment of respite but in a situation where Fijians are the political power holders, the measures of inequality aimed at another non-white group most of whom are not more well-off than Fijians smacks of overkill. It can be persuasively argued that if domination is morally reprehensible, then regardless whether it is committed by one group or another, it cannot be justified. The new system of domination reverses the role of an indigenous group diluting the claims of other similar groups to the morally unassailable position in their call for equality. Most indigenous groups in the Pacific and North America have supported the new Fijian constitution.

The unequal provisions in the new communally repressive order will constantly invite attempts at destabilization from both within and outside Fiji. With half of Fiji's population excluded from political participation and alienated, the cost of maintaining order and promoting development will be staggering. Even indigenous Fijians who are discriminated against will in time be organized by other Timoci Bavadras and join forces with other discontented elements to overthrow the new order of privilege. It seems that the new constitution has laid a time bomb under the social and political privileges of those who must rule by force and live in fear that one day at any time the germs of instability will ripen into revolutionary fire.

VIII The Elections of 1992 and 1994 and the Assumption of Power by Rabuka

In the first general elections in Fiji since the military intervened in May 1987, the main coup-maker, Lt.Col. Sitiveni Rabuka, won and became Prime Minister. For the five years from 1987 to 1992, democracy was suspended in political limbo as a military-backed interim civilian government administered the state in a rule marked by constitutionally sanctioned ethnic discrimination. Rabuka had proclaimed 'Fiji For Fijians' when he ousted the duly-elected Labour-Federation government of Dr.Timoci Bavandra from power. Under an ethnically repressive regime, Indians migrated in droves, most seeking refugee status in Australia, New Zealand, Canada and the United States. The Fiji government faced international censure and boycotts; Fiji was expelled from the Commonwealth of Nations. Under persistent international pressure, the interim government finally held elections in May 1992. However, this was done under an ethnically inequalitarian constitution which assigned electoral pre-eminence to the minority Fijians over the combined majority of Indians, Europeans, Chinese, Mixed Races, and Other Pacific Islanders. In the 1992 elections, for the first time Fijians, Indians, and the other ethnic groups were segregated into three separate communal electorates with 37 out of the 70 seats going to Fijians. The Prime Ministership, Presidency, Chief Justiceship, head of the military, police, and public service were all constitutionally prescribed exclusively for Fijians. An aura of illegitimacy loomed over the new order and the elections assumed the form not of democracy but a farce foisted on the international community.

While Fijians had regained power in the coup of 1987, the problem was to retain Fijian political pre-eminence in the face of an international community which, in the late 20th century, sympathized with governments which were democratically elected and respected individual human rights. Much of the international community perceived Fiji through the prism of the odious apartheid system in South Africa. Because of how the international community felt, Fijian leaders decided to hold elections even though they were unrepentant about their right to political pre-eminence. The elections of 1992 were therefore mainly about an exercise that was conducted to fulfil an important rite of passage to international respectability. However, in conducting the elections under a system that eliminated the role of Indians, Europeans, Chinese etc. from the political calculus of power, the Fijians made a serious miscalculation about their control of the new polity they had crafted. They had, in fact, unwittingly released into the political arena the monster of traditional intra-Fijian tribal rivalry which had been suppressed in the past by the fear of ethnic domination. In the elections of 1992, it was anticipated that a new game of political hegemony was about to be forged on the anvil of ethnic exclusion. Instead, old fissures were resurrected and in the competition for power among the Fijian political elites, the excluded ethnic elements had to be enlisted in the struggle. The elections therefore signalled not only the splintering of the Fijian community, but the re-assertion, with a vengeance, of the importance of the discriminated communities. The elections, then, had far reaching implications, not only in the restructuring of politics in Fiji, but in exposing the folly of the simple-minded calculation that the repression of political rights automatically awarded undiluted and long-lasting benefits to the claimants. This has less to do with karmic retribution than with the realities of living in interdependent multi-ethnic societies, where power sharing tends to be the most productive strategy for a just and stable order. The elections of 1992 pointed to the turmoil that inevitably comes in the wake of the pursuit of the politics of ethnic pre-eminence in a multi-ethnic state.

A. The elections of 1992

Under the new 1990 constitution, the electoral struggle was focused on the House of Assembly, which consisted of 70 seats which were divided into communal compartments. Thus Fijians were assigned 37 seats, Indians 27 seats, General Voters 5 seats, and Rotumans 1 seat. Under this system, those defined as Fijians, Indians, General Electors, and Rotumans were required to vote only for candidates of their respective ethnic communities. Together, the four rolls constituted a total electorate of 316,848 registered voters divided as follows: Fijians, 154,099, Indians, 148,546, General Voters, 10,632, Rotumans, 3,571. To understand the workings of the electoral system, it is necessary to examine the ethnic constituencies separately. The 37 Fijian constituencies were sub-divided into two regional categories of voters, provincial and urban. [Table 8.1]. The provincial constituencies contained multiple seats while the urban ones had only one seat each.

Table 8.1
Fijian Seats

a)	4 provinces with 3 seats each:	12 seats
b)	10 provinces with two seats each:	20 seats
c)	5 urban seats with one seat each:	5 seats
	Total:	37 seats

These figures concealed the skewed manner in which provincial seats were arbitrarily assigned superior weighting as Table 8.2 shows:

Table 8.2
Skewed Allocation of Voters on the Fijian Rolls

		Registered voters	% of total	per seat
Provincial Seats:	32	110,619	65	3,457
Urban Seats:	5	43,276	35	8,655

It can be observed that Fijians in the urban constituencies were weighted only half as much as those residing in the provinces. This discriminatory disparity against urban Fijians was not the only unusual feature in the allocation of Fijian seats. In the distribution of those constituencies with three and two seats, the principle of population density was ignored so that a number of smaller provinces were allocated three seats as against larger provinces given only two.

Unlike the Fijian constituencies, the delineation of the boundaries of the 27 Indian seats was not embroiled in controversy. The General Electors, the third communal group, were constituted of the residual ethnic elements outside the Fijian and Indian communities (except the Rotumans), and were assigned proportionately the greatest electoral value. Consisting of 10,632 registered voters, they were given 5 seats or 2,121 per seat compared with 5,500 for each Indian seat, and 4,159 for each Fijian seat. In the 1992 elections a total of 8 parties competed for votes. The electoral battle was conducted in the trenches of the four communal sections and the parties were free to deploy their candidates in all of the constituencies so that while the constituencies were prescriptively uni-communal, the parties could be structurally multi-ethnic. This effectively implied that the sharp and jarring edges of the system of

142

electoral apartheid could be moderated by multi-ethnic parties, which could design strategies aimed at winning a combination of seats from an assortment of communal constituencies. Probably because of the novelty of the electoral system, only two parties, the Fiji Labour Party and the All National Congress, availed themselves of the opportunity to field candidates across the imposed communal divide. Generally then the parties abided with the definition of the new electoral politics which sought to segregate the ethnic communities into exclusive communal compartments.

Among the parties, five seemed capable of winning seats. The Soqosoqo ni Vakavulewa ni Taukei (SVT) loomed largest; it was the party that was sponsored by the *Bose Levu Vakaturaga* or Council of Chiefs. It was the direct successor to the old Alliance Party which was constituted of four components: the Fijian Association, the General Electors, the Rotumans and the Indian Alliance. The Fijian Association was the most critical component, drawing its support from the Fijian community, and it was now this component which alone served as the backbone of the SVT. The SVT was clearly different from the Alliance Party in that it emerged in the crucible of militant Fijian ethno-nationalist sentiment, becoming assertively uni-ethnic, jettisoning in the process its old allies in an exclusive grab for power. The SVT deployed candidates only in Fijian constituencies. Its purpose was to discourage factionalism, unify the Fijian vote under its own umbrella, and capture all 37 Fijian seats to form the undisputed government in the 70-seat House of Assembly after the elections. In this regard the founders of the SVT had grievously miscalculated. An omnibus organization did not yield a unified party. More specifically, while Rabuka was the preferred choice for the role of leader of one section of Fijians, especially the commoners, and therefore the next Prime Minister, Josefa Kamikamica, the Finance Minister under the antecedent interim government and the protege of outgoing Prime Minister Mara was the choice of another group. The presence of the SVT did not deter other Fijian-based parties from being formed and joining the contest. Also competing was the Fijian National United Front (FNUF) which deployed 27 candidates in Fijian constituencies. The FNUF was composed of two groups, namely the Fijian Christian National Party led by Sakiasi Butadroka and the Soqosoqo ni Taukei ni Vanua (STV) led by Osea Gavidi. The FNUF was led by Butadroka, who had earlier established himself as the supreme anti-Indian Fijian nationalist, calling for the deportation of all Indians from Fiji. The FNUF was regionally based in the provinces of Rewa and Nadroga on the island of Viti Levu. Generally, the FNUF seemed to be based on the personalistic and parochial popularity of its candidates rather than on any definable, coherent set of issues. Certain FNUF candidates such as Butadroka and Ratu Mosese Tuisawau held special grievances against the Mara-Kamikamica faction of the SVT but others did not. What was clear was that the Rewa and Nadroga-based FNUF candidates were vehemently against the Mara-Kamikamica wing of the SVT and found common ground with the Rabuka faction setting up an intriguing collaboration between Rabuka and Butadroka against SVT candidates who were sympathetic to Kamikamica.

The final party which competed for Fijian seats, apart from the Fiji Labour Party, was the All National Congress (ANC) led by former Alliance cabinet minister, Apisai Tora. The ANC was formed as an anti-chief party and had a strong western bias on the island of Viti Levu around Tora's province of Ba. The ANC did not think that it was likely to win enough seats to form a government and from its inception, Tora had started to court prominent members of the General Electors with a view towards putting together a small strategic block of seats to influence the structure of the next government. The ANC was able to place only 17 candidates in the elections, none in an Indian constituency. It focused with equal attention on a combination of Fijian and General Voters seats. Together, the ANC, SVT, and the FNUF were the main parties which had enrolled to vie for the 37 Fijian seats. There were a few Independents, two of whom were from the province of Ra. This essentially meant that the contest for the Fijian seats was fought by three parties of whom only the SVT committed candidates in all 37 constituencies. The parties which challenged the SVT were regionally-based and possessed powerful local backings.

The next cluster of communal constituencies which drew multi-party competition was the General Electors who were allocated five seats. A General Voters Party (GVP) was formed on September 28, 1992 to represent this assortment of Europeans, part-Europeans, Chinese, and Other Pacific Islanders of some 10,000 voters. The GVP was an offshoot of the defunct General Electors grouping, which was a faithful partner of the old Alliance Party. In 1992 the General Voters, whose numbers included some 1,200 Melanesians (the Other Pacific Islanders), described itself as a multi-racial party of minorities.

Bestriding the Indian constituencies were two major contenders, the Fiji Labour Party (FLP) and the National Federation Party (NFP). Led by lawyer Jairam Reddy, the NFP was traditionally the representative of the Indians of Fiji. In the 1992 elections it had deployed 27 candidates to compete in all of the Indian constituencies. Until a few days prior to the close of the nomination date, the NFP seemed to be the only serious contender for the Indian seats. However, this prospect was torpedoed by the FLP which decided at the last minute to end its boycott of the elections and throw its hat into the ring. Led by prominent veteran trade union leader Mahendra Chaudhry, the FLP hurriedly assembled only 27 candidates, 23 of whom were deployed in the Indian constituencies and five in the Fijian constituencies. This meant that there was to be a contest in the trenches of the Indian constituencies by mainly two parties, one the traditional Indian Party of the Indians and the other a cross-communal party with a record of impressive achievement among sugar workers. As events would show, the struggle between the FLP and the NFP grew very bitter even though the two parties were partners in the coalition that had defeated the Alliance Party in 1987. Apart from the NFP and the FNP, two new Indian parties were formed to compete for the Indian constituencies, namely the Fiji Indian Congress (FIC) and the Fiji Indian Liberal Party (FILP). Of these two, the FIC was notable for containing a few prominent Indians who had political affinities with the SVT.

To all parties in all the communal constituencies, the main issue revolved around the constitution of 1990. But its inequalitarian features were treated differently by the partisan groups representing the ethnic communities. Unlike prior elections when a system of shared national electorates allowed for meaningful discourse of issues across communal boundaries, in 1992 the definition of the electoral struggle into ethnic compartments limited exchange to the confines of each community. This compartmentalization of issue discourse was not inevitable, had the main parties posted a full battery of candidates across the communalized constituencies. Issues were defined and debated within exclusive communal boundaries and, in the case of the Fijian and Indian constituencies, in the Fijian and Indian languages respectively.

Debate and disputations then assumed the form of intra-family dialogue. This became rancourous because in the Fijian and the Indian constituencies no single party had gained overwhelming and undivided communal support such as the Alliance and the NFP had obtained in the pre-1987 elections. Both the SVT and the NFP were challenged by potent parties within their communities. With the promulgation of the 1990 constitution, several of the old party structures collapsed and new ones emerged. Hence, in the Fijian constituencies, in place of the Alliance Party was the SVT, but it was still untested and had to compete with the FNUF, STV, ANC, and several independents for the allegiance of Fijians. Similarly, in the Indian constituencies, the old NFP was now forced to share space with the FLP and two other Indian-based parties. The 1992 elections could settle the problem of determining which parties were pre-eminent or peripheral with the greatest or least endorsement of their communities. Conversely, the results could splinter the votes regionally so as to leave the country with a variety of parties, none with enough support to command the allegiance of their entire communal sections. When the results were tallied, the SVT had obtained only 30 of the 37 seats. This was constituted of 66.6 per cent of all Fijian votes and only 43.6 per cent of all votes cast in all constituencies. The FNUF had taken 5 seats and the two other seats went to Independents. Table 8.3 shows the performance of the parties in the Fijian constituencies. In the 27 Indian constituencies, a similar sort of splitting occurred with the NFP obtaining 14 seats and the FLP

13. (Table 8.4). The General Electors constituencies had the only block of communal seats that were not split among several parties. The GVP obtained all 5 seats even though the ANC put up a stiff fight for a few of the seats (Table 8.5)

Table 8.3
Party Results in the Fijian Constituencies

Parties	No. of candidates	Votes Obtained	% of Total	Seats Obtained
1. SVT	37	154,656	66.6	30
2. ANC	12	24,736	10.6	0
3. FNUF.	27	38;359	16.5	5
4. FLP	5	2,329	1.0	0
5. INDE.	8	12,270	5.3	2
TOTAL	77	232,350	100.0	37

Table 8.4
Results in the Indian Constituencies

Parties	Candidate	Votes Obtained	% of Total	Seats Obtained
1. NFP	27	56,951	50.0	14
2. FLP	24	54,294	47.6	13
3. FIC	12	1,783	1.6	0
4. FILP	1	262	0.2	0
5. ANC	1	584	0.5	0
6. INDE	3	387	0.3	0
TOTAL	68	114,261	100.0	27

Table 8.5
General Voters Seats

Parties	Candidates	Votes Obtained	% of Total	Seats Obtained
1.GVP	5	5,079	63.4	5
2.ANC	4	2,869	35.8	0
3.IND.	2	60	0.7	0
TOTAL	11	8,008	100.0	5

In the elections as a whole, 156 candidates competed for 70 seats. The voter turnout was impressive; in the Fijian constituencies, it averaged 80.28 per cent; in the Indian constituencies, 78.49 per cent; and in the GVP constituencies, it was 78.77 per cent. The overall average was 78.77 per cent which compared favourably with previous elections. Analysis of the results in each of the communal constituencies yields some interesting insights into the new patterns of voting under the 1990 constitution. Looking at the Fijian electorate as a whole, while the SVT dominated the results, the greatest scare came from the FNUF which, while obtaining only five seats, garnered 38,359 votes or 16.50 per cent of the 232,350 Fijian votes cast. The ANC obtained 24,736 or 10.60 per cent and the Independents got 12,270 or 5.30 per cent . The two successful Independents from Ra later signalled that they identified with the FNUF, forming an important block of seats with which to bargain with other parties in forming the new government. One intriguing dimension of the seven seats consists of the fact that they came from provincial constituencies where the Fijian Council of Chiefs felt it had the greatest support, in contrast to the urban Fijian votes which were deemed unreliable. The seven seats which were lost to the SVT came from traditional rural areas while four of the five urban Fijian seats went comfortably to the SVT, contrary to expectations.

The results in the Indian 27 constituencies astounded most observers because they had not anticipated that the FLP, which entered the electoral barely a few weeks before the elections, could win 13 seats. The FLP swept the sugar belt, comprehensively winning all 12 seats located in western and northern Viti Levu and the Labasa-Macuata region in Vanua Levu. The FLP's victory plainly came from its persistent activism among sugar farmers in the tough years after the coup. The most astounding aspect of the FLP's performance came from its failure to do well in the urban seats, which were presumed to be its forte. The FLP explained its loss by reference to its late entry into the election contest and to the fact that it had an infrastructure of organized support in the National Farmers Union.

The NFP was shocked by its loss of the sugar belt, the traditional base of its support. The smaller Indian parties and the independents were wiped out entirely unlike the Fijian constituencies where there was greater fragmentation of voters.

Unlike the Fijian and the Indian constituencies, which witnessed multi-party division splits in the results, in the General Voters constituencies, the GVP won all 5 seats, but not without close calls. The GVP polled 63.40 per cent of the votes cast against 35.80 per cent for the ANC.

With no party possessing an outright majority, a coalition arrangement was compelled by the fragmenting of the 70 parliamentary seats. The SVT seats were divided thus: 20 for the Rabuka faction and 10 for the Kamikamica camp. The Indian seats were also divided into two: NFP with 14 and the FLP with 13. The Rabuka/Kamikamica split meant that interesting permutations could be created in relation to the FNUF, FLP, NFP, GVP, and the Independents. In the coalition-making process, several combinations were likely but in all cases, given the structure of the split in the SVT and in the Indian seats, whatever combination finally prevailed had to include one element from the SVT and one from the Indians. In the end, it was the Rabuka faction that won out combining with the FLP, GVP, and the Independents. How this happened is worth recounting briefly since the coalescing of Rabuka with the FLP was most ironic, given the role of Rabuka in ousting the Labour-Federation government from power in 1987.

To become Prime Minister, Rabuka needed the Indians. Rabuka personally went to see Chaudhry and the FLP leadership and accepted the three conditions of the FLP in writing - the rescinding of the draconian labour laws passed by the previous administration, the scrapping of the proposed legislation to introduce a value added tax, and a commitment to review the constitution - and with that act the first elected post coup government was inaugurated with Rabuka, the coup leader as Prime Minister and the FLP, the aggrieved and overthrown party, playing the unlikely and indispensable support role. The new Rabuka-led coalition then consisted of the SVT, the FLP, the GVP, and a few Independents. The FLP refused to accept any cabinet positions so that in the end, no Indian was present in Rabuka's official decision-making circle. About a year later, a major effort was made to establish a government of national unity across the communal divide, but this failed. The fact remained however, that Rabuka, the pre-eminent leader of the indigenous Fijians, became Prime Minister through the vital assistance of the pre-dominantly Indian-based FLP which promised to support the ruling regime to keep it in power.

B. The fall of the Rabuka Government and the 1994 elections

Under Rabuka, the SVT government inherited a rejuvenated economy and was well placed to administer the state with little turbulence. In the political area, the SVT enjoyed some cross-communal legitimacy because of its support from the FLP, even though the FLP did not accept any cabinet positions in the new government. Rabuka had publicly agreed to review the constitution and further, in his first speech as Prime Minister, he declared that he did not regard Indians as second class citizens and that he planned to govern evenhandedly on behalf of all citizens. But the SVT government also had strong pro-Fijian promises to redeem and most of these could only be met by denying equality to non-Fijians. Inherent then, in the Rabuka regime, was this tension between rival claims for policy preferences from two overlapping constituencies. A second source of challenge with which the SVT government was faced referred to the question of competence, an item which the Kamikamica faction of the SVT harped upon during the campaign. The previous Rabuka-led government of September-December, 1987 was an unmitigated economic disaster and had had to surrender power to an interim government headed by Ratu Mara in order to restore health to the economy and society. These memories haunted the mercurial Rabuka, who was known to contradict his mind as soon as he made it up. Again at the helm, this time under a new constitution and a different set of parliamentarians, he appointed a 24-member cabinet whose aim, in part, was to meet the claims of Fijians for political paramountcy. Finally, the Rabuka regime, which had made many promises to Fijians during the campaign, had to deliver under the constraints of a World Bank austerity programme which demanded a reduction of government expenditures, expanded opportunities for the private sector, and instated a new tax regime that reverberated adversely on the living standards of lower income citizens, most of whom were indigenous Fijians. Apart from these challenges, Rabuka had the unenviable task of restoring respectability to Fiji's international image.

During the first few months in office, Rabuka rode a crest of widespread approval. In time, however, he was pressured to make good on his promises to Chaudry and the FLP. Specifically, the FLP wanted the new Value Added Tax (VAT) which the previous Interim Government had agreed to pass and implement, to be scrapped. In what would emerge as a pattern of studied ambiguity, calculated hesitation and outright reneging of the promises made to the FLP, the Rabuka regime passed the VAT legislation and then neglected to do anything about constitutional review and the rescinding of the offensive labour legislation. All of the pre-coalition promises to the FLP were in ruins. Meanwhile, Rabuka was able to win over several pro-Kamikamica supporters with cabinet offers. The NFP leverage was lost and the FLP was forced into the role of an antagonist towards he government it had brought to power.

While the split between the FLP and Rabuka was being aired daily in the media, Sakiasi Butadroka, the FNUF leader, made headlines by renewing his call for the repatriation of Indians from Fiji. This created much public stir and the official government opposition, the NFP, called on the SVT government to repudiate Butadroka and clarify its own position on Indians in Fiji. Rabuka responded positively by re-affirming his commitment to Indian citizenship and asked the public to ignore Butadroka. While doing this however, Rabuka had to placate the Fijian section that his government was not too pro-Indian. Accordingly, he announced a special programme aimed at conferring increased benefits to Fijians. This included the setting up of an agency to promote Fijians into the business world, a 20-year tax free holiday to businesses in

149

which Fijians held at least 51 percent ownership, a (F)$1 million grant to each provincial council, an increase in scholarship funds for Fijian education and special priority to the Fijian owned Fijian Holdings Company in buying government shares in commercial enterprises that were privatized.

Many mistakes were made by the new regime, including the Steven's affair, which implicated Rabuka in a FNUF scam to defraud the government of millions of dollars. These and other events provided the Kamikamica faction with opportunities to deepen the divisions in the SVT parliamentary ranks. At one point, internal SVT disenchantment with Rabuka's leadership had grown so menacing that Rabuka boldly announced that he was seeking a government of national unity between the SVT and the Indian parties. This succeeded in diverting attention from the growing internal malaise within the government. When the unity proposals floundered, this again exposed the government to internal challenges. The matter reached a head during the presentation of the 1993 appropriation bill which saw the open defection of several SVT loyalists as well as Kamikamica adherents from the ranks of the government benches. The upshot was the defeat of the budget and the call for new elections.

Twice then within two years, the citizens of Fiji went to the polls to elect a new government. The new elections offered an opportunity to the electorate to sort out the question of which party in both the Fijian and Indian communities had the unambiguous mandate to represent them. The results in the February polls were much more decisive in this regard than the polls of 1992. Contrary to all predictions, the SVT, shorn of the dissidents who had voted against the budget and led again by Rabuka, secured 31 out of the 37 Fijian seats. The Kamikamica faction, expelled from the SVT, had regrouped as the Fijian Association Party (FA), winning 5 seats. During the election campaign the SVT-FA struggle had loomed large and suggestions were rife that a major split among Fijians was imminent. Not only did the FA loose heavily, including the seat of Kamikamica, but so did the FNUF which was wiped out altogether including the seat of its leader, Butadroka. The main problem with the otherwise exultant victory of the SVT was the fact that among the 5 seats won by the FA were those of the province of Lau, from which Ratu Mara came, who had ascended to the Presidency of Fiji following the death of Ratu Penaia Ganilau. The FA continued to organize supporters after the elections and is expected to continue as a major thorn in the side of the Rabuka regime. Nevertheless, the new government is based on fewer complications from that of 1992. It does not rely on an Indian party for its survival and is relatively free from internal dissident challenges. As it stood after the 1994 elections, the SVT party without an outright majority relies on only the four seats won by the GVP and the two won from Independents to govern.

In the Indian electorate, the results were similar to that of the SVT in the Fijian electorate in that the NFP won 20 out of the 27 seats, thereby acquiring an undisputed mandate to represent Indian citizens. The FLP lost several seats from its stronghold in the cane belt and suffered from the fact that it was mainly responsible for bringing Rabuka to power in 1992 with nothing to show for it. It now fell on the shoulders of Reddy and the NFP to secure for Indians a renewal of the land leases which were about to expire within the next few years. The issue of constitutional review remained as an equal priority. The problem of governance in Fiji will revolve around the challenge to reconcile the claims of Fijians to political paramountcy and increased economic benefits with the demands of other communities for equality.

IX Ethnic Conflict and Development: The Political Dimension

Having examined the course that ethnic conflict has taken in Fiji, it is now our task to evaluate the impact that persistent communal strife has had on the development of the state and its citizens. The concept of development must first be defined in relation to the environment of cultural pluralism. In the Third World, the condition of multi-ethnicity is an embedded dimension that must be incorporated in any explication of the development idea. The Fiji case demonstrates that all designs at economic and political development are ultimately entwined in the communal interests and claims of Fijians, Indians, and others. The Indian and Fijian measure a proposal for amelioration primarily from the perspective of its communal connotations. Individual interests are consciously or unconsciously subsumed under the wider umbrella of collective communal claims. In essence, this implies that planned change is made doubly difficult by the presence of the pervasive ethnic factor, rendering all ordinary political and economic calculations more complex if not more irrational and intractable. Put differently, development plans and strategies must be designed in contemplation of the interests of communal constituencies, regardless of whether such claims tend to increase costs, protract solutions, and involve 'irrational and wasteful' allocation of scarce resources. In the multi-ethnic states, policies which win legitimacy and stand a chance of implementation engage and incorporate divergent communal claims. Policies are perceived and appraised through the ethnic prism.

Nearly all available theories of development take little cognizance of the ethos of ethnicity in the typical Third World environment, often relegating it to the scrap heap of an aberrant nuisance that will, in time, dissolve and disappear. The many theories of development can be conveniently reduced to two: the modernization and the political economy schools. The modernization or developmental school is often associated with the names Samuel Huntington, Lucian Pye, and Gabriel Almond (Huntington, 1968; Pye, 1966; Almond and Powell, 1960; Almond and Coleman, 1960; Almond and Verba, 1963). Sometimes also daubed the 'systems' or 'functional' school, it stresses the need for certain systemic performances to be attained in the transformation process for the conditions of modernization to occur. Samuel Huntington best expressed these as social consensus and community, legitimacy, organization, effectiveness, and stability. In this complex of interrelated factors, it is argued that politically developed states are those that are institutionalized around the function of establishing legitimate political authority in which citizens share a common vision of the public interest. Specific modern institutions should be established around a political culture of widespread citizen participation, so that conflicting demands are well organized and articulated in an orderly fashion through a system of voluntary interest associations and political parties; a representative civilian body must be in place to dutifully receive and respond through appropriate policies to these demands; implementation of decisions should be routine and effected around de-personalized bureaucracies; political conflict must be adjudicated through recognized courts; and political succession and changes in government must be built around predictable procedures. All of this constitutes a complex of political means and ends which are to be attained in an environment of rapid political change and mobilization in which urbanization redefines the demography of the state from the dominance of a rural traditional ethos to one marked by universal achievement norms.

The stress in the modernization strategy of development is on maintaining order through evolving new norms and institutions which perform the fixed functions of a stable society. The modernization approach encapsulates its goals in a set of processes which have often been stated as a set of interlocking and sequential steps to be overcome, namely participation, legitimacy, identity, integration, penetration and distribution (Binder, 1962; Rostow, 1960). Order takes precedence over the creation of a just society; this is not, however, seen to be dependent on an economic system that is free from property disparities. Above all, in the process of transformation, the political modernization school, while acknowledging the environment of internal cultural pluralism, has tended to see this as a barrier that will be submerged and eradicated as institutionalization takes root and a new society is born. The modernization process will, in effect, impart a levelling effect over the 'distortions' erected by traditional communal attachments and, in the end, produce a new homogenous person and society. There are many sophisticated nuances which are omitted in this attempt to represent the fundamental factors of the modernization approach to development, such as the evolution of institutional differentiation and autonomy, the role of socialization and acculturation etc., but generally in terms of our analysis, it is critical to note that the integrationist and assimilationist perspectives built into this approach have tended to underestimate the arousal of ethnic group sentiment and the durability of ethnic identities and boundaries. These, as experience would show in innumerable Third World settings, are critical variables which would subvert all of the aims of development in the model. The ethnic factor tends to be resilient and cannot be swept away in the tidal wave of technological, economic and ideological change as the modernization school would have it.

The political economy school of development that contends ideologically with the modernization approach has been derived from a combination of the dependency and Marxist perspectives, even though these two orientations are not the same (Baran, 1957; Frank, 1967; Amin, 1976; Emmanuel, 1972; dos Santos, 1970; Weaver and Berger, 1984). Essentially, while the modernization school tends to stress the role of internal political, cultural and economic factors in accounting for the condition of Third World 'backwardness', the dependency-cum-Marxist approaches point to the role of imperialism and capitalism. Here, the emphasis is placed on class criteria and economic, property relations and external domination. The Marxist and dependency schools record ethnic consciousness as false consciousness that will dissolve and disappear as revolutionary transformation takes place.

From these two major schools, a number of issues and aims of political development are identified as significant even though the ethnic variable has been neglected. It is these which we shall utilize for our own analyses, giving them particular interpretations in the context of Fiji's multi-ethnic environment. In a definitional paper prepared by Rodolfo Stevenhagen presented at a conference convened by the United Nations Research Institute for Social Development in Geneva in March 1990, several development aims and issues were crystallized in the context of a communal environment for use in examining individual case histories such as Fiji (Stavenhagen, 1990). From all these sources then - the modernization development school, the dependency-Marxist perspective, and Stavenhagen's perspectives - a list of inter-related political problems are identified as salient for measuring political development in multi-ethnic states bedeviled with persistent communal strife. Much of this configuration of inter-related political issues has already been interpreted in the preceding chapters describing Fiji's experience. In this chapter, we step back with our analytic categories and criteria to comment more theoretically and generally on the political developmental impact of ethnic conflict in Fiji. The inter-related categories and criteria pertain to legitimacy, unity, order, minority and human rights, as well as institutions and various mechanisms of ethnic conflict resolution.

A. The political costs of ethnic conflict in Fiji

With the promulgation of the new constitution in 1990, marked by its discriminatory and inegalitarian features, the ethnic and communal conflict in Fiji became fully institutionalized. The new constitution, however, marks only a particular moment in the evolution of the ethnic strife. Throughout its evolutionary history, which culminated with the first military coup in 1987, the seeds of collective sectional conflict were laid in the very making of the multi-ethnic state. In the immediate post-coup period, the political costs of the ethnic conflict have proven to be extensive, including the loss of regime legitimacy, the destruction of democracy, pervasive human rights violations, and persistent instability. Many of these costs emerged as the multi-tiered ethnic fabric of the society was being laid after the signing of the Deed of Cession in 1874, especially when this was followed by the mass importation of Indian indentured labourers. When an element of popular representation was first introduced in 1904, it was communally structured. Europeans as a collective group were assigned a disproportionately large part of the seats in the earliest colonial councils. The principles of collective communal representation served to add to the separation among Europeans, Fijians, and Indians. Fijians were not allowed to directly select their representatives and Indians were offered representation significantly below what their numbers warranted. This communal structure in colonial representative institutions not only divided the population, but fostered inter-sectional fear. Fijians came to see Indians as a threat to their paramountcy in their own country. Indians viewed Europeans as usurpers who instigated Indian-Fijian rivalry and suspicion. Soon the entire society was communally compartmentalized and collective ethnic consciousness with its antagonistic propensities became pervasive. Once ethnic consciousness became the animating force that defined competition for the values and resources of the state, all political institutions - parties, voluntary associations, the electoral system, parliament, civil service, judiciary, diplomatic services, and the army and policy - became infected by it. It is as if the twisted contours of ethnic preference, antagonistically expressed against other similar solidarity groups, possessed such irresistible power, that every political structure derived its form and practice from its governing principles. Inter-ethnic suspicion and antipathy were not confined to a few select practices and separated from others. Allowed to grow on the crucible of continuing electoral competition, after universal adult suffrage was introduced in 1963, they slowly extended their tentacles to all institutions. The entire imported parliamentary apparatus was, from the very inception, of a system of representation imbued with communal motifs and was transformed into symbols impregnated with vital communal interests, dividing one citizen from the other, failing to offer any form of unity to the state.

Fijians were entirely omitted from the new equation of power. When an element of representation was first introduced in Fiji in 1904; Indians were given token representation and they persistently protested and boycotted the colonial legislature. The first major casualty stemming from the communalization of political competition in the allocation of values then has been the loss of regime legitimacy. Democratic governments are erected on the intangible factor of moral consent. The term 'legitimacy' embodies this idea; it simply suggests that governments derive their right to rule and can expect citizen compliance and cooperation, when and only when, the accepted rules of establishing and administering government are followed. Legitimacy refers then, not only to the propriety in the acquisition of power, but also to the practices of administering the state consonant with prevailing procedures and concepts of equity. Clearly, legitimacy is wrapped in the cultural and moral values of the society. In Fiji, the colonial system of government lacked all these legitimizing norms from the outset.

As a phenomenon locked into the cultural system of society, legitimacy is easily established in those polities that are undergirded and integrated by a body of shared institutions and customs. But this does not necessarily mean that legitimacy cannot be established without value consensus. These unifying values facilitate, but do not guarantee, consent and acceptance of a government and its right to rule. It is quite conceivable that in a state with a diversity of cultural systems, legitimacy can be forged through a commonly agreed-upon political regime. In such culturally fragmented situations, it is more difficult, but not impossible, to establish legitimate governments. If the cultural cleavages are constrained by systems of inter-communal cooperation at the level of the polity, then a stable and legitimate political order can be enthroned. If these culturally diverse states are permitted on the other hand to evolve so that they are marked by internal ethnically-infused antagonistic relationships, then legitimacy is bound to be lost in the attempt to erect governmental order. The Fiji case illustrates all of this. An attempt was made in 1980 by the leaders of the Fijian and Indian parties to establish a government of national unity. Had this effort succeeded, it was quite conceivable that the trajectory of intensifying ethnic conflict would have been arrested and a new order of inter-communal amity inaugurated. On the contrary, however, the two political parties not only failed to reconcile their differences but proceeded to enact a new round of rivalry that further exacerbated the division in the state.

The single most salient factor that induces the condition of inter-cultural antagonism is pervasive ethnic consciousness in the state. Ethnic consciousness means at once group solidarity as well as inter-group antagonism and conflict. Ethnic consciousness is a relational phenomenon, built on the premise of the presence of contenders for limited territory, privileges, power, etc. In itself, ethnic consciousness is not a divisive force. Once aroused, at an early stage, it can nevertheless be diverted into peaceful inter-group routines and exchanges without seriously destroying the state. However, if it is actively encouraged and protracted without much restraint, such as occurs in zero-sum electoral systems in which communally-organized mass parties compete for power and privileges, then ethnic consciousness tends to become a destructive monster (Lewis, 1965; Premdas, 1991a). Fed and reinforced by fear of domination, ethnic group activities lose all objectivity and rationality. In Fiji, these elements in the behaviour of the ethnic phenomenon were all played out. Ethnic stereotypes and suspicion were present from the start of the Indian-Fijian encounter. At first fearful of the Europeans, Fijians displaced their frustrations onto the Indian presence and came to be obsessed with potential domination. Europeans encouraged this Fijian antipathy. However, it was not inevitable that ethnic compartments persisted. In Fiji, opportunities to weld the disparate segments into a cooperative entity were never systematically exploited. In the absence of incentives and structures of inter-communal understanding, and indeed, in the midst of deliberate colonial practices of divide and rule, the division in the state became deeply embedded and institutionalized. Ethnic consciousness and boundaries soon emerged in Fiji, defining and limiting the ambit of inter-communal discourse.

The theory advanced here postulates that, at any early stage, group consciousness can actually be restrained and made into a positive force of identity formation and group solidarity. But if nurtured and systematically sustained by personal ambition, outbidding, elite interests, institutional practices, a momentum in its evolution then occurs, spreads over a widening array of institutions, and a threshold of virtual uncontrollable inter-group mass behaviour is achieved. This 'critical mass' is what imparts its first political casualty on the legitimacy of the ruling regime. (Young, 1993; Premdas, 1992). In Fiji, the critical mass was facilitated by zero-sum competition elections as well as by ethnic chauvinists such as Sakiasi Butadroka.

In Fiji, the loss of regime legitimacy was erected on the ethnically diverse structure of the population. Without the benefit of cooperative inter-communal practices and institutions, the disparate cultural segments drew further apart. The fact that the economy was characterized by specialized parts, each dominated by a particular ethnic group, meant that each ethnic community could hold the other hostage to its demands and threaten to sabotage the entire production effort as well as the political order. This emerged most starkly after Rabuka seized power. The loss of legitimacy was followed, therefore, by endemic instability and violence. In turn, this required the ruling regime to recruit new police and coercive forces which created an environment in which systemic human rights infringement occurred. However, all of this did not happen suddenly, but was progressively engrafted in the making of Fiji's multi-communal society. The issue relates to the creation of 'an ethnic state' marked by internal communal discord (Brass, 1985). In a sense, this divisive factor, laid at the outset of the founding of the Fiji state, institutionalized ethnic strife which adversely affected all subsequent effort at development. Post-colonial politics perpetuated the fragmented ethnic structure of the state and made development doubly difficult.

B. The State and ethnicity in Fiji

From the inception of the colonial state in Fiji, its operations were converted into an instrument in the service of alien planter and imperial interests. The state that was created was neither neutral nor representative. It became imbued with the priority accorded European and imperial interests and the stratification system that was implanted was plainly ethno-centric as well as racist. It presided over an order that was unequal and unjust, but more significantly, it institutionalized practices which laid the cornerstone of communal conflict. Several policies of the state founded a society which was unintegrated and conflictual. First, the colonial state deliberately implanted a multi-communal population and settled them in a manner which pitched them against each other. Second, the state anchored its routines and stability around a communal system of representation that ignored the interests of most of the population. Finally, the state was rendered into a dependent appendage of the European metropolitan centre for its survival and prosperity. In sum, the state utilized its monopoly of violence to enforce an economic, social, cultural and political order to promote the needs of the minority European interests. It enthroned a capitalist state with the pre-eminence of Europe-centric values as the measure of achievement and rewards. All of this was, however, achieved through a system of ethnic manipulation that pitched Fijians against Indians. The claims of Europeans to superordinate power could not be sustained over time, and were replaced by Fijian claims to political paramountcy but not by an arrangement that sought to reconcile Fijian, Indian and European interests. To be sure, a 'balance' in the distribution of spheres of influence and rewards was informally put in place but it was unable to withstand the challenge from outbidders.

When Fiji obtained independence, the state apparatus that was bequeathed to the local rulers tended to accentuate the ethnic segmentation in the society. A communalized variant of the imported parliamentary system fashioned on the zero-sum electoral and party system played a major role in structuring and institutionalizing ethnic conflict and competition in the state. In Britain, a body of consensual values had evolved nationally serving as a means to moderate rivalry over the values of the state. Fiji lacked such a system of settlement over basic issues. The rival parties, linked to discrete ethnic clusters, confronted each other in a manner similar to military warfare especially after the initial post-independence leadership conviviality had dissolved. Under the assault of outbidders, moderation and the 'balance' in the sharing of spheres of power yielded to strident ethnic rivalry that threatened to burst the state apart at its ethnic seams.

Apart from the fact that the state was created and marked by a system of ethnic stratification from the outset, and at independence lacked a consensus over its basic institutions, it was also in its totality the repository of jobs, contracts, and other policy opportunities. Any communal party that captured it could overwhelm the others, bringing the state to the service of its own particular interests. This in fact occurred in Fiji with Indians claiming discrimination. The main rival political parties, each representing one or the other of the major ethnic groups, recognized the value of capturing the government in its entirety. State power was so overwhelmingly powerful, concentrated, and centralized, that it could be used as an instrument for promoting personal ambition as well as ethnic domination, even genocide. In the post-coup period, all of these features assumed reality.

The cultural pluralism, the absence of overarching values and institutions, and the implanting of zero-sum political competitive institutions can, together, be conceived as the predisposing factors that laid the foundation of ethnic conflict in Fiji, with its attendant destructive effects on all development efforts. The factors which triggered ethnic conflict were clearly identifiable but occurred at different times during the evolution of the problem. These factors were: (1) colonial creation of a communally-divided state and subsequent ethnic manipulation; (2) introduction of mass democratic politics; and (3) rivalry over resource allocation. In order to understand why all of these factors which came into play at different points in the evolution of the communal conflict could be classified as 'triggering,' it is necessary to conceive of the problem cumulatively. At various times, a particular triggering factor deposited a layer of division which in turn provided the next step for the deposit of a new layer of forces to the accumulating crisis. At various points, these accumulations could have been neutralized if not entirely reversed. It is for this reason that the idea of a trigger is suggested for each stage of the evolving crisis situation. The idea is that there was nothing automatic about the transition to the next stage. To be sure, it would appear that after a number of successive reinforcing deposits of divisive forces, a critical mass in momentum had been attained so that every issue became inflammable. The state was then in perpetual crisis, expressed in perennial ongoing tensions which periodically exploded into ethnic confrontation and violence. This was often quelled and a normal poise of peaceful tension resumed until it exploded again. Ethnic conflict on Fiji as elsewhere seems to be underlaid with ongoing tensions which periodically explode into violence.

When Fiji was ceded to Britain in 1874 and Britain undertook to protect the Fijian way of life, the sugar companies' owners required an alternative source of cheap and abundant labour to sustain the profitability of their plantations. From 1879 to 1917, over a quarter million Indians from India were recruited for plantation labour in Fiji. This first important act laid the foundation of greater cultural diversity and later engendered antagonism between Fijians and Indians. Kept apart occupationally and residentially, with their own values and traditions, the Indians and Fijians soon accepted the definitions of themselves as seen through the British values and these definitions soon became dominant. Thus to the first layer of triggers that fueled Indian-Fijian antipathy was added a second layer of self-definitions forged on the Anglo-centric system of stratification. The English colonist saw the Indians as industrious, compliant and culturally superior to the Fijians. They saw the Fijians as lazy and undisciplined. These stereotypes were compounded by perceptions and evaluations which Indians and Fijians developed on their own from their own values, and from experiences with each other. Cumulatively then we witness the laying of new deposits of antipathies which will be at once become predisposing and triggering factors in the emergent ethnic malaise between Fijians and Indians.

A century later, the foundations of the ethnic boundaries were firmed up around the formation of communally-based voluntary associations and distinctively different cultural practices. Fijians and Indians were demarcated and compartmentalized by the reinforcing multiple cleavages of residence, occupation, values and stereotypes. To be sure, a few shared practices were emerging to facilitate the economic exploitation of the colony. These included the English language and, in part, an educational system which became significant after World War I. The countervailing centrifugal forces of division, however, prevailed for nearly a century without much modification.

The introduction of the suffrage by stages to enfranchise the non-white sector of the population in the colonial decision-making process provided the new layer of triggering devices that promoted ethnic conflict. The 'democratization process' can be conceived as occurring in two stages, each with a separate ethnic effect. In the first stage, Fijians and Indians were subordinated to European colonial control. But as the colonial government permitted increasing representation of Indians in the colonial councils, Fijians began openly to express fear of Indian domination and demanded political paramountcy. It would not be until the 1960s that dramatic changes would inaugurate the period of full-fledged mass democratic politics. Universal adult suffrage was introduced in 1963, bringing Fijians and Indians into head-on collision over control of the state. Political mobilization occurred along ethnic lines.

There are moments in what would appear to be an inexorable move towards establishing a tightly organized and compartmentalized communal order when opportunities for change avail themselves. There is nothing inevitable that the colonially-derived communal system should be permanent. Ethnic boundaries are notoriously fluid in rapidly changing environments; ethnically-oriented organized life can at least be modified so as to submit communal claims to cross pressures from functional class interests. In Fiji, in the early 1960s, a small effort was made by Fijian and Indian leaders to form a multi-ethnic party. This failed and a system of communally-based parties was launched and persisted to the present. At independence, the two ethnically-based parties, the Alliance Party and the National Federation Party, were drawn into very close fraternal relations. It was a moment of opportunity to re-cast, at least at the political level, the dominant role of ethnicity in giving shape to political organization and mobilization. Once the political levers were wrestled away from the colonial power, it was possible to re-cast institutions and practices so as to encourage cross-communal cooperation and co-existence. The direction of public policy under a cross-communal party could move away from ethnically-inspired employment and resource allocation practices which prevailed under the colonial power. Much of this, however, could only be achieved by a unified inter-ethnic leadership in a new popular mass-party committed to alternative paths of development. The task would have been gargantuan, flying in the face at every point of old communal habits and structural dispositions. But it could have been done. It required a vision of cross-communal unity to establish cross-communal organizations and policies that would modify and restrain the role of sectionalism in political life. This rare moment of opportunity was allowed to lapse. In a short time thereafter, ethnic outbidders appeared and exacerbated the communal divisions driving the two major parties apart. The *modus vivendi* succumbed to a deepening pattern of ethnic priorities that drew the state towards political disaster.

It is difficult to locate precisely the time when the question of ethnic shares became an issue in the struggle between the Fiji and Indian communal sections. In a sense, the entire colonially-constructed ethnic pyramid not only embodied resource allocation but explained its existence. This is credible in relation to the early European dominance of the state. However, the relations between Fijians and Indians in their later conflictual expression cannot be easily dismissed as derived from competition over scarce resources. If, however, the argument is made that economic material factors explain Indian-Fijian antipathy, the evidence to buttress this position comes abundantly from claims to jobs and privileges that Fijians and Indians have made against each other in the post-independence period. Fijians had claimed the public bureaucracy as their own preserve. Indians were cast in the role of sugar workers and business owners in the concept of 'balance.' Iincreasing numbers of Indians learnt the English language and began to pass qualifying examinations, thus earning advantageous access to the public service and to many urban-based jobs and professions. Fijians had already come to regard the public services as their own preserve. Indian-Fijian conflict can therefore be explained by this post-independence competition over public jobs and generally public resource allocation however. The Indian entry in significant numbers into the public service was seen as an unwarranted intrusion into the Fijian domain. It is clear that scarce resources and competition over jobs did play a role as a triggering factor in sustaining inter-communal conflict. It would seem justified in the light of the evidence to place this material factor in an important but not sole or dominant explanatory category in relation to the genesis and sustenance of the ethnic state.

Thus the ethnic state was created on the anvil of a combination of predisposing and triggering factors. From the very outset, a politically distorted state was fashioned. The cornerstone of the society was not laid with developmental aims in mind. The ethnic factor, founded at the outset of the Fiji state, fed into all issues and institutions in the post-independence period. Could not the communal state be reversed by a system of power-sharing? One of the deleterious effects of ethnic conflict in Fiji has been the loss of opportunity at cross-communal cooperation in government and the emergence of systematic ethnic domination and violence. This cost of ethnic conflict needs to be isolated analytically for separate but brief examination, since it is related to the undermining of those preferred values of political development. Put differently, cooperation across communities, especially where the cleavage is marked by a cultural differentiation, is an aspect of the environment vital to all efforts aimed at development. To what extent have cooperative efforts been undertaken in Fiji? Once ethnic strife has become persistent, even institutionalized in the social structure and embedded in individual behaviour, can cooperation efforts still flourish?

One of the grievous harms caused by persistent and protracted strife in a multi-ethnic society is the loss of will and capacity to reconcile. After many years of ongoing communal struggle, it appears that a sentiment of fatalism enters through the backdoor of consciousness, compelling the battered psyche to accept the ethnic battle lines and many adaptations to it as inevitable and permanent. A new socio-cultural architecture of human settlement and communal interaction emerges. A broken will, enfeebled and unprepared for reconciliation, emerges reinforced by countless symbols of old battles won and lost, as well by organizations and interests which institutionalize and structure the conflict. To be sure, at any earlier time, the leaders and elites in the various ethnic communities may have been able to communicate and beat out compromises for inter-communal co-existence. But as the conflict continues and deepens, even this upper layer becomes a victim of inter-communal intransigence. The ethnic monster devours everyone in the end.

Compromise and cooperation are the very heart of the developmental process. This is true of all social structures, integrated and divided alike. The democratic fabric itself is constituted of not only substantive give and take in beating out public policy, but this is undergirded by a culture and psychology of mutual trust in exchanges. The mortar of cooperation and compromise maintains the integrity of the edifice of society. In the multi-ethnic states of the Third World, the tension in working out mutually satisfactory exchanges is often overstrained by the fact the cleavages and differences are ethnicized. Protracted institutional ethnic conflict is the stuff out of which the culture and psychology of cooperation are undermined, rendering collective development difficult if not impossible.

Compromise and cooperation are embodied in devices for conflict resolution. In Fiji, compromise and cooperation came alive and were implemented in the system of 'balance' that was informally used by the Fijian, Indian, and European sections in sharing power and resources in the state. During the first few years after independence, an ambiance of inter-elite amity facilitated inter-communal harmony built around the 'balance.' 'Outbidding' by disgruntled ethnic entrepreneurs caused the collapse of the cooperative arrangement. Even when Indian-Fijian rivalry was again inflamed, in the midst of the ethnic division that ensued, there was a major effort in 1980 at restoring the old compromises in a government of national unity. This too broke down and the two ethnic groups and their leaders drew farther apart. The 'balance' was no longer operative and was replaced by the quest for paramountcy and power by both groups. Each group settled into its own ugly niche in an ethnically-influenced structure. But just about when it seemed that communal tension and ethnic rivalry were beyond control, a Labour-Federation party consisting of an amalgam of Indians and Fijians came to power. With this new structure, the opportunity for cross-cultural legitimacy in government was given a lease on life. This however, was quickly torpedoed by the military intervention which put an end to all pretenses at establishing a multi-cultural government. The costs are very real for they include the persistent threat of destabilization by those who are excluded. The effects are registered in a new repressive order inimical to all citizens.

The seizure of power by the Royal Fiji Military Forces to keep 'Fiji for Fijians' and the subsequent promulgation of the new inequalitarian constitution of July 1990, destroyed the basis of erecting a legitimate and stable regime. The loss of political legitimacy, the violations of human rights, and the threat of subversion together constitute the most formidable political costs that have accompanied ethnic conflict in Fiji.

X   Ethnic Conflict and Development: The Economic, Cultural and Psycho-Social Dimensions

In the long run, the ramifications of ethnic strife tend to be expressed most tangibly in the economic sphere. To some extent, the economic material effects can be measured. Less evident are the psychological and cultural repercussions of persistent ethnic problems. The environment of inter-communal malaise is fraught with tension. Every event is interpreted in terms of ethnic preferences and antipathies (Milne, 1986; Rothchild, 1986; Nevitte and Kennedy, 1986; Premdas, 1986b; Taylor and Mogahaddam, 1985). This is clearly an unhealthy environment for integral human development. In the cultural area, communal strife fosters narrow-minded and intolerant ethnocentrism and chauvinism. Cultures become cradles of hate, bigotry, and negative stereotyping (Isaacs, 1975; Premdas, 1994). Together, the economic, psychological, and cultural impact of persistent ethnic conflict can destroy the welfare, humanness, positive cultural qualities, and spiritual expression of a people. In this chapter, we briefly examine these repercussions of communal conflict in Fiji.

A. The economic dimension

To understand the economic consequences of ethnic conflict in Fiji, it will be useful to describe the unique economic structure of multi-ethnic states as a whole. Perhaps the most crucial feature of the economic environment in the typical plural society that has been created by colonization is its ethnic specialization and complementarity. The specialized parts of the economy have tended to emerge as areas of ethnic concentration so that over time each economic sector becomes the *de facto* preserve or territory of one or another ethnic section. This is clearly demonstrated in the case of Fiji. The major productive and distribution components of the economy are dominated by Fijians, Indians, and Europeans. In fact, in the case of Fiji, this system of economic ethnic specialization has evolved into a doctrine of 'balance' in spheres of predominant influence. Europeans have retained pre-eminence in large businesses such as banking and manufacturing; Indians in sugar production and in medium to small scale businesses; and Fijians in land holdings and in the public bureaucracy. To be sure, there are inter-ethnic overlaps, but generally, these spheres have evolved as predominantly separate territorial preserves. This sort of ethnic economic specialization does not exist in a vacuum but has been enmeshed in a reinforcing system of ethnic concentrations in residential, cultural, linguistic, and religious patterns.

The creation of this prototypical ethnically-specialized economy, while it initially facilitated the maintenance of political order, contained the germs of self-destruction when significant changes occurred in the society's movement from colonization to independence. More particularly, when a communal section that was hemmed into its economic and occupational niche decided to alter the terms of its participation in the informal 'balance' in the distribution of spheres of pre-eminence, it found it could do so drastically by threatening to sabotage the entire economy. This was so because each specialized part required the other in an act of coordination and cooperation for stable production and distribution to occur. If Indians withdrew their sugar production, or Fijians ceased to serve the public service or withdrew their leased lands for agricultural use, or Europeans closed their banks, the entire economy could collapse or be seriously crippled. Ethnic specialization entailed economic complementarity and dependence. This in turn required inter-ethnic cooperation as a vital pre-requisite for economic stability. Put differently, the persistence of stable economic functions resided in the socio-cultural area, for each of the major ethnic groups had the capacity to bring the economy to a halt. Bargaining intransigence in inter-ethnic conflict therefore held the state hostage to economic sabotage. When ethnic strife gets out of control and escalates into confrontation, inevitably the economic levers of dependence are unleashed by one side or the other wreaking havoc on the economic welfare of all citizens. Herein, then, resides a potent source of costs that are likely to attend inter-ethnic conflict in plural societies. This fact has been played out in Fiji as Indians and Fijians engage in intense struggle over political rights.

The creation of an economy of inter-dependent ethnic enclaves and spheres of influence also tends to result in important disparities in the distribution of material benefits. This disparity in turn feeds feelings of inter-communal malaise and provides the flammable stuff of ethnic conflagration. In Fiji, many indigenous Fijians regard their lot as unfair since on average the Fijian as compared with the Indian, European, or Chinese, was poorer. Fijians who have been socialized into a subsistence pattern of economic life do not display the same level of acquisitiveness, individualism, and competitiveness as the other ethnic groups. Consequently, over time, in a growing market economy, Fijian economic well-being has become conspicuously inferior to other groups. As was shown in earlier chapters, this disparity has provided the basis for the emergence of a breed of outbidders who have demanded that government policies be put under the control of Fijians in the design to rectify Fijian disadvantage. This has become the source of internal political upheaval.

After the first military coup in May 1987, the underlying structural characteristics of Fiji's economy, marked by ethnic specialization that demanded in its complementarity communal cooperation, came under intense strain. The costs of communally-inspired sabotage and strikes in response to the repercussions of the Fijian coup makers were drastic, attesting eloquently to the fragility of the economy to inter-ethnic pressure. The World Bank broadly summarized the immediate impact that the military coup had on the Fiji economy:

The immediate results included a sharp loss of business confidence, increased immigration, and capital flight. The sugar harvest was interrupted and tourist arrivals dropped precipitously. Investment virtually ceased and the external position deteriorated. The stance of economic policy had to shift from support for a relatively strong economy to protecting foreign exchange reserves. A large drop in government revenues led to expenditure cuts ranging from 10% to 20% in wages and salaries and 40% in capital expenditures. The budget increased nevertheless (World Bank, 1990 p.6).

It would be useful to trace out some of these general repercussions by looking at the major vulnerable sectors and areas of the economy including the sugar industry, the public service, the private business sector, tourism, land, the armed forces and the issue of inter-ethnic inequality. Sugar production is the backbone of the Fiji economy. It occupies over half of the country's arable land, employs about a fifth of the work force, serves as the principal source of foreign exchange (38 per cent in 1990), and accounts for about 13.5 per cent of GNP. The sugar industry is dominated by one ethnic section, the Indians, 60,000 of whom came as indentured labourers from 1879 to 1920 to work on Fiji's sugar plantations. Fiji's sugar production is organized on small individual private plots of about four hectares. There are some 22,000 individual small growers, three-fifths of whom are Indians who supply sugar cane to the four sugar mills in Fiji.

Table 10.1
Composition of Sugar Cane Growers, 1990

	LAUTOKA	RARAWAI	PENANG	LABASA	TOTAL
GROWERS					
number	8,445	5,793	2,573	4,849	21,660
%	39.0	26.7	11.9	22.4	100
Ethnic origin					
Indian, number	6,222	4,917	1,381	4,017	6,537
%	73.7	84.9	53.7	82.8	76.3
Fijian, number	2,172	860	1,168	812	5,012
%	5.7	14.8	45.4	6.7	23.1
Other, number	5.1	16	24	20	111
%	0.06	0.03	0.09	0.4	2.20

Source: Sugar Industry Tribunal, Register of Growers, 8 May 1990

As described in Chapter 1, the critical political fact of the Fiji sugar industry in terms of inter-ethnic relations points to the role of Indians as cultivators of sugar cane and Fijians as the main leases of the very land on which the sugar is cultivated. Further, in the harvesting of the cane, about 50 per cent of all cutters are hired labour with about 15 to 20 per cent of all this essential hired labour being Fijians. Many Indians and Fijians live in close contiguity of each other, with many Indians hiring Fijian labourers who are simultaneously the leaser-owners of the land. From the beginning, instrumental Indian-Fijian economic relations and dependence were locked into each other. When the Australian Colonial Sugar Refining Company (which practically controlled the entire sugar industry by 1973 before it was purchased by the Fiji government) commenced sugar production it did so on both freehold land and native lease with the latter emerging as the more significant (Moynagh, 1981; Fisk, 1970). The first British governor of Fiji, Arthur Gordon, oversaw the cessation of the sale and alienation of Fijian land thereby requiring sugar production on native leases. Indian-Fijian antipathy was literally grounded in an interlocking relationship between the labour of Indians and the land of Fijians, a combination that became oppositionally charged with irrational ethnic passions. Table 10.1 shows that only about 10 per cent of all cultivated sugar land is freehold. Most sugar production is under the auspices of a system of short-term lease under Fijian control. For Fiji to prosper, depending on sugar as main provider of governmental revenues, it was necessary that Indian cultivation and Fijian labour not be de-linked. The welfare of both Indians as sugar cultivators and Fijians as civil servants dependent for their salaries and wages on government revenues was entwined in uninterrupted sugar production.

All of these facts of the sugar industry have often come to bear in the ongoing conflictual malaise between Fijians and Indians. Indians have come to regard the sugar industry as their own on lands that are not under their ownership. The Indian-Fijian land relationship has been mediated by the Native Land Trust Board (NLTB), which oversees the administration of leases to Indian farmers (Lloyd, 1982). Indians have bitterly complained about their lack of tenure while Fijians have feared the permanent loss of their land. During the independence constitutional conference, Indians and Fijians traded on the land issue with Indians securing longer leases on the land in exchange for the entrenchment of Fijian ownership in the constitution. From the sugar lands, Indian families developed a measure of viability and well-being; over the years this became a visible symbol of Indian communal striving. From the sugar sector, Indians collectively gained strength. Fijians observed Indian economic growth with alarm, especially when this was coupled with strident demands for more land and political equality. Fijians felt that if Indian pre-eminence in sugar was to be respected, Fijian pre-eminence in the political domain and the governmental civil service must be also. Clearly, unless Indians and Fijians could work out a *modus vivendi* to share economic resources and power, they were each capable in the nature of the ethnicized interlocking economic order of inflicting grave costs on each other and on the country as a whole.

The threat of the withdrawal of Indian production of sugar as a leverage for economic and political demands is not new in Fiji. Indian farmers and workers had organized themselves very early into militant trade unions (Mamak and Ali, 1979). All Indian political leaders from Patel, to Koya, to Reddy, gained political ground from their ability to represent Indian sugar interests. Sugar stood as a metaphor for Indian political power. Indian leaders used the supply and withdrawal of sugar, the life blood of the country's economy, to win or redress Indian claims and complaints. The closing down of the sugar production was tantamount to the crippling and closing down of the country. In sugar inhered important political and economic power.

Hence, in 1987 when Rabuka seized power asserting 'Fiji for Fijians', the immediate response of Indian leaders was to invoke the sugar weapon as the means of counter-argument. As retraced in earlier chapters, Indian sugar farmers refused to harvest their cane in response to the eviction of the Labour-Federation Party from power. The cessation of sugar production at harvest time endangered Fiji's lucrative access to premium prices of sugar offered to Fiji under the ACP/EC Sugar Protocol and other preferential arrangements. The cessation of sugar production also had potential adverse effects on the internal Fiji food supply. About 90 per cent of all of Fiji's sugar is disposed of in overseas markets. When the sugar workers and the Labour Party successfully obtained the sympathetic support of Australian and New Zealand labour unions, this promptly stopped the shipment of a major part of Fiji's sugar to overseas destinations.

The cost of ethnic conflict cannot be better attested to than in this area of economic endeavour involving mutual Indian-Fijian interests. The Fijian military and the Taukei movement responded to Indian boycotts in the sugar industry by threatening to cancel all Indian land leases and evict Indians *en masse* from their farms. The country, caught in a grave confrontation between its two primary ethnic parts, stood on the brink of ethnic conflagration. This scenario has been enacted again and again in a ruthless game of ethnic chicken between Indian leaders and the Fijian-controlled government from 1987 to the present. As related in an earlier chapter, as recently as 1991 when Indian farmers went on a boycott, many Fijians organized a counter-protest to march into the rural areas. The Fijian government has tried a variety of methods to neutralize the Indian hold on the economy including the formation of an all-Fijian sugar union. In earlier administrations, under Prime Minister Ratu Mara, several large land reclamation projects were undertaken to increase Fijian participation in the sugar industry but with insignificant success (Watters, 1969). The sugar industry became a fierce battleground of rival Fijian-Indian political interests.

Perhaps the most startling set of measures which the Fijian-dominated government embarked upon to combat and neutralize Indian control of the sugar industry were the Sugar Industry Protection Decree and the National Economic Protection Decree of June 1991. Essentially, these decrees criminalized legitimate trade union activities threatening (F)\$10,000 in fine and fourteen years imprisonment of union leaders (Leckie, 1991). Under the Sugar Industry Protection Decree, it was a crime for any 'to interfere' with the planting and harvesting of sugar cane. Under the Economic Protection Decree, this provision was extended to other industries. To the trade union movement and its organ, the Fiji Trades Union Congress as a whole and in particular, the National Farmers' Union, both headed by Mahendra Chaudry, the new decrees struck at the heart of the trade union movement. Actually, the decrees effectively banned strikes and made union officials liable to prosecution. Further, they were contrary to several ILO conventions. The immediate target of the decrees was, however, incontrovertibly aimed at Chaudry and the sugar farmers' union.

The response from the sugar unions and the labour unions was generally massive. The country was marched to the brink of a national disaster as riot police were deployed against the National Farmers Union, which defied the decrees (*Fiji Times*,1991d). It was an inter-ethnic confrontation parading under the rubric of an industrial relations conflict. The Fiji Traders Union Congress threatened a national strike and the extremist Taukei Movement mobilized to meet strikers in what promised to be civil war. The government threatened to send in soldiers to cut the sugar harvest and even the Fijian Methodist Church wanted to recruit members to work in the sugar fields (*Fiji Times,* 1991i). The confrontation between the government and the unions was averted when the government agreed to suspend the decrees and the unions called off the strike. Subsequently, in November 1991, the government promulgated new Decrees No. 42, 43, and 44 which withdrew the mandatory check of facilities for union dues, making this negotiable with the employer and forbidding any union leader from holding official union positions in two different unions separately. This was aimed at Mahendra Chaudry, who was the leader of the National Farmers' Union and was Secretary-General of the Fijian Trades Union Congress.

In all of these actions and counter-actions, the underlying tension in the main was between Fijians in a Fijian-dominated government and Indians in the National Farmers' Union. The economic costs were registered, both in the realm of economic losses and inter-ethnic relations. The continuing threat of the loss of their leases among Indian farmers led the Landel-Miller Sugar Commission to report that 'the nature of the land tenure by lease holders does not encourage capital investments in the form of machinery and other means of capital to boost productivity because of doubts on the renewal of leases during the 1990s' (*Fiji Times,* 1991b). Most Indian leases are due, either for renewal or termination, in the latter half of the 1990s and, given the state of Indian-Fijian relations, this does not augur well for the sugar industry and Fiji's future. In the meanwhile, as the sugar unions and the government continue to struggle, sugar production, which plummeted after the coups in 1987, has progressively returned to normal and even higher production. This has occurred in the midst of the ongoing tension, which some day may well break the bounds of restraint and become violently physical and ethnically fratricidal. Many Indian farmers have already informally and formally transferred their leases to others and migrated to overseas destinations. Others are preparing to do so while most, from the evidence of field interviews conducted, are prepared to engage physically in open defense of their only means of livelihood.

One of the more dramatic and immediate costs associated with the coup and the subsequent communal repression has been the flight of people, including many cane-growing families out of Fiji. While this consisted mainly of Indians, the massive exodus was not only ethnically pronounced but occupationally biased. In a survey carried out by the World Bank, the emigration loss was especially concentrated among those with skills badly needed by a developing country to maintain its economic well-being and sustain growth. Said the World Bank report:

Fiji's quite abundant supply of skills was threatened by the political events of 1987. Prior to them, about 500 workers emigrated annually; in the years following the coups d'état, emigration rose sharply to about 2,500 or 1% of the work force. Emigration has particularly affected the supply of high-and-middle-level staff (World Bank, 1990 p.30).

According to the Fiji Bureau of Statistics, of those employed at the time of the 1986 census, about 7 per cent of the professional and technical, 17 per cent of the administration and managerial, and 8 per cent of the clerical staff had left the country by late 1988. Key professions were particularly hard hit; it is reported that 70 per cent of the lawyers, over 50 per cent of the doctors, 40 per cent of the accountants, and many architects, engineers, and technicians and teachers have recently left Fiji; vacancy rates from some key public service still range from 30 to 50 per cent (World Bank, 1990 p.30).

Nearly all theorists of economic development place a critical premium on ample supply of skilled work force and especially point to the need for middle level managers and administrators which Fiji has been losing rapidly since the coups in 1987. The haemorrhage in the loss of skills has continued and increased; the figures reported by the Fiji Bureau of Statistics gave 5,118 for 1987; 5,496 for 1988; 5,510 for 1989; and 5,650 for 1990. That is, from 1986 when the loss was 3, 0048 to 1990 when the loss was 5,650, the increase was 185 per cent (*Fiji Times,* 1991c). The ethnic composition given was 88 per cent Indians, 5-6 per cent Fijians, and 5-6 per cent others. In a typical month in July 1990, of the 470 who emigrated, 420 were Indians, 20 Fijians, and 26 others. For 1990, the skills composition was of a total of 5,650, some 169 were teachers, 128 architects and engineers, 57 medical, dental, and veterinary doctors, and 63 accountants. Altogether, about 40,000 persons had emigrated by 1992 (Ibid.).

While for the coup makers, the emigration of Indians served to equalize the ratio of Indians to Fijians in the population and reduced the size of the Indian presence in the population, the effects of the mass emigration were not confined to the loss of gross numbers alone. The loss of skills in which the country had invested was monumental, reverberating at all levels of economic well-being in the society. More critically, these losses included not only persons who were skilled, but many were investors and entrepreneurs that included Indians, Chinese, and Europeans who found that the atmosphere of ethnic tension was not conducive to investment. The modern monetary sector in the Fiji economy is built on private investment, an area that became the predominant domain of non-Fijians. When the first coup occurred, investors withdrew their funds from banks in droves and transferred them overseas, creating a crisis in the balance of payments. In the wake of this loss, Fiji devalued its currency twice in 1987, reducing the value of the currency by 30 per cent. Investor confidence plummeted and the economic repercussions were devastating. Reported the World Bank: 'The immediate results included a sharp loss of business confidence, increased emigration, and capital flight' (World Bank, 1990 p.3). The healthy trajectory of economic growth that was projected for Fiji prior to the crop quickly evaporated: 'Incentives for foreign and new domestic investment were more effective in 1986 and 1987, when a number of new projects, mainly in tourism and production for export, were approved. Many investments were postponed, however, when the political crisis occurred' (Ibid.). By 1994, while some investors had returned and new ones from Asia and Japan came, the loss of business confidence persisted.

Fiji needed investment to maintain its economic strength and to cope with its unemployment problems. Unemployment in urban areas by 1990 was about 10 to 12 per cent, and among indigenous Fijians between the ages of 20 and 24 years, it was about 49 per cent (Ibid., p. 8). Economic policies aimed at solving the unemployment problem and facilitating growth as well as at increasing revenues for a Fijian-controlled government under severe pressure to meet the increased demands of Fijians for more and better services and benefits required a return to private investment. The area of private investment that seemed to have the greatest long-term potential for growth was manufacturing, especially export manufacture (Ibid., p. 9). This was especially so because of the improved and preferential access that Fiji manufactures offered by New Zealand, Australia and the EC. The main constraint in this sector had been the supply of needed skills (Ibid., p. 11). Hence, to some extent, the problem of availability of investment came back to the issue of loss off skill as well as the lack of investor confidence. Said the World Bank in 1991: 'Currently, the most serious constraint is the lack of investor confidence; a potentially more important limitation is that of human resources' (Ibid., pp.12-13).

In the final analysis, all of this cost revolved around the shortages of capital and skills that occurred in the wake of persistent conflict in Fiji. Investment for economic growth is not necessarily confined to the private sector. Fiji's mixed economy has grown in the past under the stimulus of an active government involvement in the production process. This has led to the expansion of the public bureaucracy, which provided new employment opportunities for the indigenous Fijian population in particular. Public sector employment in Fiji accounts for about one-third of all continuous employment; about two-thirds of all wage employment between 1976 and 1986 occurred in the public sector (Ibid., p. 2). The heavy involvement of the government in the economy was facilitated by remarkable growth in the pre-1980 period, especially between 1965 and 1973, but also continued at a slower rate between 1973 and 1980. Both sugar and tourism flourished well between 1973 and 1980. After 1979, however, when oil prices increased dramatically and the industrialized countries were experiencing a recession, significant

172

deterioration occurred in Fiji's balance of trade and inflows of capital. This impacted adversely by increasing government deficits as export earnings decreased and economic growth slowed. To compound these effects, Fiji was repeatedly buffeted by cyclones that wreaked havoc on sugar and copra production and by the concessions to public servants for increased pay. While the economy did rebound in the mid-1980s, the pattern was set that attested to wide fluctuations of the economy in response to external and internal investment conditions. When cyclones and recessions from outside hit Fiji, the government sector suffers deficits. This event is cyclical. However, to the role of cyclones and external recessions, has now been added the loss of business confidence attendant on the ethnic conflict and the military coups. Facing multiple stresses, the public sector, serving as the preserve of indigenous Fijians is, today, compelled to contract. The new emphasis in an age of structural adjustment guidelines issued by the International Monetary Fund and the World Bank is to rely on private investment to guarantee economic recovery and growth (Eleck, Hill, and Taylor, 1991). This new economic doctrine demands that Fiji decrease its role in the economy through privatization and diminish and destroy its manifold subsidies, restrictive trade barriers such as tariff barriers, price supports, quotas, etc., and establish a policy environment conducive to promoting a more competitive market economy. Prescribed the World Bank:

A sustained recovery in investment and growth will require major shifts in economic strategy. The deregulation of activity within the economy should receive high priority, to provide more freedom for entrepreneurs to engage in informal as well as more structured enterprise, to compete more effectively andto produce goods and services more efficiently (Ibid., p.12).

While this prescription is appropriate for a country with a unified set of values and traditions, in Fiji where a multi-ethnic society exists, such prescription can impact very adversely on one community more so than on others (Milne, 1986). To deregulate the Fiji economy means that the Fijian sphere of employment and power will have to shrink. Conversely, this entails that non-Fijians as the group with investment capital and skills, stand to benefit most. The need to maintain an atmosphere conducive to private investment then flies in the face of political calculations to diminish the size of the Indian population and its role in the economy. Non-Fijians have been excluded from equal participation in the polity but are now called upon to provide the means of maintaining the viability of the economy as a whole. Yet, non-Fijians and Indians in particular, are not in the best strategic position to dictate the political terms of their survival in Fiji. They nevertheless need Fijian land and labour to exist and prosper. While inter-communal cooperative behaviour is clearly required, it is this commodity above all that is most sadly lacking.

To counter the loss suffered as a consequence of Indian and non-Fijian emigration, the government embarked on a variety of policies which in many ways added fuel to the fire of inter-ethnic malaise. The new constitution of Fiji has prescribed that at least 50 per cent of all jobs in the public service be reserved for indigenous Fijians. This discriminatory policy, while in itself offensive, did not necessarily injure other sectional interests fatally since many Indians, Chinese and Europeans were employed in small businesses and agriculture. However, with the lid placed on government expenditures affecting the size of the public service, Fijian claims for jobs could only be denied at great risk to the ruling regime in an era of ethnic chauvinism. In practice, in the post-coup period in the public service, more Fijians were employed and promoted than other groups. By July 1991, a pattern had emerged, evidenced by official Public Service Commission data showing that only about 34 per cent (not the 40 per cent set forth in the constitution) of appointments were allocated to Indians, with 42 per cent of these acting appointments; only 38 per cent of all promotions were gained by Indians (Chand, 1990). While many Indians protested about these figures, the fact remained that Indians were not excluded altogether and many had abandoned their posts and migrated. Indian presence in the public service had become suspect since they were least likely to stay and offer their best support. In turn, this affected the relations between Fijians and Indians at the work place. It became safer to promote Fijians who were more likely to remain in their jobs. It amounted to less of an ideal situation for job performance, attesting to the subtle ways in which ethnic conflict and discrimination undermine the collective effort so vital for development.

To offset non-Fijian pre-eminence in business, the Fijian-led government embarked upon a series of affirmative action measures to encourage Fijians to enter into the private sector. Special programmes aimed at enabling Fijians to establish private businesses are not new in Fiji (Hailey, 1985). Under the Prime Ministership of Ratu Mara, several schemes were initiated by the government but generally they failed to become anchored so that today no sizable group of independent Fijian entrepreneurs has emerged. There have been various reasons advanced to explain this problem, including the 'numerous regulations that for example prevented them from borrowing more than a specified sum of money, placed numerous conditions on those who wanted to opt out and become independent farmers, etc (Chand, 1990).

Subsistence and communally oriented, and unfamiliar with the ways of communal competition in an economy of private enterprise, the Fijian was rendered institutionally unprepared after independence to enter into the arena of business. To make the Fijian a successful business person, however, required more than just the supply of capital, accompanied with a modicum of training courses and even a degree in business administration. The Fijian link to the collective values of his/her community locked in an economy of love and mutual sharing remained the most stubborn bulwark against success in the individualist and acquisitive world of commerce. Even in the area of cooperatives, Fijians have floundered, yielding to communal demands in priority to individual gain. Overall, then, the record of Fijian accomplishment in private business has been dismal for a variety of historical and customary reasons.

Despite this, the current Fijian-run regime has embarked even more vigorously on lavish programmes to facilitate Fijian entry into the business world. Prospective and actual Fijian business persons jave organized themselves into the 'Viti Chamber of Commerce.' The allocation of public funds for three sets of programmes has been established which has evoked strident protests by non-Fijians. First, the Fijian Development Bank, a statutory body of the Government established to grant loans for development, announced that of a total of (F)$62.8 million available for loans between July 1991 and June 1992, (F)$13.1 million could be exclusively set aside for Fijians under special concessional terms (Chand, 1990; *Fiji Times*, 1990b). Under the 'Special Loan Scheme for Fijians,' each prospective Fijian entrepreneur would obtain about (F)$200,000 at 5.5 per cent interest. Apart from this special scheme, Fijians also had access to the bank's normal lending schemes. Under its practices, and especially in the post-coup period when the bank's board of directors became staffed exclusively with indigenous Fijians, the Fijian Development Bank emerged in the public consciousness as an indigenous Fijian bank where unlimited access was available for funds for all purposes (Ibid.).

While non-Fijians, and especially Fiji Indians, decried the special loan programmes, in part because of the very large losses the government suffered from these business failures connected to loans given to Fijians, Ratu Mara, the Fijian Prime Minister in the interim government, stoutly defended government policy. He argued that 'for too long Fijians have been commercial outsiders with limited access to the real wealth of the country' (*Fiji Times*, 1990a). He felt that in the din of charges of discrimination against non-Fijians that these complaints were 'usually one sided reflecting the fears and concerns of only one community' and that in fact 'many criticisms and protests seem to be oblivious to the discrimination which stares Fijians in the face every day' (Ibid.). Mara pointed out that it was not true that Fijians did not like nor wanted to be in business; he argued that on the contrary, Fijians 'want to compete in business and in other sectors of the community too but the system works against them' (Ibid.). He therefore defended 'the government's policies aimed at rectifying all of this' (Ibid.).

The second scheme that the government embarked upon to put Fijians into the business sphere was through financial participation in the purchase of shares in companies. Through Fijian Holdings Ltd., a holding company formed originally in 1984 by fourteen Fijian provinces, the Fijian Affairs Board, and the NLTB, an interest free loan of (F) $20 million was secured from the government to purchase shares in ten private companies (Ibid.; *Fiji Times,* 1991k). This holding company has been the recipient of substantial profits which in 1990 amounted to (F)$1,906,259 and paid a 10 per cent dividend. The company sought additional government loans and intended to expand the area of Fijian ownership in the private sector. Many analysts have contrasted this mode of indirect ownership by Fijians with direct forms of ownership of companies such as those owned by NLTB which became bankrupt incurring great loss to the government.

Finally, the government has accelerated its programme of allocating sums of money to secure a quota of scholarships and places at the University of the South Pacific and other training institutions. Because of the loss via emigration of Fiji trained graduates, mainly Indians, who were trained in tertiary institutions in Fiji such as the University of the South Pacific, the Fiji School of Medicine, and the Fiji Institute of Technology, the government has felt justified in heavily tilting scholarships in favour of Fijians. The problem of manpower losses has become especially acute because of the brain drain of engineers, teachers, doctors, lawyers, accountants, etc. from Fiji. Government expenditures have increased dramatically in recruiting replacement staff from Sri Lanka which has supplied judges and magistrates, from Taiwan and Malaysia which have supplied doctors and dentists, and from other parts of the world. Indigenous Fijians find themselves under immense pressure to fill the gap created by the losses in the areas of business investors, professionals, and farmers. The cost of training and replenishing the loss has been more than anticipated reverberating in the fall of public services facilities, medical attention, and health services. Without an adequate government public infrastructure of roads, communications, education, etc. private investors would be deterred from entering Fiji. The economic cost of ethnic conflict has come back to haunt the coup makers. The massive economic dislocation has been partly concealed by the resurgence of tourism and even sugar production. The structural costs are however likely to persist as the ethnic conflict continues to smoulder. In the short run, it is unlikely that economic disparities between Fijians and Indians will be bridged so that the basis of another round of discriminatory policies is being laid for ethnic outbidders to capitalize upon.

B. The socio-cultural and psychological dimensions

A general tendency exists to evaluate a Third World country's well-being mainly on the basis of aggregate per capita and GNP data. These indices are often useful as broad country characteristics but they are too abstract and intangible. Behind the array of aggregate statistical data are people, their lives, how they survive, suffer, cope, fail, succeed, etc. Ultimately, development devolves on the well-being of the individual in society. Social well-being is the micro-dimension of development change; it orients and measures the impact and effects of political and economic structures and strategies on the welfare of the very subject of all directed development activities. Social development is multi-faceted, but in the last analysis, derived from economic, political, and cultural aggregate sources, it holistically addresses the dignity, welfare, and personal development of the human creature. This, however, is not always easy to specify without reference to the norms and customs of a society, for the cultural system defines the meaning of such critical categories of development as dignity; self-hood; material, spiritual and ethical values. Despite this, we cannot relativize the fundamental needs of the human person, tangling it in a thicket of ideological and cultural debate and jargon. We can proceed *de negativa* to a fruitful discovery of what features are not involved in social, ethical, psychological, and spiritual development. We know at a minimum what is not acceptable: torture, starvation, domination, isolation, dependence, discrimination, etc. That is a useful starting point for a programme of action as well as an evaluation of the meaning of social development. Having specified what cannot be accepted, we can then proceed to establish minimal levels and optimizing ideals in a critical list that define human need, In this part of the chapter, both the negative and positive approaches to social development will be used inter-lockingly to examine and evaluate the impact of ethnic conflict on development in Fiji. Most of the materials in this section of the chapter are distilled from data previous descriptions.

(i) Violence, terror and personal security

It is essential to the normal survival of the human creature that its security is not threatened. That is, on an elementary day to day basis, it is a necessary condition for wholesome survival that physical life not be threatened, especially for collective irrational reasons. A reasonable measure of predictability about one's continued safety and survival is essential and a pre-requisite to all of the remaining basic needs of life. Physical insecurity disrupts and destabilizes all aspects of life, and distorts every province and pursuit of behaviour, especially social and psychological existence. Terror and anxiety tend to overwhelm all behavioural dispositions breeding its own pathologies.

The omnipresent hovering threat of personal injury even death often paralyses the will to function especially in contexts of helplessness and open vulnerability.

In the wake of the first military coup in May 1987, widespread ethnic violence erupted in Fiji, concentrated mainly in the capital city, Suva where masses of Fijians attacked and injured Indians, their stores, and threatened their homes. The Fijians who attacked the Indians did not know each other but had a view inculcated from their youth that made the Indians their main adversary in life. To Indians, Fijians were inferior and thus held them in contempt. Through negative stereotyping built into their cultural upbringing, the lenses of collective antipathy were imparted to Fijians and Indians. It dehumanized each side, but equally significant it laid a body of pre-disposing prejudices which made every day in the mind of every Fijian and Indian an invitation to civil strife. To be sure, rituals of avoidance and minimal courtesy are everywhere evident in daily inter-communal interaction, but below the veneer of civility and indifference lurks the monster of collective ethnic suspicion and hate. In the privacy of the homes and communities, Fijians and Indians openly utilize denigrating epithets to describe each other's behaviour. It is a case of 'we' versus 'them' in an ongoing contest over territorial space, land, jobs, politics, and just about everything.

After a system of popular representation was first introduced in 1904 and onwards to 1963 when universal adult suffrage was conceded to Fiji by Britain, politics became the main arena of inter-ethnic rivalry. Fijians asserted their claim to paramountcy in their own land; Indians countered with a demand for equality. On the anvil of protracted ethnic conflict over time emerged a total engagement involving practically all Fijians and Indians. In the tightening vice of the contest between the two major ethnicized parties that came to represent Fijians and Indians, a rigid sectionally compartmentalized society evolved, breeding a spiral of tensions that periodically erupted into violence. In one notable event after the 1968 elections when the two communal groups confronted each other, the country was brought to the brink of civil war. Commented Ratu Mara on these events: 'those were the days when we sailed so close to the rocks...we came so near to the edge of the abyss that we could see with unmistakable clearness the dangers that lay there if we did not change course. So we changed course' (Milne, 1975 p.420).

Like most ethnically segmented states, Fiji is perpetually at war with itself (Young, 1976). Surrogates for physical violence suffuse the system. These encompass such forms as rivalry in the celebration of their respective religious holidays, competition in business and government, etc. Stereotypes belittle and separate entire communities serving as a sort of quiet victory of the mind over the opponent. They tend to dehumanize ethnic enemies and set the stage for violence against the collective opponent. When mass politics were introduced and ethnically based parties emerged, these underlying stereotypical antipathies were harnessed into instruments of mass action. The parties accentuated inter-communal hostilities. Competition at elections provided the occasion for these antagonisms to be vented openly; often political campaigns seemed like military engagements (Lawson, 1991). All of this brought the society periodically to the brink of mass violence.

The logic of confrontation between government and opposition bringing the country to the border of bloody communal conflagration has been decried by the leaders of the sectional parties. In 1980 when a government of national unity was first proposed, Ratu Mara warned that the persistence of ethnic conflict was paid in the price that threatened the 'destruction of what was already achieved' for the society lived in tension of racial confrontation (*Fiji Times,* 1980 p.1). He described these conditions as 'crisis prone' and pointed to the failure of government 'to weld into a nation peoples with strong ethnic allegiances' (Ibid.). The Indian leader, Jai Ram Reddy, underscored Mara's admonitions about the 'divisiveness' of communal rivalry and 'warned against the dangers of polarization' (Ibid.). Both Mara and Reddy predicted that if current trends continued, they would inevitably telescope to open violence. While they share a consensus then that collective communal policies and rivalry were divisive, wasteful, and prone to instability and violence, the sectional leaders have not hesitated to use the inflammatory materials of inter-ethnic stereotyping to campaign for votes. Playing with ethnic fire which threatens the entire house in which both communal groups lived has become a routine mode of conducting political life. It is a game of deadly self-deception and hypocrisy.

To some extent, violence and the threat of violence have derived from the gross physical features of Fijians and Indians. Fijians tend, on average, to be taller and more muscular than Indians. In the games that they play, such as very robust Australian Rules rugby and boxing, Fijians have demonstrated prowess. The Royal Fijian Military Forces, mainly constituted of indigenous Fijians, embody the military traditions of ancient Fijian warfare, a fact that has made the military forces a special preserve of prominent Fijian families and clans. Above all, on a day to day basis, this physical elan among Fijians is paraded as a point of Fijian pride and is conducted in the immediate shadow of the proverbial puny Indian who is cowardly and prone to agricultural pursuits and clerical jobs. In inter-communal contact, this physical distance has created much strain. This is a part of the psychology of Fijian-indian interaction that enacts a script of aversion in daily civil intercourse.

Played out on a larger level of national politics, the physical differential translates into Indian fear of collective slaughter in the event of an openly violent confrontation. Many Fijians and Indians, from the evidence of years of field work conducted by this researcher, have entertained visions of civil war

179

in which the Indians would be routed brutally and comprehensively. The fact that Indians hold Fijians in such low cultural esteem regarding them as *'jungli'* or barbarian easily invites Fijian desire to retaliate physically. Some militant Indians do talk of organizing for defence but generally concede that they stand little chance of survival in a civil war. The talk of such an event is not a sketchy or sporadic event in Fiji. In the vice of tightening ethnic tensions, often experienced at election time, the bounds of tolerance are broken by quiet talk of communal violence including the prospects of genocide. Fijian extremists such as Sakiasi Butadroka, who spoke of eliminating Indians through mass eviction from Fiji, merely express a variant of outright liquidation. Talk of collective inter-communal violence is pervasive in Fiji.

From time to time, such talk has become intensely threatening. Butadroka often wears a red tie as a symbol of the bloodshed that must follow, should Indians not leave Fiji. In 1977, he was convicted and jailed for using racially inflammatory language in public. Indians have reacted by migrating and discriminating against Fijians at every opportunity. In shops and stores, courtesy and credit extended to Fijians fluctuate with the state of ethnic relations. In effect, in many subtle ways violence and its threat are perpetuated by each community on each other. The war is conducted in underlying idioms that are understood well by each other.

When Fijians attacked Indians in May 1987, after the first military coup, it was merely a more overt and physical expression of another war that had been conducted in many millions of ways every day, everywhere, for a long time in Fiji. Indian mass emigration from 1987 onwards has been only the intensification of a pattern of departures that was practised for over a decade earlier. The brinkmanship that marked the overt use of violence in 1987 had often been conducted by political leaders on both sides. With the coups in 1987, the restraints were practically all let loose. The army and police, placed in sole control of the coercive arms of the state, as well as the Taukei extremists and gangs of roving Fijian youths, established a garrison state that placed all non-Fijians in virtual custody. Lt. Colonel Rabuka argued that he had carried out the first coup in part to protect Indians from being slaughtered by plans hatched by the Taukei. There can be little doubt that the military did constrain the excesses of violence after the coup. However, the military and police themselves became the source of widespread terror, house break-ins, arbitrary arrests, and intimidation, all ethnically guided (Singh, 1991). In an earlier chapter, the record of the repression and discrimination by the post-coup regime was detailed. What has emerged is a 'new reality' forged on superior Fijian military and physical might. The foremost fear of the Indian is liquidation either through mass migration or internal violence. Whether this is real or not is not as significant as the fact that this is so perceived. The cost of this aspect of the communal strife enacted in the threat of physical harm is immense. It creates a level of malaise that deeply poisons the humanity of both Fijians and Indians. Indigenous Fijian compassion and welcome for which they are justly famous have been submitted to their own kind of internal contradictions. Fijians as well as Indians have been hurt in communal violence. The environment of inter-ethnic distrust continues resulting in the persistence of personal affront to human dignity that offends and distorts both Fijians and Indians.

The garrison state that the Fiji constitution has created is manifested in a 'new reality' that violates the rights and well-being of all citizens. The establishment of the Fijian Intelligence Service with un-restricted license to burgle, open private mail, eavesdrop, etc. can be used against all opponents of the regime, Fijian and Indian alike. Like in other places with similar criminal conflicts such as Guyana, a repression at first directed against one communal section and applauded by the other soon spreads to engulf all citizens who are critical of those who wield power (Milne, 1981; Premdas, 1992). Fear of expressing open criticisms pervades the post-coup Fiji. This fear constrains freedom of expression of all citizens regardless of ethnic origins. The constitution forbids criticisms of Fijian chiefs, a fact that binds both Fijians and Indians. The widespread use of Fijian civilians to report on the behaviour of Indians after the coups has established a form of terror that extends to all citizens who dare to oppose the ruling regime. As time passes, the new Fijian-dominated governments are bound to incur the anger and wrath of citizens of all ethnic stripes; in time repression is bound to become universalized. A number of indigenous Fijians have already migrated in fear of their lives and future.

The costs of the universalitzation of fear and terror of a regime that lacks legitimacy and is upheld by indirect coercion are likely to be resistance, non-cooperation, and sabotage which in turn causes a ruling regime to expand its security system and divert resources from development to the maintenance of order. A vicious cycle of ethnic-directed state violence countered by citizen violence (sometimes communally organized, as in Sri Lanka) can throw the entire society onto a path of Lebanese-like self-destruction. Communal violence is an especially virulent form of irrational behaviour that can rarely be restrained once civil war breaks out. In Fiji, the persistence of the regime of inequality, discrimination and repression provides the incendiary raw materials for a protracted, system-wide struggle. In time, external sympathetic actors with money and arms join the fray, expanding the scope of the struggle, intensifying its effects, and rendering reconciliation and conflict resolution more complex and intransigent (Premdas, 1990b.). With large numbers of Fiji Indians living in concentrated overseas enclaves, many of them having lost their careers and properties, the internal ethnic violence in Fiji is bound to breed unending plots with local conspirators to destabilize the Fiji government. There has already been one attempted hijacking of an aircraft in Fiji, an attempted shipment of arms into Fiji, and several plots to overthrow the government. More of this is likely to be spawned compelling the ruling regime to resort to more intense levels of repression and breeding similar responses in kind, in a spiral of unending irrational waste.

(ii) Culture and social participation and the psychological dimension

The polarization of ethnic politics has pervaded all aspects of life and all issues, creating intolerance for the cultures of Fijians and Indians. Fijians regard Indians as 'heathens,' 'unchristian,' and 'idol worshippers.' Indians similarly depreciate Fijian culture regarding it as inferior to the Indian. The rich heritage of each cultural section is not enjoyed mutually, but has instead become part of the artillery of confrontation between the sections. Generally, Fijians and Indians do not speak each other's languages even though in some parts of Fiji many do so. English is the *lingua franca*. A powerful cultural veil separates the Fijian from the Indian in the areas of religion, language, and values. Few cross-cultural norms that are sufficiently strong have evolved to offer common ground for political discourse. The main medium of communication is blind collective antagonism often expressed in intransigent claims and counter-claims. The cultural barriers that have evolved render inter-ethnic Fijian-Indian marriages and liaisons infrequent and rare. In a real sense, cultures have become incubators of inter-ethnic racism fostering prejudices and preparing the ground of inter-sectional antipathy and outright violence. Cultural practices in an ethnically segmented state at war with itself have led to the social compartmentalization of individual lives and to personal isolation and distorted identity formation.

In its most general sense, participation refers to membership of a person in all aspects of society. It at once eliminates isolation and confers identity. It attests to the idea that the human personality is formed relationally in the ways of social interaction which mould the mind and confer value on existence. Participation then is not just about political rights to vote and involvement in collective decision-making, but about social self-definition and community identity. Further, it refers not only to being a part of anything, however negative in structure, but to being a member of a wholesome system of relations that does not distort human dignity and promote personality deformation.

In Fiji, as in most unintegrated multi-ethnic societies, personal identity is fragmented, derived from the norms supplied by the separate communities. In itself, this is a positive fact since it confers belonging and identity on the human person providing essential cultural anchorage and a point of collective reference. Membership confirms religion, custom, and role. It provides a structure of meaning, eliminating existential isolation. All of these advantages of social participation are, however, conditional on the existence of peaceful relations with other similar communal sections which share the same territorial state. In Fiji, a small state where inter-communal and cross-sectional interactions are inevitable and frequent, a condition of inter-communal malaise that deteriorates into open and prolonged conflict can distort all the advantages of group participation. Each communal section has become a virtual military garrison, suffusing all of its activities with social self-assertions built on the dehumanization of ethnic opponents. Persistent ethnic struggle tends to sharpen the negative stereotypes which communal groups hold of each other. The stereotypes extend to derogations that border on outright racism. In time, one factor above all - the ethnic enemy - assumes the centre stage of intense group assertion. It occupies the very centre of the soul with an obsessive preoccupation, assigning to it all manner of causes of every conceivable social problem. Apart from shaping attitudes of intense collective hate, the basis of any future inter-communal co-existence is consequently crippled. At the level of voluntary associations, a *de facto* uni-ethnic membership persists in Fiji. Following the coups, increasingly ethnic compartments were created into which all normal emotions were expressed.

A collective spirit constrains membership only to certain uni-ethnic associations and penalizes persons who dare to join groups that are cross-communal. Personal autonomy, essential to individual development is lost. Old cross-cultural networks and friends erode. It would seem that a new form of social pathology sets in. In Fiji, if development means liberation and freedom to grow in healthy relationship to others, then ethnic conflict hampers, if not eliminates this avenue of personal growth. In effect, in the tightening claims of group loyalty, social participation of a particular pathological type becomes prominent. Extremist and militant behaviour aimed at belittling the ethnic enemy has been rewarded.

In sum, especially after the seizure of power by one of the ethnically-based parties in Fiji and the ensuing implementation of a regime of ethnically-oriented discrimination and repression, the persistence of inter-ethnic malaise has severely constrained cross-cultural interaction and participation as a legitimate form of social behaviour. The new governmental system has created a new political hierarchy in inter-ethnic relations. It has marginalized one communal section without meaningfully benefitting the other in Fiji's bi-polar state. The thoroughgoing nature of the oppression destroys the freedom to choose one's friends. It creates powerless people in all the ethnic sections. It encourages invidious forms of inter-ethnic rivalry which distort the friendship and love that people are capable of. It places a premium on hate and dehumanized inter-communal perception in communications. New generations of Fiji citizens are nurtured in this environment. The social personality that evolves is suspicious, and incapable of inter-communal trust and fellowship. In those situations, where inter-ethnic conflict persists, it has bred forms of social hypocrisy which parade as peaceful inter-ethnic co-existence. Under the veneer of civil order, a socially deformed population enacts a script of inter-ethnic antipathy that continues the ethnic war by other means in the dark recesses of the soul. A stressful environment has been created unconducive to healthy human development. It is marked by hate, jealousy, and simple-minded obsession to overcome the ethnic enemy.

It has been argued that one of the few positive effects of inter-ethnic rivalry is the imparting of a sense of ethnic community and identity. Ethnic identity, to be sure, had been affirmed. But this raises the fundamental question about how much ethnic or communal identity is enough for imparting a sense of psychological belonging. Is there a threshold of too much ethnic solidarity when it becomes pathological and suffocating? I believe that protracted ethnic conflicts can engender a level of solidarity that over-saturates the need for belongingness. It brings into play, in diminishing returns, after a certain threshold of solidarity intensity is attained, a new set of adverse effects which negate the initial value of group cohesion. That threshold to which I refer can be called 'the collective insanity threshold.' When group consciousness attains a certain critical mass, usually in conditions of confrontation, it thereafter destroys the carriers themselves. This clearly appears to be happening in Fiji and in many other places including Bosnia and Rwanda. Ethnically-inspired collective insanity destroys the human perceptual apparatus, distorts all messages, and breeds a system of behaviour that destroys adaptation for a healthy fulfilling survival. In Fiji, human creatures who were capable of love and spiritual sharing have been turned into mass instruments of hate. From this environment, have arisen several apocalyptic personalities and extremist groups which have exploited the tensions in Fiji.

What kind of personality is suited for development? It is clear that the crippled personality that is born of protracted ethnic conflict is not in any way appropriate for bringing into being a wholesome society. Integral human development is therefore denied in societies caught in the vice of ethnic strife.

Bibliography

Ali, A. (1972), 'The Fiji General Elections of 1972', *Journal of Pacific History*, Vol.8.

Ali, A. (1973), 'The Indians of Fiji', *Economic and Political Weekly*, Vol.7, No.36, 8 September.

Ali, A. (1975), 'The Arrival of the Communal Franchise', *Journal of Pacific Studies*, Vol.1, No.1.

Ali, A. (1980), 'From Plantation to Politics', *Fiji Times Publications*, Suva.

Alley, R. (1973), *The Development of Political Parties in Fiji*, Doctoral dissertation, Victoria University, Wellington, New Zealand.

Almond, G. and J. Coleman (eds.) (1960), *The Politics of Developing Areas*, Princeton University Press, Princeton.

Almond, G. and B. Powell (1960), *Comparative Politics: A Developmental Approach*, Little, Brown and Co., Boston.

Almond, G. and S. Verba (1963), *The Civic Culture*, Princeton University Press, Princeton.

Amin, S. (1976), 'Unequal Development', *Monthly Review Press*, New York.

Amnesty International (1990), *Amnesty International Report*, London, 18 January.

Andersen, B. (1983), *Imagined Communities*, Verso Books, London.

Anthony, J. (1969), 'The 1968 Bye-Elections in Fiji', *Journal of Pacific History*, Vol.4.

Armstrong, A. (1982), *Nations before Nationalism*, University of North Carolina Press, Chapel Hill.

Ashan, S.A. (1988), 'Relative Deprivation and Begali Secession', *Canadian Review of Studies in Nationalism*, Vol.15, Nos.1-2.

Balawanilotu, J. (1989), 'The Church and I', *Pacific Islands Monthly*, Suva, September.

Banton, M. (1967), *Race Relations*, Tavistock, London.

Banton, M. (1983), *Racial and Ethnic Competition*, Cambridge University Press, Cambridge.

Baran, P. (1957), 'The Political Economy of Growth', *Monthly Review Press*, New York.

Barr, K. (1990), *Poverty in Fiji*, Pacific Conference of Churches, Suva.

Barry, B. (1975), 'The Consociational Model and its Dangers', *European Journal of Political Research*, Vol.3, No.4, December.

Barth, K. (ed.) (1969), *Ethnic Groups and Boundaries*, Universitetsforlaget, Bergen, Norway.

Bavadra, T. (1989), 'Draft Constitution', *Fiji Times*, 19 May.

Belshaw, C. (1964), *Under the Ivy Tree*, Routeledge, Kegan and Paul, London.

Binder, L. et al. (eds.) (1962), *Crises and Sequences in Political Development*, Princeton University Press, Princeton.

Bolaria, B.S and P. Li, (eds.) (1988), *Racial Oppression in Canada*, Garamond Press, Toronto, Canada.

Bonacich, E. (1980), 'Class Approaches to Ethnicity and Race', *Insurgent Sociologist*, Vol.10, No.2.

Brass, P., (ed.) (1985), *Ethnic Groups and the State*, Crown Helm, London.

Breuilly, J. (1982), *Nationalism and the State*, University of Manchester, Manchester.

Brookfield, H. (1972), *Colonialism, Development and Independence*, Cambridge University Press, Cambridge.

Burns, A. (1960), *Report of the Commission of Inquiry into the Resources and Population Trends of the Colony of Fiji*, Legislative Council Paper No.1, Suva, Fiji.

Burns, A. (1963), *Fiji*, Her Majesty's Stationery Office (HMSO).

Carens, J.H. (1992), 'Democracy and Respect for Difference', *University of Michigan Law Reform*, Spring and Summer.

Chand, G. (1990), 'Race and Regionalism in Fiji, Pacific and India', *Economic and Political Weekly*, 20 January.

Chick, J. (1972), 'Fiji: The General Elections of 1972', *Pacific Perspective*, Vol.2., No.1.

Cole, R. and H. Hughes (1991), *The Fiji Economy, Problems and Prospects*, Centre Development Studies, Policy Paper No.4, Australian University, Canberra, Australia.

Contact (Fiji's Catholic newspaper) (1989), 'Father Rouse Leaves', 30 April.

Contact (1989), 'PM: Fijian Provision Need Not Be Argued', 21 May.

Connor, W. (1972), 'Nation-Building or -Destroying?', *World Politics*, Vol.24, No.3.

Connor, W. (1973), 'The Politics of Ethno-Nationalism', *Journal of International Affairs*, Vol.27.

Commonwealth Secretariat (1987), *Notes on the Commonwealth*, London.

Coulter, John W. (1967), *The Drama of Fiji*, Paul Hesch and Co., Melbourne.

Cox, O.C. (1948), *Caste, Class, and Race*, Routeledge, Kegan and Paul, London.

Dalton, J. (1990), *Ethnic Soldiers: The Army as a Political Institution in Fiji*, Paper presented to the conference sponsored by the Research Committee for Ethnicity and Politics of the International Political Science Association held at Brigham Young University, Laie, Hawaii Campus, 9-10 August.

Davies, J., (ed.) (1971), *When Men Revolt and Why*, Collier MacMillan Ltd., London.

Dawkins, R. (1976), *The Selfish Gene*, Oxford University Press, London.

Dean, E. and S. Ritova (1988), *Rabuka: No Other Way*, Oceania Publishers, Suva.

Delaibatiki, N. (1987), 'Challenge to Coalition', *Fiji Sun*, 24 March.

Delaibatiki, N. (1987), 'New Cabinet Designed to Keep Fijians Happy', *Fiji Sun*, 19 April.

Derrick, R.A. (1966), *The Fiji Islands*, Government Printer, Suva.

Despres, L. (1967), *Cultural Pluralism and National Politics in British Guyana*, Rand McNally, Chicago.

Despres, L. (ed.) (1975), *Ethnicity and Resource Competition in Plural Societies*, Moughton and Co., Paris.

Deutsch, K. (1966), *Nationalism and Social Communication*, Harvard University Press, Cambridge.

Durutalo, S. (1985), *Internal Colonialism and Unequal Regional Development: The Case of Western Viti Levu*, M.A. Thesis, University of the South Pacific.

Durutalo, S. (1986), *The Paramountcy of Fijian Interests and the Politicization of Ethnicity*, South Pacific Forum, Suva.

Eleck, A., H. Hill and S.R. Tabor (1991), *Liberalisation and Divestment in a Small Island Economy: Fiji Since the 1987 Coups*, Working Paper, Australian National University, Economics Department, Canberra, Australia.

Emerson, R. (1966), *From Empire to Nation*, Harvard University Press, Cambridge, Massachussetts.

Emmanuel, A. (1972), *Unequal Exchange*, Monthly Review Press, New York.

Enloe, C. (1973), *Ethnic Conflict and Development*, Little and Brown, Boston.

Enloe, C. (1980), *Ethnic Soldiers*, Penguin, Harmondsworth.

Esman, M., (ed.) (1977), *Ethnic Conflict in the Western World*, Cornell University Press, Ithica.

FCC (Fiji Council of Churches) (1989), 'Introduction' in *The FCC's Statement on the Proposed Draft Constitution*, Fiji Council of Churches, Suva (mimeo).

Fiji Youth Association (1991), 'Only 34% of Civil Service Appointees Indians', in *Sangharsh*, Vol 3., No.7.

FINS (Fiji Independent News Service) (1990), 'Mara-Rabuka Brawl over Army Budget', in *Fiji Voice*, Sydney, Australia, December.

FINS (1990a), 'Bashed and Bruised But not Defeated', December.

FINS (1990b), 'Kami Kamica Threatens USP Funding', December.

FINS (1991), 'Expanded Army Budget', March.

FLP (Fiji Labour Party) (1984), *The Fiji Constitution of 1990 : A Fraud on the Nation*, Oceania Publishers, Suva.

Fiji Sun (1987a), 'Gutter-level Politics: Bavadra to Alliance', 28 March.

Fiji Sun (1987b), 'Nitya Reddy Slams Politics of Race', 28 March.

Fiji Sun (1987c), 'The Truth about Employment' (Alliance Advertisement), 28 March.

Fiji Sun (1987d), 'Twelve-Point Plan to Secure the Sugar Industry', 28 March.

Fiji Sun (1987e), 'Bavadra: I am Ready', 13 April.

Fiji Sun (1987f), 'Fijian Uproar', 24 April.

Fiji Sun (1987g), 'U.S. Has Duty to Protect U.S. South Pacific Interests', 2 May.

Fiji Times (1980), 'Ratu Mara Speaks on Government of National Unity', 2 September.

Fiji Times (1987a), 'The People's Day' (Editorial), 28 March.

Fiji Times (1987b), 'Coup', 15 May.

Fiji Times (1987c), 'Bavadra-Government Exchange of Letters', 4 July.

Fiji Times (1989a), 'Don't Legislate on Religion : Churches', 1 January.

Fiji Times (1989b), 'The 70 Constitution Had Major Flaw', 11 January.

Fiji Times (1989c), 'P.M.: Law Backs Special Rights', 11 May.

Fiji Times (1989d), 'Western Group Unhappy with Draft Constitution', 22 May.

Fiji Times (1989e), 'Rakka Accuses Government of Preaching Racism', 26 June.

Fiji Times (1990a), 'Government for Press Freedom - PM', 6 September, .

Fiji Times (1990b), 'Five Million Dollar Loans for Fijiian Businesses', 19 September.

Fiji Times (1991a), 'Fijian Ownership for Woko, says Mara', 16 January.

Fiji Times (1991b), 'Sugar Industry at Crossroads', 8 April.

Fiji Times (1991c), 'Fiji's Emigration Still on the Rise', 13 April.

Fiji Times (1991d), 'One Hundred Riot Police Deployed in the West', 1 June.

Fiji Times (1991e), 'Coalition Hits New Decrees', 4 June.

Fiji Times (1991f), 'Soldiers to Cut Cane?', 5 June.

Fiji Times (1991g), 'National Farmers' Union Barred from Holding Meeting', 5 June.

Fiji Times (1991h), 'Unions on Alert for Showdown', 7 June.

Fiji Times (1991i), 'Church Force to Cut Cane', 7 June.

Fiji Times (1991j), 'Revoke Decrees NFU Tells Government', 8 June.

Fiji Times (1991k), 'Fijian Holdings Invests', 6 August.

Fisk, E.K. (1970), *The Political Economy of Independent Fiji*, Australian National University Press, Canberra.

France, P. (1969), *The Charter of the Land*, Oxford University Press, Melbourne.

Frank, A.G. (1967), *Capitalism and Underdevelopment in Latin America*, Monthly Review Press, New York.

Froman, C.W. (1962), *The Island Churches of the Pacific*, Orbis Books, Mary Knoll.

Froman, C.W. (1986), *The Voice of Many Waters*, Lotu Pacifica Productions, Suva.

FTL (Fiji Times Limited) (1988), 'Back from the Brink', *Pacific Islands Monthly*, Suva, January.

Furnivall, J.S. (1948), *Colonial Policy and Practice*, Cambridge University Press, London.

Garrett, J. (1983), *To Live among the Stars: Christian Origins in Oceania*, Institute of Pacific Studies, University of the South Pacific, Suva, Fiji.

Gaunder, H. (1987), 'Civil Disobedience', in *Fiji Sun*, 26 April.

Geertz, C. (1963), 'Primordial Sentiments and Civic Politics in New States: The Integrative Revolution', in C. Geertz (ed.), *Old Societies and New States*, Free Press, Glencoe, Illinois.

Gellner, E.(1983), *Nations and Nationalism*, Basil Blackwell, Oxford.

Ghai, Y. (1990), 'A Coup by Another Name? The Politics of Legality', *Contemporary Pacific*, Vol.2.

Gillion, K.C. (1962), *Fiji's Indian Migrants*, Oxford University Press, Melbourne.

Gillion, K.C. (1977), *The Fiji Indians Challenge to European Dominance 1920-1946*, Australian National University Press, Canberra, Australia.

Glaser, N. (1975), *Ethnicity: Theory and Experience*, Harvard University Press, Cambridge.

Glaser, N. (1977), *Affirmative Discrimination*, Harvard University Press.

Grocott, Paul (1976), 'Fiji: Politics of Communalism', in P. Grocott, (ed.), *Readings in Pacific Politics*, University of Papua New Guinea Printery, Waigani.

Gurr, T. (1970), *Why Men Rebel*, Princeton University Press, Princeton.

Hagen, Stephanie (1987), 'Race, Politics, and the Coup in Fiji', *Bulletin of Concerned Asian Scholars*, Vol.19, No. 4, October-December.

Hagen, Stephanie (1987), The Party System, the Labour Party, and the Plural Society Syndrome in Fiji', *Journal of Comparative and Commonwealth Studies*, Vol., 25, No.2, July.

Hailey, J. (1985), *Indigenous Business in Fiji*, East-West Centre, Honolulu, Hawaii.

Harder, C. (1988), *Guns of Lautoka (Kahan's defense)*, Sunshine Press, Aukland.

Hayes, C.J.H. (1931), *The Evolution of Modern Nationalism*, Unwin, New York.

Hecter, M. (1975), *Internal Colonialism*, University of California Press, Berkeley.

Herman, J. (1990), 'Censorship versus Responsibility: A View of the Media in Post-Coup Fiji', *Pacific Perspective*.

Hince, K.W. (1971), 'Trade Unionism in Fiji', *Journal of Industrial Relations*, Vol.13.

Hobsbawm, E.J. (1992), *Nations and Nationalism since 1780*, Cambridge University Press, Cambridge.

Horowitz, D. (1986), *Ethnic Groups in Conflict*, University of California Press, Berkeley, California.

Howard, M. (1991), *Race and Politics in an Island State*, University of British Columbia Press, Vancouver.

Huntington, S. (1968), *Political Order in Changing Societies*, Yale University Press, New Haven.

IBI (Islands Business) (1990), 'Chaudry', *Islands Business*, July.

Isaacs, H.R. (1975), *Idols of the Tribe*, Harper and Row, New York.

Iyer, K. (1987), 'No Bias for Lau', in *Fiji Sun*, 28 March.

Jenkins, R. (1988), 'Social Anthropological Models of Inter-Ethnic Relations', in J. Rex and D. Mason., (eds.) *Theories of Race and Ethnic Relations*, Cambridge University Press, Cambridge.

Johnson, C. (1967), *Revolutionary Change*, Little and Brown Ltd., Boston.

Johnson, M. (1990), 'The Part of the Constitution that Enables them to Sweep Aside all those Guarantees', *Islands Business*, August.

Kedourie, E. (1960), *Nationalism*, Hutchinson, London.

Keith-Reid, Robert (1987), 'Pacific Loses its Jewel: Rabuka Strikes', *Islands Business*, June.

Keith-Reid, Robert (1988), 'Intriguing Questions of the Fiji-Saw', *Islands Business*, January.

Keyes, C.F. (1981), *Ethnic Change*, University of Washington Press, Seattle.

Kohn, H. (1944), *The Idea of Nationalism*, MacMillan, London.

Korpi, W. (1974), 'Conflict, Power, and Relative Deprivation', *American Political Science Review*, Vol.68, No.4.

Knapman, B. (1987), *Fiji's Economic History 1874-1939*, Australian National University, Pacific Research Monograph No.15, Canberra, Australia.

Koroi, M. (1987), 'One House, 31 Seats, Chiefs', in *Fiji Times*, 29 July.

Kumar, V. (1987), 'Why Alliance Lost Key National Seats', in *Fiji Times*, 13 April.

Lal, B. (1983), 'Girmityas: Origins of Fiji's Indians', in *Journal of Pacific History*, Australian National University, Canberra, Australia.

Lal, B. (ed.) (1986), *Politics in Fiji*, Allen and Unwin, Sydney.

Lal, B. (ed.) 'Emergence of the Fiji Labour Party', in op.cit.

Lal, B. (1987), 'The Elections of 1982: The Tidal Wave That Never Came', in *Journal of Pacific History*, Vol.18, No.2.

Lal, B. (1988), 'Power and Prejudice: The Making of the Fiji Crises', *Journal of Pacific History*, Australian National University, Canberra, Australia.

Lal, V. (1990), *Fiji: Coups in Paradise*, Zed Books Ltd., London.

Lawson, S. (1991), *The Failure of Democratic Politics in Fiji*, Clarendon Press, Oxford.

Lasaqa, I. (1984), *The Fijian People*, Australian National University Press, Canberra.

Leckie, J. (1990), 'From Localisation to Politisation: The Fiji Public Service Association', in Moore, J. Leckie and D. Monroe (eds.), *Labour in the Pacific*, University of Queensland Press, Queensland, Australia.

Leckie, J. (1991), 'State Coercion and Public Sector Unionism in Post Coup Fiji', *New Zealand Journal of Industrial Relations*, Vol.16.

Legge, J.D. (1958), *Britain in Fiji, 1858-1880*, MacMillan, London.

Lewis, A. (1965), *Politics in West Africa*, Allen and Unwin, London.

Lijphart, A. (1985), *Democracy in Plural Societies*, Yale University Press, New Haven.

Lloyd, D.T. (1982), *Land Policy in Fiji*, Cambridge University Press, Cambridge.

Lustick, I. (1979), 'Stability in Deeply Divided Societies:Control v. Consociation', *World Politics*, Vol. 3, No.3, April.

MacGarry, J. and B. O'Leary (1993), 'The Macro-Political Regulation of Ethnic Conflict', in J. MacGarry and B.O. O'Leary (eds.), *The Politics of Ethnic Conflict Regulation*, Routeledge, Kegan and Paul, London.

MacNaught, T. (1982), *The Fiji Colonial Experience: A Study of Neo-Colonial Rule under British Rule prior to WWII*, Australian National University Press, Canberra, Pacific Research Monograph No.7.

Mamak, A. (1978, *Color, Culture and Conflict: Pluralism in Fiji*, Pergamon Press, New York.

Mamak, A. and A. Ali (1979), *Race, Class and rebellion in the South Pacific*, George Allen and Unwin, Australia.

Mara, Ratu (1988), 'Our Great Challenge', *Pacific Islands Monthly*, May.

Mayer, A.C. (1963), *Indians in Fiji*, Oxford University Press, London.

Mayer, A.C. (1973), *Peasants of the Pacific*, University of California Press, Berkeley.

Meller, Norman and J. Anthony (1967), *Fiji Goes to the Polls*, University of Hawaii Press, Honolulu.

Melson, R. and H. Wolpe (1988), 'Modernisation and the Politics of Communalism', *American Political Science Review*, December.

Miles, R. 'Race, Class and Ethnicity: A Critique of Cox's Theory', *Ethnic and Racial Studies*, Vol.3, No.2.

Miles, R. (1982), *Racism and Migrant Labour*, Routeledge, Keagan and Paul, London.

Milne, R.S. (1975), 'The Pacific Way - Consociational Politics in Fiji', *Pacific Affairs*, Summer.

Milne, R.S. (1982), *Politics in Ethnically Bi-Polar States*, University of British Columbia Press, Vancouver.

Milne, R.S. 'Ethnic Aspects of Privatisation in Malaysia', in N. Nevitte and H. Kennedy (eds.), *Ethnic Preference and Public Policy in Developing States*, Lynne Reiner, Boulder, Colorado.

Ministry of Information (1949), *Report of the Commission of the Inquiry into the Natural Resources and Population Trends of the Colony of Fiji*, Government of Fiji, Suva.

Ministry of Information (1966), *Census Report*, Government of Fiji, Suva.

Ministry of Information (1967), *Report of the Public Service Commission*, Government of Fiji, Suva.

Ministry of Information (1969), *Annual Statistical Abstract-Fiji*, Government of Fiji, Suva.

Ministry of Information (1975), *Report of the Royal Commission Appointed for the Purpose of Considering and Making Recommendations as to the Most Appropriate Method of Electing Members to the House of Representatives*, Government of Fiji, Parliamentary Paper No.24.

Ministry of Information (1988), *Draft Constitution for the Republic of Fiji*, Government of Fiji, Suva.

Ministry of Information (1989a), 'A Proposed Constitution for Fiji', in *Focus on Fiji*, Government of Fiji, Suva, Vol. 1, No.2, Special Issue.

Ministry of Information (1989b), *Constitutional Inquiry and Advisory Committee Report*, Government of Fiji, Suva.

Moynagh, M. (1981), *Brown or White? A History of the Fiji Sugar Industry 1873-1973*, Pacific Research Monograph No.5, Australian National University Press, Research School of Pacific Studies, Canberra.

Murray, D. (1978), 'The Governor-General in Fiji's Constitutional Crisis', *Politics*, Vol.13, No.2.

Naidu, V. (1980), *The Violence of Indenture*, University of the South Pacific, World University Series, Fiji Monograph No.3., Suva, Fiji.

Naidu, V. (1986), *The Fiji Labour Party and the By-Elections of 1985*, Institute of Social and Economic Studies, University of the South Pacific, Suva, Fiji.

Narayan, J. (1982), *The Political Economy of Independent Fiji*, South Pacific Review Press, Suva, Fiji.

Narsey, W. (1979), 'Monopoly Capital, White Racism, and Super Profits in Fiji', *Journal of Pacific Studies*, Vol. 5.

Nation, J. (1978), *Customs of Respect: The Traditional Basis of Fijian Communal Politics*, Research School of Pacific Studies, Australian National University, Canberra.

Nayacakalou, R.R. (1975), *Leadership in Fiji*, Oxford University Press, Melbourne.

Norlinger, E. (1972), *Conflict Regulation in Divided Societies*, Institute of International Affairs, Harvard University, Cambridge, Massachussetts.

Norton, N. (1978), *Race and Politics in Fiji*, University of Queensland Press, Queensland, Australia.

Overton, J. (ed.) (1989), 'Fiji Since the Coups', *Pacific Viewpoint*, Vol. 30, No.2.

Pacific Islands Monthly (1975), 'Party Leaders Fall Out', Vol. 46, No. 12, December.

PJT (Pacific Journal of Theology) (1989a), 'Fiji Coup: Church Statements', Vol. 2, No.1, January.

PJT (Pacific Journal of Theology) (1989b), 'Fiji Council of Churches Statement on the Sunday Decree, March 11, 1988', Vol. 2, No.1, January.

Plange, Nii-K. (1992), 'The Three Fijis Thesis: A Critical Examination of a Neo-Empiricist Naturalistic Analysis of Fiji's Polity', *Journal of Pacific Studies*, Vol. 15.

Prasad, S., (ed) (1988), *Coup and Crisis - A Year Later*, Arena Publications, Victoria, Australia.

Premdas, Ralph (1972), *Racial Politics in Guyana*, University of Denver Press, Denver, Colorado.

Premdas, Ralph (1977), 'Ethno-Nationalism, Copper, and Secession : The Case of Bougainville', *Canadian Review of Studies in Nationalism*, Vol. 4.

Premdas, Ralph (1978), 'Fiji: Communal Conflict and Political Balance in the South Pacific', *Caribbean Affairs*, Vol. 4, No.1.

Premdas, Ralph (1980a), 'Elections in Fiji: Restoration of the Balance in September, 1977', *Journal of Pacific History*, Vol. 14, No.1.

Premdas, Ralph (1980b), 'Constitutional Challenge: Nationalist Politics in Fiji', *Pacific Perspective*, Vol. 9, No.2.

Premdas, Ralph (1981), 'Towards a Government of National Unity', *Pacific Perspective*, Vol. 101, No.2, November.

Premdas, Ralph (1986a), 'Politics of Preference in the Caribbean', in N. Nevitte and C.H. Kennedy (eds.), *Ethnic Preference and Public Policy in Developing States*, Lynne Reiner, Boulder, Colorado.

Premdas, Ralph (1986b), 'Ethnic Conflict Management: Fiji', in B. Lal (ed.), *Politics in Fiji*, Allen and Unwin, Sydney.

Premdas, Ralph (1987), 'Fiji: Elections and Communal Conflict in the First Coup', *Ethnic Studies Report*, Vol. 5, No.2, July.

Premdas, Ralph (1989), 'Fiji: The Anatomy of a Revolution', *Pacifica*, Vol. 1, No.1, January.

Premdas, Ralph (1990a), *Balance versus Dominance: The Protection of Ethnic Interests in Fiji*, paper presented to the conference sponsored by the Research Committee for Ethnicity and Politics, of the International Political Science Association, held at Brigham Young University, Laie, Hawaii Campus, 9-10 August.

Premdas, Ralph (1990b), 'The Internationalisation of Ethnic Conflict: Theoretical Perspectives', in R. May and K.M. de Silva (eds.), *The Internationalisation of Ethnic Conflict*, Frances Pinter Publishers, London.

Premdas, Ralph (1990c), 'Problems of Establishing Labour Parties in Communal Societies', in C. Moore et al. (eds.), *Labour in the Pacific*, University of Queensland Press, Queensland, Australia.

Premdas, Ralph (1991a), 'The Politics of Inter-Ethnic Accomodation: The Lewis Mode', in R. Premdas and E. St. Cyr (eds.), *Sir Arthur Lewis: An Economic and Political Portrait*, Institute of Social and Economic Research, University of the West Indies, Mona, Jamaica.

Premdas, Ralph (1991b), 'The Political Economy of Ethnic Strife in Fiji and Guyana', *Ethnic Studies Report*, Vol. 9, No.2.

Premdas, Ralph (1991c), 'Fiji: Ethnic Conflict and Indigenous Rights in a New Political Order', *Asian Survey*, Vol. 30, No.6.

Premdas, Ralph (1992), *Ethnic Conflict and Development: The Case of Guyana*, Discussion Paper No.30, UNRISD, Geneva, January.

Premdas, Ralph (1993a), 'Balance and Ethnic Conflict', in McGarry and B. O'Leary (eds.), *The Politics of Ethnic Conflict Regulation*, Routledge Publishers, London.

Premdas, Ralph (1993b), 'The Anatomy of Ethnic Conflict', in R. Premdas (ed.), *The Enigma of Ethnicity*, Extra-Mural Studies, University of the West Indies, Trinidad and Tobago.

Premdas, Ralph (1993c), 'Ethnic Conflict in a New Political Order', in R. Premdas (ed.), *The Enigma of Ethnicity*, Extra-Mural Studies, University of the West Indies, St. Augustine, Trinidad.

Premdas, Ralph (1994), 'The Church and Ethnic Conflicts in the Third World', *Ecumenist*, Vol. 1, No.4, May-June.

Premdas, R., A. Andersen, and S.W.R. de Samarasinghe, (eds.) (1990), *Secessionist Movements in Comparative Perspective*, Pinter, London.

Premdas, R. and P. Hintzen (1982), 'Guyana: Coercion and Control in Political Change', *Journal of Inter-American Studies and World Affairs*, Vol. 24, No.3, August.

Premdas, R. and M. Howard (1985), 'Vanuatu's Foreign Policy in the Pacific', *Australian Outlook*, August.

Premdas, R. and Nyamekye (1979), 'Papua New Guinea-Indonesia Relations over Irian Jaya', *Asian Survey*, Vol. 19, No.10.

Premdas, R. and J.S. Steeves (1984), *Decentralisation in Melanesia*, South Pacific Forum, Suva, Fiji.

Pye, L. (1966), *Aspects of Political Development*, Little and Brown, Boston.

Rabushka, A. and K.A. Shepsle (1972), *Politics in Plural Societies: A Theory of Democratic Instability*, Charles E. Merrill Co., Columbus, Ohio.

Rae, P. (1979), 'Ethnic Politics in Trade Unionism in Fiji', *Pacific Perspective*, Vol. 1, No.1.

Ratuva, S. (1993), 'Post-Coup Nationalism: The Rise and Demise of Taukeism', *Review*, Vol. 20.

Ravuvu, A. (1988), *Dependence and Development*, Institute of Pacific Studies, Suva.

Ravuvu, A. (1991), *The Facade of Democracy*, Oceania Printers, Suva.

Rex, J. (1958), 'The Plural Society in Sociological Theory', *British Journal of Sociology*, Vol. 10, No.2.

Rex, J. (1983), *Race Relations in Sociological Theory*, Cambridge University Press, Cambridge.

Rex, J. and D. Mason, (eds.) (1986), *Theories of Race and Ethnic Relations*, Cambridge University Press, Cambridge.

Robertson, R.T. (1985), 'The Formation of the Fiji Labour Party', *New Zealand and Monthly Review*, October.

Robertson, R.T. and A. Tavanisua (1987), *Fiji: Shattered Coups*, Pluto Press, Canberra.

Robie, D. (1987), 'Death of the "Pacific Pacific"', *Islands Business*, June.

Rokotunivuna, A. et al. (1974), *Fiji: A Developing Australian Colony*, International Development Action, Melboune.

Rostow, W. (1964), *The Stages of Economic Growth*, Cambridge University Press, Cambridge.

Rothchild, D. (1986), 'State and Ethnicity in Africa' in N. Nevitte and C.H. Kennedy (eds.), *Ethnic Preference and Public Policy in Developing States*, Lanne Reiner Publishers, Boulder, Colorado.

Routledge, D. (1985), *Matanitu: The Struggle for Power in Early Fiji*, Institute of Pacific Studies, University of the South Pacific, Suva, Fiji.

Runciman, W.G. (1966), *Relative Deprivation Theory and Social Justice*, University of California Press, Berkeley.

Sanday, J. (1989), 'The Coups of 1987: A Personal Analysis', *Pacific Viewpoint*, Vol. 30, No.2.

dos Santos, T. (1970), 'The Stuctures of Dependence', *American Economic Review*, May.

Scarr, D. (1988), *The Politics of Illusion: The Military Coups in Fiji*, New South Wales University, Kensington, Sydney.

Schermerhorn, R.A. (1970), *Comparative Ethnic Relations*, University of Chicago Press, Chicago.

Sharma, D. (1987), 'Labour's Socialism Perilous, Voters Warned', *Fiji Sun*, 28 March.

Sharma, H. (1989), 'Draft Constitution', *Fiji Times*, 26 May.

Shibutani, T. and F.M. Kwan (1965), *Ethnic Stratification*, MacMillan, New York.

Shrimpton, J. (1987), 'Coalition Government Will Have a Significant Effect in Pacific', *Fiji Sun*, 13 April.

Singh, A. (1991), *Silent Warriors*, Institute of Applied Studies, Fiji.

Smith, A.D. (1979), *Nationalism in the Twentieth Century*, New York University Press, New York.

Smith, A.D. (1981), *The Ethnic Revival in the Modern World*, Cambridge University Press, Cambridge.

Smith, A.D. (1986), *The Ethnic Origins of Nations*, Basil Blackwell, London.

Smith, A.D. (1991), *Ethnic Identity*, Penguin, London.

Smith, M.G. (1965), 'Institutional and Political Conditions of Pluralism' in L. Kuper and M.G. Smith (eds.), *Pluralism in Africa*, University of California Press, Berkeley.

Smith, M.G. (1993), 'Race and Ethnicity' in R. Premdas (ed.), *The Enigma of Ethnicity* Extra-Mural Studies, University of the West Indies, Trinidad and Tobago.

Smootha, S. (1980), 'Control of Minorities', *Comparative Study in History and Society*, Vol. 22, No.2.

Spate, O.A.K. (1959), *The Fijian People: Economic Problems and Prospects*, Government Printery, Suva.

Stavenhagen, R. (1990), *Ethnic Politics: An Agenda for Research*, paper read at conference convened by the United Nations Research Institute for Social Development, Geneva.

Stone, J. (1977), *Race, Ethnicity, and Social Change*, Duxbury Press, North Seituate.

Sutherland, W. (1992), *Beyond the Politics of Race: An Alternative History of Fiji to 1992*, Institute of Political and Social Change, Monograph No.15, Australian National University, Canberra, Australia.

Tajfel, H. (1974), *Intergroup Behaviour, Social Comparison and Social Change*, Katz-Newcomb Lectures, University of Michigan, Ann Arbour, Michigan.

Taylor, M., (ed) (1987), *Fiji: Future Imperfect*, Allen and Unwin, Sydney, Australia.

Taylor, D.M. and F.M. Mogahaddam (1985), *Theories of Inter-Group Relations*, Praeger, New York.

Thompson, B. (1968), *The Fijians: A Study of Decay of Custom*, Dawsons, London.

Thornley, A. (1974) 'The Methodist Mission and Fiji's Indians 1879-1920', *New Zealand Journal of History*, Vol. 8, No.2.

Tilly, C. (1975), *The Formation of the National State in Western Europe*, Princeton University Press, Princeton.

Tinker, H. (1974), *A New System of Slavery*, Oxford University Press, Oxford.

Unispac (1969), 'Cane Farmers: Fiji's Unrewarded Peasants', University Student Papers, Vol.7, No.5.

Van den Berghe, P.L. (1978), *Race and Racism in Comparative Perspective*, John Wiley Co., New York.

Van den Berghe, P.L. (1981), *The Ethnic Phenomenon*, Elsevier Press, New York.

Vasil, R.K. (1972), 'Communalism and Constitution-Making in Fiji', *Pacific Affairs*, Vol.45, No.23, Spring.

Vasil, R.K. (1984), *Politics in Bi-Racial Societies*, Vikas Press, New Delhi.

Walsh, A.C. (1978), 'Fiji's Changing Poulation: Implications for Race Relations', *Unispac*, Vol. 8, No.1.

Ward, R.G. (1965), *Land Use and Population in Fiji*, Her Majesty's Stationery Office (HMSO), London.

Watters, R.F. (1969), *Koro: Economic Development and Social Change in Fiji*, Clarendon Press, Oxford.

Weaver, J. and M. Berger (1984), 'The Marxist Critique of Dependency Theory', in C. Wilber (ed.), *The Political Economy of Underdevelopment*, Random House, New York.

Williams, E. (1964), *Capitalism and Slavery*, Andre Deutsch, London.

Wilson, E.O. (1975), *Sociobiology: The New Synthesis*, Harvard University Press, Cambridge.

The World Bank (1990), 'Fiji: Challenges for Development', *World Bank Report*, Washington, D.C., May.

Yelvington, K. (ed.) (1993), *Trinidad Ethnicity*, MacMillan, London.

Young, C. (1976), *The Politics of Cultural Pluralism*, University of Wisconsin Press, Madison, Wisconsin.

Young, C. (1993), 'The Dialictics of Cultural Pluralism: Concept and Reality', in Young and Crawford (eds.), *The Rising Tide of Cultural Pluralism: The Nation-State at Bay*, University of Wisconsin Press, Madison, Wisconsin.

Research in Ethnic Relations Series

The Migration Process in Britain and West Germany
Two Demographic Studies of Migrant Populations
Heather Booth

Perceptions of Israeli Arabs: Territoriality and Identity
Izhak Schnell

Ethnic Mobilisation in a Multi-cultural Europe
Edited by John Rex and Beatrice Drury

**Post-war Caribbean Migration to Britain:
The Unfinished Cycle**
Margaret Byron

**Through Different Eyes: The Cultural Identity of
Young Chinese People in Britain**
David Parker

**Britannia's Crescent: Making a Place for Muslims
in British Society**
Danièle Joly

Religion, Class and Identity
The State, the Catholic Church and the Education
of the Irish in Britain
Mary J. Hickman

**Migration, Citizenship and Ethno-National Identities
in the European Union**
Edited by Marco Martiniello

Ethnic Conflict and Development: The Case of Guyana
Ralph R. Premdas